THE CREATIVE DEALMAKER

A Fable on Creative Business Buying

BY

CARL ALLEN

Copyright © 2024 by Carl Allen.

All rights reserved. No part of this publication may be reproduced, distributed, or transmitted in any form or by any means, including photocopying, recording, or other electronic or mechanical methods, without the prior written permission of the author, except in the case of brief quotations embodied in critical reviews and certain other non-commercial uses permitted by copyright law.

Ordering Information: Quantity sales. Special discounts are available on quantity purchases by corporations, associations, and others. Orders by U.S. trade bookstores and wholesalers.

DREAMSTARTERS

www.DreamStartersPublishing.com

Table of Contents

Dedication 5
Introduction 6
Cast of Characters 8
Prologue 10
Corporate Frustration 12
The Empty Nester 20
Defining the Buy Box 24
Not All Buyers Are Created Equal 27
The Buy-Side Process 34
The Sell-Side Process 39
Broker Sites 43
Pushing the SELL Button 47
Bottom of the Fifth 50
The Annuity Deal 55
Welcome to Protégé 58
Jacqueline Calls the Brokers 62
Terence Hits the Deal Origination Machine 66
Jacqueline Meets Jeremy for Lunch 71
Terence's First Seller Call 74
Terence Receives Three More Deals 78
The Buyer List 83
Terence's RLGL Submission 87
Impromptu Meetings 91
The Big Meeting 97
More Seller Meetings 104
Terence Values JAT 107
Terence Prepares JAT for the RLGL Call 114
Jeremy and Jacqueline Set the JAT Valuation Range 116
Carl's RLGL Review of JAT 120
Terence Makes His Offer for JAT 122
Terence Reviews All His Other Deals 126
Terence Talks to the Banks 128
Jacqueline and Jeremy Review the Offers 131
Charity Fundraiser with Jack 134
Jacqueline Makes Her Decision 138
Best and Final 141
The LOI 143
Due Diligence 146
Four Weeks Later 149
Jacqueline Gets Cold Feet 150
Terence Gets Cold Feet 154
Date Night 159

Jacqueline Addresses the Team	161
Terence Takes the Interview for the Partnership	164
The Decision	168
Updating Calls with Legal and the Bank	171
Government Shutdown	175
Pivoting the Deal	179
The Annuity Purchase Option	181
Jacqueline Takes the Deal	186
The Closing	190
Terence Resigns from Creative	193
The Handover	195
Jacqueline and Jack's First Weekend Date	197
Terence Spends the Day with His New Team	199
The One-Page Business Plan	204
Federal Budget Signoff	207
The SBA Reopens	210
The Next Acquisition	213
Closing Luxe	219
Terence Needs More Capital	221
The Medical Deal Model	227
The Upper Echelon Mansion	229
Carl's Equity-Raising Masterclass	231
Deal Synergies	236
The Pitch Deck and Forecast Model	240
Medical PR Goes Under LOI	245
Terence Pitches to Equity Investors	247
Double Closing	251
Two Years Later	254
The First Seller Call for JAT	259
The Proposal	262
JAT Is in Play	265
Empire Visits JAT	268
Empire Makes an $87 million Offer to Buy JAT	271
A Smooth Closing	274
Epilogue	276
About the Author	280

Dedication

I dedicate this book to my family, friends, business partners, investors, customers and employees who are supporting me on my dealmaking journey. And to all my amazing Dealmaker Protégé students who go out every day to originate deals, meet sellers and make offers to buy profitable small businesses. I salute you all and hope you enjoy my very first novel.

Introduction

The Creative Dealmaker isn't a technical business book. It's a fable—a story about a buyer and seller who meet and transact on a business acquisition. It's a gritty tale of a motivated buyer and seller who embark on their first-ever business acquisition and exit.

You'll meet Jacqueline, a retiring 60-year old owner of a successful PR agency she founded over 20 years ago. She's tired, burned out and looking forward to spending more time with her grandchildren.

You will also meet Terence, a 40-year old executive in one of the USA's largest PR agencies. He knows the industry and, after a 20-year career in corporate America, yearns to own his own business. Rather than start a business from scratch (and struggle), he wants to acquire (and grow) an existing, successful business that already has customers, employees, premises, a substantial cash flow and a solid reputation.

Both Jacqueline and Terence have never bought or sold a business before, so the book conveys not only the process involved in transferring business ownership but also the drama, emotions and psychology that both buyers and sellers typically go through, especially with that first deal.

At the start of the book, we learn all about Jacqueline and Terence and their motivations for transacting a deal. Eventually, they meet and begin the lengthy process of both setting up the transaction and closing the deal. Both buyer and seller receive advice and educate themselves throughout the process.

The book contains several business buying frameworks, including a 10-step business buying process, various methods of originating leads and generating dealflow, multiple methods of structuring and financing a transaction and, finally, the closing portion of the transaction, which covers due diligence, legal contracts and what happens on the final day at the closing table.

I hope these realistic characters and familiar situations will inspire you as a potential buyer to seek out your own dream business (either as an operator or an investor). Or, if you're a potential seller who's been putting off the sale of your business, let this book be your inspiration and guide to finally make it happen.

Over the course of my corporate and entrepreneurial career spanning three decades, I've been part of more than 400 acquisitions—as a buyer, seller, investor, partner, advisor, coach and mentor. I've seen pretty much everything there is to see in a business acquisition. I could have easily written a technical book about the many lessons I've learned, but those kinds of books are a dime a dozen, and they don't capture the intense drama, emotion and psychology of closing a deal, all of which is crucial to understand. Hence, the fable.

When I was a big-time corporate mergers and acquisitions (M&A) executive doing massive deals, the transactions were all about the numbers. Financial engineering. Share swaps. Complex legal structures. However, on Main Street where most of us live and do business, the numbers and technical aspects of a deal are less important. Buyer and seller psychology play a much bigger role.

When people start and build businesses over many years, these businesses become part of them. When, eventually, the owner and business have to part ways, the emotions involved can be like sending a child off to college or watching them leave the nest to marry and start their own new life. You may be surprised to learn through this fable that many sellers care more about their legacy, brand, culture, and the protection of their employees, customers and vendors than they do about the cold, hard cash at the closing table. Many times in the pages that follow you'll read the phrase "a safe, trusted pair of hands" describing what the seller sees as the ideal buyer.

Following the Prologue below, the book consists of three parts. Part I is the *dance*. It's how Jacqueline and Terence meet and agree to the terms of the transaction. Part II is the *deal*. It's the process both buyer and seller go through to consummate and close the transaction. Part III is the *denouement*, or how everything turned out following the deal . . . including developments up to present day.

For downloads, free tools and additional resources, please visit ...

http://www.creativedealmakerbook.com.

Enjoy the story and the rollercoaster ride.

My best regards,

Carl Allen
Viera, Florida

Cast of Characters

The Seller: JAT (Jacqueline Ann Turley) PR LLC

Jacqueline Turley - Owner
Phillip Fouts - General Manager
Barbara Wicks - Executive Assistant
Jeremy Brown - CPA and fractional CFO (Jeremy Brown & Associates LLC)
Lucy Vaughn - Financial Controller
Jack Beech - Advisor, confidante, friend and future husband to Jacqueline Turley

Herb Sanders - M&A Attorney (for the seller)
Anthony Marks - SBA Financing Broker
Bill Frisk - Business Broker 1
Martin Crowther - Business Broker 2
Leanne Deakins - Business Broker 3
Beau Harding - Business Broker 4
James Brock - Business Broker 5

The Buyer: Creative PR, Inc

Terence Turner, Senior Account Manager, Creative PR, Inc

Peter Hitchen - CPA (PH Financial LLC)
Brittney Anderson - M&A Attorney (for the buyer)

PR Empire Inc.
Ross Thompson, President & CEO
Jess Thompson, COO
Chris March, SVP Marketing
Sarah Lewis, CFO
David Gifford, Legal Counsel

The White House
President Gerald Booth (Democrat)
Larry Moss, White House Chief of Staff
Josh Parker, Deputy White House Chief of Staff
Kevin Drexler, Speaker of the House of Representatives (Republican)

SBA (Small Business Administration) and Financiers

Felix Walker - Senior Loan Officer, SBA
Marlyn Day - Assigned Closer, Live Stem Bank
Lisa Trammel - Head of Sponsored Lending, Live Stem Bank
Kevin Hart - Legal Counsel, Live Stem Bank

Dealmaker Wealth Society, LLC

Carl Allen - CEO Dealmaker Wealth Society, business buying coach
Tracey Topping - Protégé enrollment coach, Dealmaker Wealth Society

Prologue

Jacqueline Turley and Jack Beech gazed into each other's eyes. The weather at the exclusive Phoenician resort in Scottsdale was amazing. Perhaps a little too warm for December, but both of them were dressed casually and comfortably. When people get married in their 60s (and not for the first time), tradition tends to be a bit more relaxed.

Jacqueline and Jack had been dating for almost four years. They had been friends from the Chicago business roundtable, and Jacqueline had taken advice from Jack on the sale of her business almost four years ago. In fact, the courtship started during the closing of the deal.

The officiant commenced the brief ceremony, and both Jacqueline and Jack recited their prepared vows.

"I now pronounce you husband and wife. You may kiss the bride."

Jack locked in for a long kiss, to the delight and cheering of the crowd of attendees.

Moments later, Terence Turner hurried forward to congratulate them. He had acquired Jacqueline's business almost four years prior. She had retained a 10% equity stake and, following significant business growth and some strategic acquisitions, had just recently exited the business to a major trade buyer.

Terence strenuously pumped Jack's hand and gave Jacqueline a big hug and a kiss on both cheeks. He reached into his pocket and pulled out a plain white envelope, handing it to Jacqueline and making her promise not to open it until tomorrow.

Terence's wife Julie and their two children quickly followed and voiced their congratulations to the couple as well. All had become firm friends in the past four years since the deal had closed. They had even twice gone on vacation together—sizable affairs that had included members of Jack's and Jacqueline's extended families.

The wedding party sat down on the shaded veranda and ate dinner just as the sun was edging into the horizon. Appetizers of tuna sashimi and lobster claws were followed by mouth-watering prime rib. Wines from Burgundy, France and Napa Valley topped off the feast.

Jacqueline excused herself to visit the ladies room. While there, when nobody was watching, she opened the envelope. Inside, to her amazement, she found a check for $5,199,619, representing the proceeds from her 10% retained stake in the business she had sold to Terence. The check was made out in her new married name. What a lovely touch.

Combining her initial exit, the profit distributions and now this final exit check, she had amassed more than $8,500,000 from the sale. It had been her first and only time to go through an exit before she retired. Terence had insisted she sit on the board over the past three and a half years, retain the 10% stake and enjoy the wild success of the PR business she had founded many years before.

Now, here she was married. As the sun set over Camelback Mountain, she considered herself blessed.

Chapter 1

Corporate Frustration

Four years earlier…

    Terence Turner woke up in his modest, Chicago-suburb home at his usual 6 a.m. The beeping of his iPhone seemed louder than normal, and he groaned as he reached over to silence it. After gingerly kissing his sleeping wife, Julie, on the cheek, he slipped into his cycling gear and went into the next room to get ready for his Peloton workout.

    He logged in, selected his favorite coach, Leo, and connected his headphones by Bluetooth so as to not wake his sleeping family.

    "Let's go Peloton!" shouted Leo.

    Terence couldn't manage to generate quite the same level of gusto as Leo, but he pushed himself all the same throughout the 30-minute session, sweating more than usual. After the session, he showered, dressed and fixed his usual coffee and wheat toast with jam.

    At 7:30 a.m., Terence climbed into his Tesla X and drove 20 minutes into downtown Chicago to start his day. He worked for Creative PR, Inc., a Fortune 1000 PR agency on Michigan Avenue.

    Terence wouldn't say he hated his job, but he was certainly frustrated. He had graduated from college almost 20 years ago, and this was his third job in the PR industry. He actually enjoyed the work itself. He was the senior account manager for several brands, including Nike, Starbucks and the high-end grocery chain, Publix. He also donated five hours a month pro-bono to his son Joshua's baseball team generating publicity and raising money for their uniforms, travel and other expenses.

Terence's frustration came down to compensation. He was reasonably well paid at $150,000 per year plus the occasional bonus, but he had no equity in the firm, no stock options and no real path to partnership or higher levels of management.

As the time approached 8 a.m., Terence parked his Tesla in his usual contract lot space and walked the 300 yards to his office, picking up a Starbucks Caramel Macchiato en route. He opted for the sugar free vanilla today, that Peloton session still burning his calves.

"May as well spend money with my own client," he muttered under his breath.

Terence walked into his well-appointed office and slumped into his chair. He plugged in his laptop and sighed. *Am I going to be sitting here, doing the same thing 10 years from now?* It wasn't the first time he had wondered this to himself. He still hadn't been promoted at this firm, and he had only left his previous, smaller PR firm because he hit a glass ceiling and realized he wasn't going to be made partner.

This was, however, a big day. Terence and his team had been working for months on a new advertising and PR campaign for Nike's wearables technology division, and today was the day for making the pitch. Nike had launched a new wearable product to compete with the Apple watch, and Creative PR, Inc. had been tasked with launching the product into the market.

As Terence checked his keynote presentation and pitch notes, he could feel the nervous excitement in him building. When the time for the meeting neared, he walked down the hall to the boardroom, where Nike VP of Marketing Glenda Burrows was waiting somewhat impatiently with her team. Terence's deputy on the account, Mike Moore, and his assistant, Sam Smith, were still setting everything up.

Mike was the junior account manager on the Nike account. He had done most of the research, product-market fit and competitor analysis on the new product launch. However, as typically happens in large PR firms, the account manager (Terence) was expected to make the pitch. Terence felt prepared and energized by the workout and the coffee. He was good to go. *You've got this*, he thought to himself.

He began the pitch, went through each point of the launch strategy and felt confident he'd nailed it. When Glenda followed up with questions, Terence handled them like a pro. The meeting ended and Glenda seemed pleased. She clearly loved the PR strategy and launch schedule, and she was thrilled with the customer-group trials, which Mike had managed.

Shortly after the meeting broke up, Terence's wife Julie texted to ask him how the meeting had gone. While he was typing his response to her, Terence noticed that Mike was walking Glenda back to the elevators. He didn't think anything of it at the time, however. He returned to his office and went about the rest of his day.

At 4 p.m., the managing partner of the firm, Rudy Jones, sent Terence a Slack message. "Please come and see me as soon as possible." More intrigued than concerned, Terence put on his jacket, rode the elevator up three floors and announced himself to Rudy's secretary, Janice Keel, in the outer office.

"He's on the phone," she responded, "but he'll be with you in a minute."

When Terence walked into Rudy's office, he could immediately see all was not well.

Not getting up to welcome him, Rudy frowned and said, "Terence, we need to talk about Nike."

Terence's throat tightened.

"Sounds like you guys did a great job on the pitch," Rudy continued.

"Glenda called me earlier to say she's thrilled with the work we've done. However, she did have one request."

At this point Rudy paused, as if choosing his next words carefully.

"She asked me to promote Mike to Senior Account Manager."

Terence couldn't believe what he was hearing, but he tried not to show it.

"Now," Rudy continued, "I know Nike is your largest account, and you've done some great work on it, but let's have Mike step up to the plate on this one. It'll give you more time to focus on Starbucks and Publix, and I hear Universal Studios is shopping for a new PR agency. In fact, I'd like you to get on a plane over to California later this week if you can. Here's the contact details for Derek Kron."

Rudy handed him a piece of paper with handwriting on it.

"He's the VP of marketing there, and he's expecting your call. Go get 'em, tiger."

Terence took the paper, managed to mumble out some generic words of appreciation for the opportunity, and went back to his office, completely deflated over losing top spot on the account.

Nike was *his* account. He had won it, nurtured it and fought really hard for the expansion into the wearables division. Mike was a great team member and must have just caught Glenda at the right time. *But did Mike actually ask to run the account?* Terence wondered. *Could he have tried to claim credit for the work that went into preparing the meeting?* Terence felt he should speak to Mike about it, but he knew that Glenda was stubborn. There was no way he could get the account back now.

To make matters worse, Terence hated the long flight to California, especially given that since COVID, the firm had stopped all first class travel, meaning he had to fly coach. And he was out of air miles after taking the Bermuda trip with his wife for his wedding anniversary earlier in the year.

His day, which had started out so promising, had turned into a disaster.

Terence went home early, threw a softball in the backyard with his son for a while and listened to his daughter play the piano before dinner. He was in a dark mood, and his wife knew it. They put the kids to bed then settled in the den with a glass of Shiraz—a fine import from Argentina. It was his favorite.

"What's up, my love," asked Julie.

Terence initially clammed up. Professional pride. How could he admit to his wife he had been demoted? But at the same time, he loved and trusted his wife. She was his soul mate. Nobody in the world knew him as much as her. So, he unloaded. Full bore.

Julie was shocked at how angry he was over the situation. Her husband was normally such a placid guy. Apart from a drunken spat with a waiter at a restaurant in Bermuda, she had not seen him lose his temper in the 15 years of their union. But there in the den that evening, with a half-full glass of Shiraz sloshing in his hand, Terence was pissed.

"What are you going to do, my love?" She asked the question with compassionate concern.

"I don't know," Terence responded, calming down a little after having let out the pent up anger.

"I'm flying to Los Angeles the day after tomorrow to meet Universal, so let's see how that goes."

"I do have plenty of work to get on with, and Starbucks really likes me. But I'm starting to wonder if I have a future in this firm. I really want to be a partner, but I have no idea what the buy-in will look like, how I would get financing or even if I have a realistic shot. Brian is five years younger than me and was hired a year after me, but he's making partner next month. I just don't think my face fits here anymore, and I'm tired of switching firms . . . working my nuts off and not getting a shot at a partnership."

"Then why don't you start your own PR agency?"

The question hit Terence with surprising simplicity, and in that moment, something switched in his brain that would change his life forever. The words sank in, and Terence knew he could never return to the corporate world.

Julie drained the last of her glass and rose to go up to bed, "Don't be too late, my love."

Terence stayed behind in the den and, over the next half hour, emptied the bottle of wine, lost in his thoughts. Eventually, he dozed off in the chair, where he woke the next morning, having never made it to bed.

He decided to skip the Peloton that morning so he would still have time to eat breakfast with the kids. He didn't let it bother him that he left the house later than usual, and he even offered to drop his son off at the charter school five blocks from the house on the way to work. His son had a baseball game scheduled that day after school, and Terence had missed the last six games because of work. "I'll definitely be there, watching from the stands," Terence assured him as his son was getting out of the car. "I want you to play hard but fair. Go hawks!"

Work was a shit show. Terence had lost all motivation. He pushed paper around his office desk for an hour, attended several boring Zoom meetings, then canceled his regular Wednesday lunch with Mike so he could take a walk instead. He just couldn't face Mike, not today. Terence was still too raw over the demotion, especially when he saw Mike prancing through the office that morning sporting a brand new $10,000 Rolex. *His reward to himself for getting the Nike account promotion*, Terence thought.

Let him celebrate. None of this will matter to me much longer anyway. Terence knew his own days in corporate America were quickly winding down, now that he intended to strike out on his own.

Terence slipped out of the office, walked down Michigan Avenue past the Wrigley building, over the river and into Millennium Park. There, he bought a hot dog from a stand and sat down on the nearest bench.

What he saw made his heart sing. Families playing together, laughing, having fun.

It then suddenly hit him hard. He had sacrificed so much family time to chase his career, yet he had still felt trapped, under-appreciated, stale, unfulfilled and destined to never make partner. He had hardly seen his children for weeks, and seeing these families enjoying a summer day together caused the craving for freedom, for work-life balance, for self-respect and confidence to rise inside him with a force he hadn't felt before.

"I ... am ... *done*," he said aloud to himself. Yes, he was scheduled to make the trip tomorrow to Los Angeles, but that would be his last trip.

He walked slowly back to the office then endured an afternoon of boredom, constantly checking his watch for the time. At exactly 5 p.m. he left the office, drove home and made a point to spend the entire evening with his family.

The following morning, his car service collected him at 5 a.m. for the 40-minute drive to O'Hare. He checked in early for the American Airlines direct flight to Los Angeles, and as he had an AAdvantage Platinum card, he decided to pass the time in the executive lounge. After fixing himself a coffee and grabbing a muffin, he browsed Spotify for a podcast to download and listen to on the four-hour flight.

Terence always enjoyed making deals—winning new accounts then growing them. He was great with numbers and great with people. Starting a business would be a walk in the park for him. He had $100,000 saved up in the rainy day fund, and his wife was 100% supportive of using that money to fund the new venture. He had dreamed about his new start-up overnight.

Searching Spotify, he came across Carl Allen's Creative Dealmaker podcast. *Interesting*, he thought. *I'm creative ... I work in PR, after all .... and I absolutely am a dealmaker*. He browsed the many episodes listed until he came to one titled,

"Why you should never start a business ... Buy one instead and use other people's money to do it."

Is this guy for real? thought Terence. Only Wall Street guys buy businesses. That's not for us mere mortals. And what's this "other people's money" shit? Sounds like a sleazy real estate investing commercial.

But Terence was intrigued. *Could I buy a business?* he asked himself. Just then, the boarding call came over the loudspeaker, so Terence quickly downloaded the episode onto his iPhone and waited to board the plane. Minutes later he was settling into his coach seat near the back while the flight attendants performed the mandatory safety briefing. As the plane began to roll down the tarmac, he put in his ear phones and settled into the flight and the podcast.

The Airbus A320 was soon at its cruising altitude. Terence hated paying the $8 for a cocktail, so he just went with the free coffee, water and cookie. He had been only distractedly listening to the podcast when suddenly Carl said something that hit him like a Mike Tyson punch in the jaw.

"96% of start-ups fail within 10-years."

This statistic both shocked and baffled Terence—until Carl went on to explain why: Start-ups, by definition, start out with no customers, no credit, no cash flow, no credibility, no employees, no vendors, no premises, and no equipment, among other things.

But it was Carl's car analogy that really hammered the point home.
"Do you have a car?" asked Carl.
Sure, I do, thought Terence. Doesn't everyone?

"So," Carl continued, "if you own a car, did you . . .

"A . . . go to eBay and buy all the components (the battery, the windows, the engine, the wheels, the cables and the thousands of other pieces), then find a YouTube video on how to actually put it all together in your garage?

"Or B . . . rock up to a dealership, buy a car someone already built for you, then finance the purchase using other people's money (dealer financing, your bank, etc.)?"

The logic of Carl's words hit Terence hard. *He's exactly right.*

We buy things every day that people build for us, then we finance them. Cars, houses (although some people do build houses from scratch), iPhones, technology. Terence was even leasing his Pcloton. He hadn't built it or even bought it for cash—he had used Peleton's handy $150 per month lease option and gotten the bike for zero dollars down.

"You can do the same thing by buying businesses," Carl assured.

Terence was so jolted by the realization that the tight confines of his coach seat and tray table almost made him spill his coffee.

So, let me get this straight, thought Terence. Instead of starting a PR agency, I can just go buy one—one that already has customers, employees, cash flow, credit, and a solid reputation. And I can just find an owner who wants to sell, negotiate a fair deal then finance the acquisition using other people's money. Just like what I did to own my Tesla, my house, my iPhone and my Peloton.

Terence finished the rest of the podcast, but, sadly, the Wi-Fi wasn't working on the plane (does it ever?), so he took a nap for the rest of the flight, waking up only as the A320 was starting its descent into LAX.

At the baggage claim, he logged onto the free airport Wi-Fi and started downloading all Carl's other episodes, including deal origination, meeting and negotiating sellers, the art of establishing rapport (*Is this business acquisition training or advice on how to get laid?* wondered Terence), deal valuation, deal structures and the closing process.

There's a methodical process behind all this, thought Terence. This guy has figured it out.

In the back seat of the Uber to Universal's HQ in Universal City, San Fernando Valley, Terence started a Google search for Carl Allen. He found the fellow's Youtube, Instagram and website, Dealmaker Wealth Society.

I like that name, thought Terence. I'm a dealmaker too. I like the fact there's wealth involved and that it's a society, a community—a collective of hard-charging dealmakers doing deals.

Carl had the chops. A Wall Street background, retired at 37, went into micro private equity on Main Street deals and had built a coaching empire on the art and science of closing deals.

Terence was engrossed, and in what seemed like minutes, the Uber pulled up at Universal HQ. Terence got out, grabbed his bag and walked into the foyer.

A Buzz Lightyear character asked him if he needed any help.

"I'm here to see Derek Kron."

"Please take a seat, grab a drink and Derek will see you shortly."

The meeting was eventful. Universal was planning on opening a third park in Florida and was also expanding in other countries. The various franchises Universal had invested in were paying off big time. This would be a major account and would even eclipse Nike, but Terence realized his heart just wasn't in it any more. He was consumed with the idea of quitting corporate America and having his own business. He wanted to be an employer, not an employee. Labor day was round the corner. "This is going to be my last Labor day working for someone else," Terence muttered under his breath as he rode the elevator back down to the foyer.

On the Uber ride back to the hotel, he went back to Carl Allen's podcast. "Defining your buy box." *This one sounds fun*, thought Terence. He tapped the screen and quickly became immersed in the topic.

Chapter 2

The Empty Nester

     Jacqueline Turley was a 60-year old baby boomer, one of the 76 million living inside the United States. She was also one of the 12 million who own a small business, 70% of which will transition ownership in the next 20 years—a more than $10 trillion transfer of wealth.

     She woke very early that day. She was fighting a cold. *Probably caught from one of the grandkids*, she thought, germs being rife in kindergarten. Jacqueline had lost her husband of 35 years only 18 months before, and she missed him . . . badly. Yes, they had four amazing children and seven grandchildren, and the family rallied around her all the time. Vacations, Thanksgiving, Christmas—even a weekend trip to Disney World with the grandkids for the upcoming Labor Day weekend.

     Jacqueline shed a tear remembering all the amazing times she had with her dear husband, Bill. Both of them were entrepreneurs, they had shared a great life. Bill had been a real estate developer in Chicago, and when he passed, he had no exit strategy, no one to take over the business. The four children had their own careers and passions. Leo was a dentist in Bethesda, Cameron a football coach at UCLA, Tina a midwife at the Cook County Medical Centre in Chicago and Lola was a JAG in the military, based in Texas. All of them loved their careers, and none had any desire to follow their father into real estate or their mother into PR.

     Jacqueline and the kids had been forced to close her husband's business down. Bill had left no plan. He *was* the business. He had kept all the systems and processes in his head, and he personally owned all his customer relationships. This meant there was no longer any value to Bill's business. It had all been in his head and was completely lost when he passed.

For her part, Jacqueline had grown tired of her PR business. It had been doing well for over a decade, with great customers (not the major brands like the big guys in town but some loyal, happy and growing customers) and a strong cash flow. Jacqueline felt blessed to have a loyal team. But she was also feeling the weight of the years, and she knew in her heart that she couldn't keep the momentum up indefinitely.

Contemplating all this over her morning coffee, she suddenly felt anxious. What's my exit strategy? Who's going to buy my business?

After Bill's death, Jacqueline had made major changes to her company. The pain of erasing Bill's legacy had forced her to hire a general manager, Phillip Fouts, to run the business. Phillip wasn't particularly dynamic, and he certainly wasn't a visionary, but he ran the business competently enough from day to day and was a solid operator.

With Phillip's help, Jacqueline had created an operating manual for the business and developed improved systems, processes and KPIs (key performance indicators). Installing a GM who could operate the business day to day for her allowed her to work *on* the business, strategically, instead of *in* the business, technically. She had begun attending all management meetings and meeting with her key clients once a month for lunch along with her new GM, who had shaken things up quite a bit in the business. Phillip had hired a fractional CFO to oversee the financials, and the business was humming better than ever. The account managers knew exactly what the game plan was, and the fulfillment team was young, sharp, motivated and hungry. Phillip had also convinced Jacqueline to install a profit-share plan which paid employees an average of $2,000 per quarter each in bonuses. Everyone loved the business, loved Phillip and adored Jacqueline.

They even loved the name. JAT PR LLC.

Jacqueline Ann Turley . . . JAT.

Funny, isn't it, she thought.

Many business owners name their business after themselves.

Pete's Plumbing
Barry's Fish Fry

Lucy's Orthodontics

I'm no different, although it's just my initials, laughed Jacqueline. It was the first time she had laughed or even smiled that morning.

Perhaps Phillip would want to buy the business, she mused.

Phillip was young, early thirties. He didn't have much in the way of savings and wasn't really a leader. He was great at the day-to-day, but Jacqueline was still responsible for strategy, vision, culture and making the big moves in the business—the ones that move the needle.

If I do sell the business to him, thought Jacqueline, he will need some help.

Jacqueline picked up her iPhone and tapped out a text to Phillip. Across town, Phillip was already in the office preparing for a pitch that morning with a local, thriving dental practice. They were franchising their operations and needed a solid PR strategy.

"Phillip, good morning. Good luck with the pitch today. I'm taking my granddaughter out this morning, but I will be in by lunchtime. Let's grab lunch offsite at the Grill at noon. There's something I want to discuss with you."

Phillip glanced at the text when it came in and quickly replied. "Roger that. Meet you at the Weber Grill at 1pm. I'm dying for a burger."

It was confirmed. Jacqueline blocked the time off in her diary and texted her assistant, Mary, to make the reservation.

Phillip bounded into the Weber Grill promptly at noon. He had that swagger you get when you've had a big win. The pitch had gone well. He had crushed it and signed up the new client on the spot. Not only was he commissioned on the personal accounts he signed, he also had a profit interest partnership alongside the rest of the employees.

They shook hands at the table and both sat down. After water, menus, and drink and food orders, Jacqueline went straight to the point.

"Phillip, I think the time has come for me to sell the business. You're a great operator, and, naturally, I want to consider you as the buyer. I have no idea what the business is worth, but I'll get with my CPA later today and figure it out. Would you be interested?"

Jacqueline was surprised to see the blood drain from Phillip's face. He started nervously fidgeting in his chair.

"Well, this is definitely out of the blue," Phillip said with some hesitation. "Why are you thinking of selling? Things are going so well, and we're set for a record year. Why on earth would you want to sell?" He was genuinely puzzled.

"This isn't just a whim—it's an idea I've had brewing for a while. I have to be honest, ever since I lost Bill, and his business wasn't sellable, I've wanted to put things in place so my business could work without me. You've done an amazing job, Phillip, running the day-to-day. It seems like it would be a natural transition for you to go ahead and take over, right?"

"I'm flattered you'd think that, and thank you for the vote of confidence in me," Phillip responded. "But I have to be 100% honest with you too: I don't think I'm ready. Maybe in two or three more years. But I'm just now getting a handle on the team and the growth plan. I'm not ready to assume full responsibility for the business and be responsible for everything. And besides, I don't have a lot of money. I'm going great, mind you, but I just have no idea where I could get the capital together to make a deal work for you."

With Jacqueline's proposal seemingly shot down, they continued their lunch, but Phillip (although starving) hardly touched his burger. He played a game of pushing his fries around the plate, but he had clearly lost his appetite.

As they strolled back to the office, Jacqueline promised to speak to her CPA and catch up with Phillip tomorrow for his final decision. But she already knew the obvious: Phillip was not her buyer. Still, he would be an excellent operator to assist the new owner in taking over.

It's a shame, she thought, but she understood. When she started the business 20 years before, she had been filled with the fear and trepidation she now saw in Phillip's face.

He was a solid operator but not an entrepreneur.

Chapter 3

Defining the Buy Box

Terence checked into his hotel downtown, near the USC Campus. He could see the LA Memorial Coliseum. He was barely born in 1984 when Carl Lewis won four gold medals for the United States in that very arena.

He ordered dinner in his room, opened the shiraz from the mini bar and pulled out his laptop to start making notes.

Earlier, Carl had told him on the podcast episode to focus on his "buy box."

The buy box is your unique, dream-deal specification.

During the podcast, there was a phrase Carl must have repeated 100 times.

"Stay in your lane."

What that means is to buy businesses in sectors that you understand, are passionate about, and can have meaningful conversations with business owners, financiers and deal intermediaries (CPAs, attorneys, etc.) about. When you "stay in your lane," you stick to businesses you can actually add value to through your skills, experience and network.

And if you decide to pursue a business where you don't have this stuff, then be sure to partner with someone who does.

Simple.

Bingo, Terence thought. *I love PR. I know PR. I have clients I can onboard for growth. I know people who can come and work for me. I understand the industry, know all the players. That's my sector. I've got this.*

Next, Carl said to buy businesses with between $1 million and $5 million in annual revenue. He explained that buying a business below $1 million in annual revenue is tantamount to buying a job. Terence would be happy to be the owner-operator of the business, but he definitely wanted a management team in place to assist him. Clearly, small businesses below $1 million don't have that—as there just isn't the revenue to support employing those people.

On the other hand, above $5 million in revenue and certainly at anything over $10 million, businesses become more sought after for acquisition, which in turn causes their valuations to inflate and spike higher. Why? The simple economics of supply and demand: If a $50 million business wants to acquire other businesses to grow, why buy a $2 million business when it can buy a $10 million or above business? Doing larger deals is actually faster because the quality of management information available is higher and banks and investors typically prefer larger deals, as there is more redundancy and diversification.

So, the savvy Main Street buyer will look for a business in the $1 million to $5 million range. Potentially a bit higher. Terence felt a PR firm in the $3 million to $5 million range would be ideal for him, as there would be some good-sized clients in there (not Nike and Starbucks, mind you, but some worthwhile clients for sure).

Next, Carl had talked about the differences between being an owner-operator and an owner-investor. Owner-operators run the day-to-day operations. They "drive the bus." Owner-investors don't drive: they're the GPS. They provide leadership, vision, strategy and culture. They also do deals. Mergers, acquisitions, exits (when selling the business) and joint ventures.

Terence was torn. He wanted to operate his own business but was also very attracted to the owner-investor duties of strategy, vision, leadership and culture. *Well*, he thought, *if I found a business with a great operator that isn't the seller, that would be the perfect setup for me because as an owner-investor I can support them and focus on the growth.*

Regarding location, Carl had said that owner-operators need to buy a business where they live or want to live. Owner-investors, on the other hand, don't work in the business day to day, so the deal for them can be anywhere.

Regardless, even if he were to be an owner-investor, Terence preferred a business close to home in Chicago or perhaps elsewhere in Illinois. He might also consider Michigan and Ohio as well.

Finally, Carl had talked about cash flow.

"Cash flow is everything," he said. He quoted someone famous who once said, "revenue is vanity, profit is sanity, cash flow is reality."

Carl recommended buying a business with at least $250,000 in annual cash flow (sometimes called EBITDA or SDE—we'll get to that later) or a minimum 15% profit margin. That amount would give the business some headway and the ability to ride out any storms.

Terence typed his buy-box requirements into his Google sheet.

Business: PR agency but can also include marketing and advertising services

Location: Chicago, wider Illinois, Michigan and Ohio
Size: $3 million to $5 million in revenue
Profit: $450,000 to $750,000 (15% margin)
Role: Owner-investor but need a solid GM in place to drive operations day to day

    Terence closed his laptop and began getting ready for bed. The next question on his mind was where to find such deals. He picked up his phone, opened the podcast app and saw that this very topic was next on Carl's playlist.
    Good, thought Terence. *That's my listening for tomorrow morning.*

Chapter 4

Not All Buyers Are Created Equal

Jacqueline put a call into her CPA, Jeremy Brown, to discuss selling the business. Jeremy was also the fractional CFO of JAT PR LLC.

"Hello, Jeremy, this is Jacqueline. How are you?"

"I'm fine, Jacqueline, thanks for asking. If you're calling to chase up your quarterly financials, they should be with you by the end of this week. I can tell you revenue growth is solid, and your cash flow looks fantastic."

"That's great news, thanks. But, actually, I'm calling on a different matter." Jacqueline paused a moment for effect, then announced, "I'm thinking of selling my business." Before Jeremy could respond, she proceeded to explain. "Honestly, I think it's time for me to retire. I mentioned this to Phillip to see if he'd be interested, but I don't think he's ready. Still, he'd be a great asset to a buyer. Can we meet to discuss what would have to be true for me to be ready to sell?"

Jeremy gulped. He knew this day would come, and the question that immediately came to his mind was whether the new owner would retain him as the CPA and fractional CFO. JAT PR was one of his largest accounts. He would hate to lose the business. *Maybe I can stall her*, he thought.

"Yes," he answered. "This is a complex topic; we should meet and discuss. Are you free at 10 tomorrow morning?"

"I am, thanks." Jacqueline ended the call and texted her assistant with the meeting details. Moments later she heard the reliable ping of her iPhone when the appointment entered her calendar.

All Jacqueline could think about the rest of the day was the "afterlife." Retirement. Freedom. More time with the grandkids. A safe, trusted pair of hands that could continue her legacy through the business. Someone that would embrace Phillip, the team, her amazing customers and the other vendors and partners JAT had.

Jacqueline went for dinner that evening with her oldest friend, Mary Thompson. They had both been on the varsity swim team at college. Mary was the same age as Jacqueline but wasn't an entrepreneur. She had taken many jobs over the years but for the last five had worked at the DMV. The two ladies chuckled over cocktails as Mary recounted an incident from earlier in the day when she had to test a British man who recently moved to Chicago on a green card. He needed an Illinois license but was mystified that even though he had been driving for 35 years, he still needed to take the tests. "But they drive on the wrong side of the road over there, don't they?" laughed Jacqueline.

Mary was in her second marriage, with a younger man who was a firefighter. He loved the work and the service.

Mary wasn't really the type to give advice; however, she told Jacqueline to follow her heart. "That's what has always served you so well," Mary said.

That night Jacqueline slept like a baby, dreaming of retirement. Something was different now. She still adored the business, her team and her clients, but a psychological shift had occurred in just the last 24 hours. She was itching to do this deal and knew in her heart Phillip wasn't her buyer. But she was flooded with questions and with a measure of anxiety. How much was her business worth? Who would buy it, and where would she find them? Would the buyer treat her business with respect? Would Phillip and the team embrace the new owner?

As she drove to see her CPA the next day, she realized this was going to be her most important meeting of the year.

Jeremy was waiting for her in the foyer of his small office. The receptionist fixed Jacqueline an iced latte, and she and Jeremy walked into the conference room together. On the table was a neatly printed set of accounts. As Jacqueline picked them up, she could feel the warmth of the printer still on the paper. The sensation gave her a pleasant feeling that all would work out for her.

Jeremy quickly went through the accounts with Jacqueline. "Your trailing last 12-months financials look fantastic," he reported.

Revenue $3,460,200
SDE (seller's discretionary earnings) $814,500
Net working capital $912,000
Cash on hand $540,000
Non-current liabilities $137,000 (this was a line of credit from the bank Jacqueline had used to upgrade all the technology in the office and the furniture)

Jeremy was nothing short of thrilled.

Jacqueline was dismayed to not see a valuation report.

"Jacqueline, you're on a roll," Jeremy said. "Phillip is doing a great job. I don't think you should sell your business for at least another two years. At this pace, you'll hit $1 million in SDE next year, and that will make the business even more valuable. I don't want you leaving money on the table here."

"Thank you," Jacqueline said politely. "But I'm ready *now*. I know the business is performing well, but I really do think it's time for me to hand the business over. Phillip isn't ready, I can see that in his eyes. But *I'm* ready, and I have questions for you."

She then proceeded to articulate three questions, making clear that she expected Jeremy's best answer to them then and there in the conference room.

"How much is my business worth?"

"Who do you think will buy the business?"

"How can I make sure I find the right buyer who will protect and nurture this wonderful business?"

Cornered, Jeremy no longer attempted to evade her clear intent. "Those are all great questions," he said. "Let me answer them." And at that, he leaned back in his chair and began a lengthy, detailed explanation.

First, business valuation isn't an exact science. It's actually more of an art form.

There are four primary drivers that affect the valuation of a business:

1. First, there is financial valuation. This is my wheelhouse. Businesses are typically worth a multiple of their profits. The SDE number you can see in the accounts. But sometimes buyers look at a profit measure called EBITDA. It's essentially the SDE number less what you as an owner take from the business (salary, bonuses, benefits, etc.). It doesn't include distributions, though, which we know you've enjoyed in the past few years. Most buyers take an average of the last three years and make adjustments for things called "add-backs" and "take-backs," adjusting for working capital and non-current liabilities. That's an easy calculation, but remember, it's only one of the four valuation drivers. Multiples are published online via platforms like Dealstream. You can pick a sector and profit size and see the comparative (range of) multiples similar businesses are selling for; however, these numbers will reflect drivers two through four that I'm going to explain to you now.

2. The second driver is your deal structure. If you find a buyer who is prepared to pay you all (or most) of the cash at closing, then they—or the bank, if the deal is to be financed—are taking all the risk. They will, therefore, want a discount. Conversely, if a buyer wants to place a large part of the deal consideration into seller financing—where the seller receives payments over time—then the valuation increases because you, as the seller, are sharing some of that risk now, and you need to compensate for that through a higher valuation.

3. Third, we need to understand how seller psychology affects valuation. Imagine two identical businesses. They have the same revenues, SDE, balance sheet, customers and employees, and they offer the same product or service. The businesses are identical. The only difference is the owner and, more importantly, the owner's selling psychology. If an owner is happy, not motivated to sell and quite content continuing to own and/or operate the business, then the valuation will be very high. Conversely, if the owner is highly motivated to sell the business, is sick, burned out, tired, distressed, has run out of ideas, has taken the business as far as they can, or a combination of all these, the valuation will be lower, to reflect that higher motivation.

4. Finally, there is the transfer of value. Buyers will typically value a business based on how they can monetize it. We'll talk about the

different types of buyers in a minute, but for now imagine two businesses. One has recurring revenue, low customer concentration, the owner is not the operator, there are systems, processes, KPIs in the business, and it has a solid culture, brand and external reputation with raving-fan customers. That business is worth a premium. We call that "best in class," or BIC, and it commands a best-in-class valuation—a premium over the average market multiple. Everyone will want to buy that business, right? So, simple supply versus demand economics creates a higher valuation through a bidding war. Remember the frenzy when the new Playstation 5 came out? Demand radically outstripped supply, so people were paying double the retail price (and more) to have one. It's the same in a business. Conversely, if the business has high customer concentration, the owner is the operator and works in the business in a highly dependent role, all the customer relationships are personally held, there's no operating manual for the business (all the systems and processes are in the owner's head) and the external brand is relatively weak, with some less-than-happy customers and a poor internal culture, then all this erodes value and in some cases makes the business worth only it's liquidation value (the value of the balance sheet when the business is closed down)."

Wow, thought Jacqueline. Her brain hurt with the sudden influx of information. She knew numbers . . . revenue growth, profit margins, working capital, balance sheet, etc., but she was astounded at just how much other "stuff" goes into valuing a business.

She sat pensively as the information sank in, and neither of them said more for the next few minutes. You could hear the birds chirping in the trees outside over the eerie silence. Finally, Jeremy broke the silence.

"The good news, Jacqueline, is that your business is definitely more "best in class" than liquidation-only value. You have all the right attributes."

Jacqueline nodded and smiled but didn't otherwise respond. Taking this as his cue, Jeremy continued. "Next, let's talk about your dream buyer."

"There are three types of buyer for your business: individuals or teams, trade buyers (competitors), and financial buyers."

Individuals or teams are usually the safest bet, although these buyers typically have lower valuations. Why? Because they're rarely paying cash. Instead, they're working with banks through the SBA (Small Business Administration) 7a loan scheme. The buyer puts down about 10% of the deal, the bank puts in 80% and the seller is left with a 10% seller financing note. These deals take longer to close because you're dealing with Federal Government bureaucracy and banking protocols.

The bank will appraise the value of the business and—like in real estate—will not fund above that appraised value, so often you'll see lower valuations. The benefits of individual buyers, though, is they are a safer pair of hands and will acquire the business 'as-is', then grow it, maintaining the employees, the culture and treating the customers and vendors as they're treated today.

If Phillip *did* buy the business, that would be called an MBO (management buy-out), as he's already working in the business. If an outside person acquires the business, it's called a MBI (management buy-in). Sometimes a buyer will come into the business for a period of time to figure things out (often with a minority investment) then buy it, and that's called a BIMBO (buy-in, management buy-out).

Next, you have trade buyers. These typically pay the highest valuations, but there are some risks involved. First, they tend to be much heavier and longer on due diligence (that's the buyer vetting the business and the deal). Second, they'll operate your business just like their own. They will typically be larger and think they know best. Your culture will change, and not all your employees will survive. Trade buyers will aim to cut costs as quickly as possible to create shareholder value, and they'll cross-sell their existing products and services to your customers and vice versa. Those deal synergies allow trade buyers to pay higher valuations.

Finally, you have financial buyers. Think private equity, family offices, etc. These people are not operators. They'll typically buy a percentage of the business up front (say 40% to 70%) then expect you to stay for a few years as they grow the business with you, typically via additional acquisitions (this is called a "roll-up"), and then you cash out the second part of the deal later at a much higher valuation. Many business owners go down this route if they want to generate some cash now but aren't ready to fully exit."

Jacqueline could feel a migraine coming on. She had taken in so much information in the past ten minutes, and she was now way outside her comfort zone.

"I need a minute, Jeremy," she said. "I need some time to process this."

"No problem," he replied. "Why don't we stop for now and let you digest what we've talked about. We can catch up again later."

Jacqueline agreed, left the meeting and began walking the nearly half mile back to her own office. The sun was shining and the air was a cool breeze. Her head was spinning with all the information that had just been poured into it.

She stepped into a Starbucks, ordered a chai cinnamon latte, sat down in the window seat and pulled out her journal.

On the next available clean page, she wrote out three major points.

"The right buyer is critical. I want a good price for my business, but I want the best buyer—not necessarily the best deal."

"My valuation is very subjective. I may need multiple offers to find the right balance of buyer and deal."

"I have no clear understanding of the process and the timeframe. Will this take a month? A year? Longer? Can Jeremy run this process for me? He seems to know what he's talking about, and there's no way I can go through this on my own."

Jacqueline reread what she had just written, then closed the journal and took another sip of her latte, lost in thought.

Chapter 5

The Buy-Side Process

Terence woke up at 6 a.m. Although his sleep was restful, he didn't really like hotel rooms. As comfortable as the bed was, he missed his wife and his adorable French bulldog, Ralph, who always slept on the bed with them, snored like a trooper and explored every conceivable position in which to nestle up to them.

Once Terence owned a PR business with local clients, he wouldn't have to take business trips like this. He would have sales reps and account managers who would travel to meet out-of-state clients and attend networking events. "I'm not going to be the guy that does that," proclaimed Terence to himself.

He had one more follow-up breakfast meeting with Universal, then he'd be flying back to Chicago. The flight, taking into account the two-hour-forward time difference, would rob six hours total from the clock, but, fortunately, he would be home in time for dinner.

Terence opened the Carl Allen Creative Dealmaker Podcast series again and scrolled through the episodes. Instead of jumping into deal origination (which was currently at the top of his mind), he ended up deciding to check out an earlier episode that focused on what Carl called his "10 step process."

In this episode, Carl talked about deals as being like a recipe. If you want to bake a truly great cake, you need a proven recipe and the best ingredients. Combine these at the right time and you have the perfect cake. Similarly, when all the proven components of a successful business acquisition are carefully taken into account, you can expect amazing results.

ACQUISITIONS

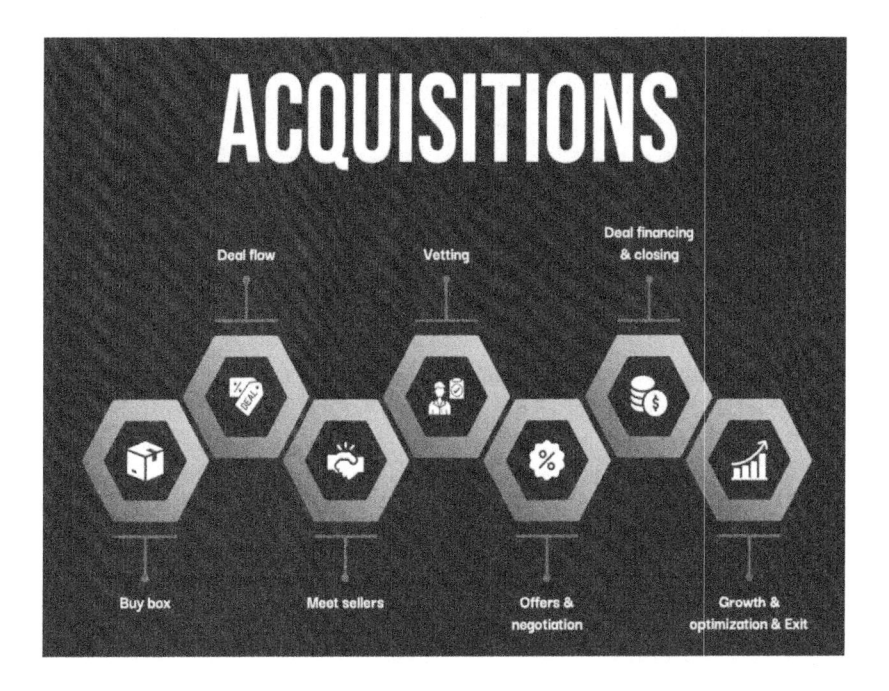

Deal flow | Vetting | Deal financing & closing

Buy box | Meet sellers | Offers & negotiation | Growth & optimization & Exit

As Terence became more and more intrigued in the podcast, Carl detailed the business buying process as follows.

1) *Developing your dealmaker mindset.* This involved, first, believing in yourself, determining your "why"—your passion or purpose—and committing to doing the work. Carl spoke of your "why" as the fuel that would push you forward. "Who are you fighting for?" he asked. Fight for something or someone bigger than yourself. Elaborating, he said that nobody really wants to own or buy a business, per se. Those are just surface features, symptoms of a deeper need. What we truly want are the profound emotional benefits that come from owning a small business. Freedom. Passion. Work-life balance. Cash flow. Wealth creation (even generational wealth in some cases). Insurance. Assurance. Even ego. His words resonated with Terence. Yes, he wanted all those things and more. The second aspect of having a dealmaker mindset, Carl said, was the actual execution. He claimed there are three things you must do consistently to win as a dealmaker: Originate deals, meet sellers and make offers. It was essentially a numbers game. Dealmaking was like going to the gym to build muscle. If you go there three to four times per week, do your reps and sets, and put the proper fuel into your body, then it's biologically impossible not to build muscle. Likewise, if you originate deals every day, meet with sellers and make offers consistently,

you simply cannot fail to eventually successfully buy a business. Terence was pumped at this idea. He just knew he could do it, and he had found a mentor to show him the path.

2) *Defining your buy box.* Terence had already thought this through, but, to summarize Carl's advice: (a) Do deals that are "in your lane." That is, buy businesses you know something about, can add strategic value to and can potentially inject your network into after you've acquired the business. (b) Figure out whether you want to be an owner-manager or owner-investor (which Terence had done . . . Investor for sure). And (c) focus on deals at least $1 million in revenue with healthy margins and great cash flow. No point buying a beat-up business that needs intensive care. Terence imagined walking immediately into cash flow, and his heart beat that much faster.

3) *Deal origination.* Carl mentioned that deal flow primarily comes from four different places. One is on-market (primarily business brokers) and three are off-market (no brokers involved). Carl didn't sound too thrilled with the broker network. They tend to overprice deals and prevent you from building rapport with the seller, he said. But some broker deals could work, he added; you would just need to be really watchful with them. The off-market deal options were direct approach letters, building a relationship network with attorneys, CPAs and wealth managers, and leveraging social media, particularly LinkedIn. *I'm really looking forward to that podcast episode*, thought Terence.

4) *The seller meeting.* Carl talked about the importance of dividing the first seller meeting into four parts. Part one was simply to build rapport with the seller. Forget the business for a few minutes and just concentrate on getting the business owner to know you, like you and trust you. A lot of the businesses Carl owned, he said, had undergone massive growth in the previous few years. He and his business partner Chris were whiz marketers, and they credited much of their growth to understanding how knowing, liking and trusting are critical to business growth. Second, talk about the business and ask the five killer questions. *That will also be a very enjoyable podcast episode*, thought Terence. Third, sign an NDA (non-disclosure agreement). Terence knew all about these. Nike had made him sign one when it showed him the design for the new wearable technology his current company was promoting. Terence knew NDAs were actually not worth the paper they were written on, but he

understood them to be a mandatory legal tool prior to seeing business information. Fourth, get the business data. This should include the last three years of financial accounts and tax returns, interim financials for the current year, the shareholder list and any other key information that would allow you to (a) vet the deal and (b) calculate a valuation and deal structure.

5) *Deal vetting.* Carl discussed here the importance of understanding the income statement, balance sheet, business valuation, financing options and the various methods of structuring a deal. Terence had flunked math in college and hated this part of business. "I'm going to need some help with this," he grunted to himself. His personal CPA (who prepared his taxes) would crush this, though, Terence thought. *Maybe he would consider becoming my fractional CFO?* Terence was on a roll now.

6) *Offers and negotiations.* In this section, Carl mentioned things like a "two offer structure" and an "offer sequence." It all sounded like legitimate mind-control techniques to always stay two or three steps ahead of the seller during the negotiation. *This guy is smart*, thought Terence.

7) *Financing.* Carl explained that some deals need closing payments, whereas others do not, but in a case where a seller wants some (or all) of the cash at the closing table, there are multiple ways of raising that capital: from banks, debt funds, investors, family offices or by leveraging the resources of the business. Terence chuckled. *So, it sounds like you can actually use the business itself to raise the capital that will finance someone buying it.* Terence had some capital, but the sound of using someone else's money to finance the purchase sounded amazing. When a financier (debt or equity) pledged capital to the deal, they would issue you with something called a "term sheet." *Sweet*, thought Terence.

8) *Deal execution.* Carl emphasized that you don't do this yourself. You hire a CPA to vet all the numbers in a process called "due diligence" or DD. He likened it to a real estate deal (Terence had done some of these in his time). In real estate you order a home inspection report. In a business, the CPA verifies the numbers and the attorney checks all the legal aspects of the business to make sure it's safe to buy. Financing is also locked up during this stage as the capital provider moves from term sheet

to actual financing documents and funds get placed in escrow. The attorney handles all that, Carl said.

9) *Closing*. A monumental day, mused Carl. The day you rock up to the seller's attorney's office, sign a bunch of forms, then take over the business. Sometimes, this happens virtually via a tool like DocuSign. You sign the docs, then the funds move from escrow and suddenly you're the new business owner. Terence could taste it. What an amazing day that would be. He was really starting to get excited.

10) *Growth*. Carl said that as the business owner, you can sometimes take some cash out of the business at closing. As the owner you now control the cash flow every month (after debt service), so that money is legitimately yours if you want it. But, he added, the big money is made when you grow the business, amortize the capital you used to buy the business in the first place and then sell the business in the future. That could be one year, five years or even longer. Terence wanted to own his new business for at least ten years and potentially acquire others to make it larger.

Terence was mesmerized by this point. Almost salivating. It all made perfect sense to him. All he needed to do now was to execute each of the different steps, and he was thrilled to know that each section had its own podcast episode.

I'm going to be busy this weekend, he thought. Also, there would be his son's baseball game, his daughter's piano recital and his usual Saturday night date with his wife.

Bring it on, he thought.

Chapter 6

The Sell-Side Process

Jacqueline woke up unusually early for a Saturday morning. It was still dark outside at 5 a.m. She threw on her nightgown, donned her slippers and gingerly walked down the wooden stairs to the breakfast nook to make coffee. "Amazing, these Nespresso machines," she remarked out loud, breaking the early morning silence of the house. This machine was the new version. It knew what type of capsule was inserted by reading the barcode around the rim, so the machine could distinguish an espresso from a long black, for example, and it detected the size of the drink. Jacqueline was a creature of habit, so she predictably put in her long black spiced arabica, poured the almond milk into the frother and hit the button. The noises coming from the machine settled into a perfect hum. *This is a system for making coffee*, she observed. *Now, all I need is a system to sell my business.*

Her CPA had been a solid advisor over the years on bookkeeping, taxes and even the financial optics he looked at daily to get an overview of the business's performance. Now, Jacqueline needed him to walk her through the process of selling the business, since she really didn't have a clue.

She knew from her late husband's real estate business that transactions involved buyers and sellers, financiers and various forms of due diligence and legal contracts. *How much harder can it be to sell a business?* she wondered.

After coffee, a walk around the local park, a hot shower and getting dressed in her power suit (*This is the day to step up my wardrobe*, she thought with a smile), Jacqueline fired up her Apple MacBook and logged into the Zoom account.

Despite it being first thing in the morning, her trusty CPA was already waiting. Jacqueline noticed he looked nervous, however.

I wonder why? Am I really going to have to convince him all over again that I'm serious about doing this?

"Good morning Jacqueline," Jeremy said, interrupting her thoughts and flashing a plastered smile. "How are you?"

"I'm good, thanks. Looking forward to better understanding the process."

"Great, then, let's begin. Last time, I walked you through the three different types of buyers: individual buyers, financial buyers and trade buyers. Regardless of who you want to buy your business (or who actually does), the process is the same."

"First, I will spend some time updating your financials for the year to date, create a full year-end forecast and also a financial projection of revenue and income for next year."

"I'll also compile a data room of all your financial documents, tax returns and the details throughout the balance sheet, namely, an asset list, depreciation schedule and up-to-date statements of accounts receivables, accounts payables and any prepaid and accrued expenses."

"Then we need to decide on a valuation range. Some people selling their businesses list an asking price, while others declare the business "open to offers." I recommend the latter. Since you told me finding the right buyer was equally as important (if not more) than the actual price and terms, I want us to get multiple offers. I'll give you my opinion on what the business is worth so we have that as guidance, and you'll likely want to set a pricing floor."

Seemingly without stopping for breath, Jeremy plowed on. "I'll then create three documents:

1) A "one sheet." This is an anonymous summary of the business, including highlighted financials.
2) A "full confidential information memorandum" (CIM), which is like a prospectus or sales brochure for the business. It charts the history, tells the story of the business, maps out your unique differentiators, your customers, team, systems, processes and KPIs, together with the multiple growth options we've previously spoken about to make buyers excited about the opportunity.
3) And, finally, a non-disclosure agreement (NDA).

We'll circulate the one sheet to interested parties, and for those who want access to the full CIM, they'll sign the NDA, and we'll give them access to it and the data room. Some parts of the data room will be reserved for full due diligence (we'll get to that shortly); however, buyers need a certain amount of information to (a) vet the business, (b) determine if it fits their buy box, and (c) form their opinion on both valuation and likely options for the deal structure.

As part of this step, you'll need to give a management presentation, either over Zoom, or some prospective buyers may want to meet you in person, especially if they're local.

After the first round of presentations, we'll narrow the field down to the best three to six options, then after additional information requests, we'll solicit offers. Once we've ensured we have proof of financing or capital for at least the closing payment, we'll decide on which deal you like the best.

After that, you'll enter into a letter of intent (LOI) with your chosen buyer. That gives the buyer a period of exclusivity, so we aren't allowed to solicit other buyers at that time. This is exactly how it works in a real estate transaction. Like putting a house under contract; it's the same in a business acquisition.

The LOI sets out the primary deal points. We'll agree on what liabilities (if any) you're leaving in the business and the amount of working capital you'll leave behind. You'll also lay down any continued involvement you want after closing and any other major points you want to be part of the main legal contract.

Once we're under contract, the buyer (and his or her financier, if appropriate) will conduct financial, legal and commercial due diligence. Like an inspection report on a property, the buyer wants to make sure the business is exactly how we're presenting it.

At the same time, your attorney and the seller's attorney will negotiate the main deal legals. This is called a "stock purchase agreement" (SPA) if you are selling your stock or an "asset purchase agreement" (APA) if you're selling your assets. Most trade buyers want to only buy assets via an APA; however I would strongly recommend selling your legal entity—your stock. It's more tax efficient for you, and although you'll give disclosures, representations and warranties in the deal, the buyer inherits the business, lock, stock and barrel. Warts and all, as we sometimes say; however, you have an excellent business with no warts that I'm aware of.

Jacqueline had been struggling to keep up for several minutes, but with the mention of "warts" she burst out laughing. Her dear old granny had carried around a giant wart on her nose, and the mental image brought back fond memories of her grandma's antics (she had been quite a character) and of Jacqueline's childhood on the lake.

At this, Jeremy finally paused, appearing perplexed by Jacqueline's sudden fit of laughter.

"It's fine . . . I'm fine," she said, grinning broadly and waving her hand back and forth in the air before her, as if to dismiss the interruption. "I'm sorry; go ahead."

Jeremy looked unsure, but then jumped back into his monologue. "Once due diligence is complete and the legals are ready to sign, the buyer will lock up any financing contracts that are relevant, and then we close the deal. As times have evolved, it's now more common to sign remotely using a tool like Docusign. However, I do like the old-fashioned way of buyer and seller meeting at the seller's attorney's office and hand signing all the documents, then going out together for cocktails to celebrate.

Depending on who the buyer is and the requirement for financing, the entire process takes between two and six months. Sometimes shorter and sometimes longer. It all really depends on who the buyer is and the type of deal structure you agree to.

"So, in short, that's the process. Any questions?"

Jacqueline was feeling overwhelmed with information again, but she had to admit Jeremy's whirlwind tour of selling a business had been enlightening. "Not right now," she said, "but this was very usefuL. I'll give my attorney, Herb Sanders, a call later today and put him on standby."

"Also, I want to chat with Phillip this afternoon and explain my decision to him. Then, we can get the ball rolling. Just let me know what you'll need from me to kick this off."

Jacqueline and Jeremy closed down the Zoom. With her head still spinning from all the new information, Jacqueline gathered her purse, keys and cell phone and climbed into her car to drive downtown to the office.

Chapter 7

Broker Sites

Terence was thoroughly enjoying the process so far, but he knew it was still in the very early days. He took comfort knowing this would be very similar to his selling role at the PR agency. Scout potential opportunities, vet and qualify them and bring some of them to fruition.

Terence was really dialed in on his mindset, although he knew there would be periods in the coming months where his dedication and commitment to the process would be tested. Carl's words on a podcast episode last night were still echoing in his ears. "This isn't hard," proclaimed Carl. "It just takes hard work."

Terence now had his "what," "why" and "how."

- *What?* The buy box. Buy a PR agency to maybe include marketing and advertising services, in Chicago or within a few hundred miles, with $3 million to $5 million in revenue and minimum 15% margins. Terence absolutely wanted to be an owner-investor and inherit a solid team.
- *Why?* Because he was tired of corporate America. He wanted more freedom, more control and a better work-life balance. He didn't want to just be the sales guy any more. He wanted predictable cash flow that would only go up in the years to come, and he wanted to build a business and asset that would provide significant wealth generation within five years.
- *How?* Carl's podcast was teaching him the "system," a step-by-step process he could follow. Carl also had a mentorship option that Terence was interested in joining to really make this a no-brainer venture. "The

system is simple and effective," muttered Terence under his breath. Originate deals, meet sellers, make offers.

Terence hadn't gotten to the section yet that covered the seller meeting. His immediate focus was to start originating deals related to his buy box.

He was a shortcut guy. One of the foundations for his success was his ability to quickly figure out the fastest, most efficient way to do anything. For him, that meant involving business brokers. Carl talked a lot as to why he didn't particularly like most brokers. They overvalue deals, stop you from building one-to-one rapport with the seller and can (sometimes) just be a pain in the butt. Carl preferred off-market deal origination; it seemed like he would say this every 30 seconds on his podcast. *I'll leave that for later*, thought Terence. *I'd first like to hit all the broker sites quickly and see what's out there.*

Carl had mentioned that businesses were typically valued on a multiple of profit and that for smaller deals (which is where Terence was focused) the multiples would range from 2X to 4X the profit. Some industries (like technology, SAAS and healthcare) could demand even higher multiples; however, since Terence was laser-focused on professional services, he would only entertain deals in the 2X to 4X range.

Terence Googled "PR businesses for sale in Chicago" and received tens of thousands of hits.

He then clicked the top related search and found one of the major MLS sites for business brokers. He clicked the link to www.sellingmybusiness.com and found a search box for industry and location.

"This is so cool!" Terence blurted out. It was early Saturday morning in the Turner household. Terence's wife, Julie, was up and had at that moment just sleepily walked into Terence's ground floor study with a fresh cup of coffee. "What's cool, hun?" Julie almost yawned the words. Terence was dialed in and just grunted in response. Julie half smiled at his enthusiasm, knowing he had kept her up most of the night with the bright glare from his cellphone, lying right beside her. Now he was absorbed in some podcast, frantically using his iPad to take notes and run Google searches. Julie knew he was starting his process of buying a business. *Better get myself an eye mask*, she thought as she went back upstairs to get the children up. Both had activities this morning.

Terence selected "professional services" as the business category and "Illinois" as the search State but also selected "within 100 miles." *Let's stay narrow for the first run*, he thought.

The laptop completed its search and 116 results showed up. *Wow*, thought Terence. *Why are there so many businesses for sale?* he wondered, almost syncing the words to the music playing from his boombox on the opposite side of the study.

He started scrolling through the search results. One of the "cool" features of this website is that it lists both the asking price ... and ... something called the "SDE." Carl hadn't mentioned that term yet (however, Terence remembered the business financials and valuation chapter was next up on his list to listen to).

He opened another tab and Googled "SDE." The trusty "Investingpedia" website gave him a simple definition:

SDE means seller's discretionary earnings. It's the amount of cash flow the business generates annually before the owner makes decisions about what to do with it. Salary, bonuses, distributions, personal expenses, benefits, etc.

Sounds like profit, Terence surmised.

What initially surprised him was the multiples. Although these were not listed, Terence was good enough at arithmetic to do the mental math of dividing the asking price by the SDE number to calculate the approximate multiple.

Deal 1 had a $3M asking price and $600k in SDE. That's a 5X multiple. Too high. The next page was similar.

Deal 9 had a $1.5M asking price and $150k SDE. 10X! *Are these guys for real?* he thought. Whatever happened to Carl's 2X to 4X range? Terence really liked other features of the deal, though. It was in Chicago and focused purely on PR. Management team in place. Retiring owner. *Worth a punt,* thought Terence.

Deal 23 was more sensible. $2.4M asking price and $800k SDE. Bingo, a 3X multiple. "Right down the fairway!" exclaimed Terence, who then suddenly found himself thinking about the last time he'd actually had time to play golf. It had been almost a year ago, and he had gotten crushed by his buddies, both of whom owned a business and always seemed to find time for golf. Terence smiled as he dreamed of frequenting the country club two or three times a week while his management team ran the business for him.

Julie was calling Terence to go clean up and get ready to take the children to their respective Saturday morning activities. Terence was Baseball dad, and his son was set to play in 45 minutes. Terence quickly clicked the "send me more information" button on deals 9 and 23, filled in his email address and phone number, and saved the search, vowing to return later to scout out some other deals.

He literally bounded up the stairs, two steps at a time, and skipped into the bathroom to shower. *This is going to be fun,* he thought as he undressed, turned the shower to medium-hot then brushed his teeth as the steam built up in the bathroom.

Just before jumping in the shower, he used his index finger to write "Dealmaker" on the bathroom mirror, with a big smiley face underneath. He could just make out his goofy grin through the foggy reflection.

Chapter 8

Pushing the SELL Button

Jacqueline arrived at the office a little later than normal, in light of her earlier Zoom with the CPA and given that it was the weekend. Phillip, it seemed, had arrived before her and was awaiting her arrival. Before her MacBook had even had time to boot up, he walked in her office and shut the door behind him. He looked pained. Almost frazzled. He hadn't shaved, and his eyes were puffy. Phillip wasn't the crying type, so Jacqueline knew it wasn't tears. He just looked dead tired.

"What's up Phillip—you okay?" Jacqueline queried in her usual cheery voice.

"I'm fine, thanks for asking, but I didn't sleep a wink last night. I'm just worried about my future here. I know you want to retire and sell the business, and I absolutely know I'm not ready to take full ownership, but I'm just very conscious of a new owner coming in, and I'm wondering what my role will be."

Jacqueline didn't answer immediately, but motioned for Phillip to take a seat while she herself sat down at her desk. "It's good we're having this conversation, Phillip. I spoke to Jeremy last night and again literally this morning, if you can believe it. He walked me through the entire process and explained to me the principles of valuation and, importantly, that I actually get to decide who to sell the business to."

"Okay, so please explain that to me," said Phillip.

"Sure, I'll try." Jacqueline immediately began reviewing the rather jumbled mental notes she'd been storing in her head since last night. It felt almost like sitting for an end-of-semester exam that one isn't quite ready for. But then Jeremy's words began to come back to her.

"Jeremy said there are usually three types of buyers. One is an individual or team of individuals. They offer a 'safer pair of hands.' Then, there are financial buyers who tend to be used when a seller wants to exit in stages but stay on working for a period of time. Third, there are trade buyers, who're usually competitors or other businesses looking to enter a new market or location."

"I'm potentially open to all of the above at this stage," she said. "However, my gut is telling me right now that an individual or team would probably be the best bet; I'm just not sure that would be the best deal structure, though. Until I receive offers, I won't know."

"I'm expecting Jeremy to have a target range of valuations over to me sometime next week."

Phillip didn't look much relieved by Jacqueline's short "buyer's" lesson. "Well, I really want to stay with the business," he said. His next words sounded as if he'd been rehearsing them. "And I just want you to know I fully support your decision and will give whoever the buyer is my full support both during the transition and after closing, if I'm still needed."

"Phillip, let me assure you right now that you're critical to the recent success of this business, and any buyer would be a fool not to see that and to not have you continue in your role. But as I said, it's early days, so let's just see how this plays out. And I promise I'll protect you through this process to the best of my ability."

Phillip's expression now changed dramatically. It was like a weight had been lifted from his shoulders. He bounded out of the office and back to his own.

Later in the day, Jacqueline called her attorney, Herb Sanders, to put him on notice. Herb was running between meetings but promised to call back first thing tomorrow morning to take instructions.

Jacqueline also took a few minutes to sit down with her financial controller, Lucy Vaughn. Lucy was a stalwart, a solid employee who kept her fingers on every dime that went through the business.

Lucy was less than optimistic about the news of the intended sale. To convey her concern, she told Jacqueline a story of her college roommate who had been let go from a similar-sized business immediately after its acquisition by a larger competitor that had its own central finance function.

Jacqueline smiled. "Well, trade buyers are my least favorite option. My CPA walked me through the different buyer types earlier, and I really like the idea of passing the baton onto an individual or group of buyers. But you never know, we may find a friendly trade buyer who doesn't want to shake the tree too hard."

"I'm really going to need you and Phillip on this transaction", Jacqueline added. "The buyer will be doing due diligence and will need a lot of financial information from us. I'm going to position you both as mission critical to the success of this business—because you are."

"Why doesn't Phillip want to buy it?" asked Lucy.

"Because he's not ready."

"Well, I do love this business, Jacqueline, and I just want it to fall into the best, safest pair of hands."

Strange, thought Jacqueline. *That's something Jeremy said earlier too.* It appeared that Lucy was going to be a strong sounding board and advocate for the deal.

As soon as Jacqueline left her office, Lucy placed a call to Jeremy's CPA firm and spent the next 30 minutes making a list of the documents she would need to upload to the new data room Jeremy was setting up. *I hope Jacqueline knows what she's doing*, thought Lucy. She also made a note in her daily planner to start calling recruiters. *I want a backup plan in case I don't survive the deal*, she thought.

Chapter 9

Bottom of the Fifth

Youth baseball games are typically only six innings—shorter than the nine innings in the pro leagues.

Joshua was on his game today. A solid baseman with a wicked swing, his team was up 11-3, and the game was almost over.

As Terence sipped a now-cold Starbucks in the stands, his phone buzzed in his pocket.

"Hello, is this Terence Turner?" a gruff, north-eastern voice barked into Terence's ear.

"Yes," replied Terence cautiously. "Who is this?"

"Bill Frisk from Central Park Brokers. You enquired about one of our listings, a PR firm in Chicago." This had been deal #9 on Terence's list.

"Ah, yes," Terence pivoted, realizing what the call was about. "I'm a corporate PR executive in one of the big firms downtown, and I want to own my own business."

"Hope you have plenty of cash available," laughed Bill. He laughed like one of those evil cartoon characters his son Joshua watched. "This listing is red hot—my email's blowing up with inquiries."

"Okay, perhaps I should leave it be then," Terence said. "I don't have my financing strategy figured out yet. I only started looking for deals this morning."

"Look, pal, let's not waste each other's time." (Terence hated being called "pal," especially from someone he didn't know.) "Let me send you an NDA, and before I send you all the information about the business, I'll need proof of funds for the asking price of $1.5 million. Oh, and I'll also need your blood type and a DNA sample."

It took a moment for Terence to realize that Bill was joking about the last two requests.

A little flustered, Terence agreed. Bill said he should expect the NDA later that afternoon. *Strange that these guys work on a Saturday*, Terence thought.

As he collected his son, Terence gave him a high-five for (again) being awarded Player of the Match. That was four MVPs in a row. "Certainly qualifies for a Pizza Hut lunch," Terence announced to Joshua.

Terence placed the order on his app, buying enough to feed four, as he always liked to get extra for Julie and his daughter, Lily, who would need extra brain calories after her two-hour piano lesson that morning. Father and son climbed into the car and began the two-mile drive to Pizza Hut. As he drove, Terence's mind drifted back to the broker conversation.

How can I provide proof of funds? he thought. He and Julie had agreed to use $100,000 of their savings on the purchase, but that would leave him $1.4 million short, with zero clue who would give him that money. Terence's earlier high over the fun of the process was quickly dissipating. *There's just so much I don't know.* He also quickly realized a podcast alone wasn't going to give him all the answers. He needed expert coaching. He needed someone in his corner who knew how to do this.

The family of four destroyed the two delicious pizzas in the breakfast nook. Julie was a vegetarian, and she and Lily shared the veggie supreme. Terence and Josh were carnivores and annihilated the double pepperoni with BBQ sauce. Josh ate most of it. Terence only managed two slices. His mind was preoccupied with deals.

Joshua went out on his bike around the leafy neighborhood and promised to be back for dinner around six. Julie and Lily left to go shopping for new dresses for a family wedding coming up in a few weeks. The second Julie reversed the car out of the driveway, Terence bolted for his office and turned on his boombox and computer. Foo Fighters' "Everlong" filled the entire ground floor of the large detached house. He was home alone, so why not? *The neighbors are practically deaf anyway*, he thought.

He googled "Carl Allen" and found Carl's YouTube channel, Instagram account (*Wow! 200,000 followers . . .*) and saw a link to book a strategy call with "one of Carl's coaches." Terence scheduled a call for later that afternoon with Tracey Topping. She had just one 30-minute slot still available, and Terence figured out quickly she was on the West Coast. *May as well strike while the iron is hot,* he thought.

As soon as the calendar invite and Zoom link popped into his calendar online, Terence's email pinged. Bob had emailed him an NDA, a detailed buyer

51

profile sheet and a 14-page personal asset and liability template. *Jeez*, thought Terence, *these guys are ruthless.*

He replied to say he had received the information and would get back to Bill early next week.

Bill replied almost immediately. "This is a hot listing, pal. You snooze, you lose."

Terence opened the rest of the listings and continued to plow through them. Within a couple of hours, he had extended his search and had selected almost 20 listings for additional information.

Once he was done, he started prepping for his call with Tracey, from Carl's team.

The top three questions he planned to ask were,

- "How do I provide proof of funds to brokers?"
- "What other methods are there for originating deals that don't involve brokers?"
- "What's the price and terms of working with Carl?"

Terence logged into the Zoom link Tracey had provided. Tracey was a middle-aged marketer and mindset coach who also worked for Carl as an enrollment coach. She was also doing deals herself in the commercial cleaning industry with other dealmakers in Carl's program, Dealmaker Protégé. In addition, she was part of Carl's Upper Echelon Mastermind—his top 1% of dealmakers. The best of the best.

A cancer survivor, Tracey's life skills and pure grit just beamed through the computer. Terence immediately liked her.

She gave a really cool answer to the broker question.

"Terence, buying business deals is like buying real estate deals. You can fund most if not all of the purchase using bank finance, investors and other creative financing strategies that Carl will teach you. Once you have the business information and you've initially vetted the deal, Carl will show you how to value the business and structure the deal. If it requires financing, he'll point you in the right direction. There are equity investors and debt financiers within Protégé, and we review student deals as a group every Thursday."

Tracey then walked Terence through the three, primary off-market deal origination methods.

First, she explained what she called the "direct approach": "With this method, you generate a list of businesses you like in a particular industry and geographic region, then use a special letter template Carl has created and tested to approach them. You'll research each business (or have a virtual assistant do it for you) to find unique differentiators for each business, then find the seller on Facebook and LinkedIn and interject something about them that relates to you—sports team, vacations, cuisine, family, pets, anything that will build rapport." Terence thought that was super cool even if a little creepy, but Tracey said other Protégé students were getting great results with this approach. She also mentioned a cool new AI service that was being used by Protégé students. He wrote down the name and promised to check it out.

Then there was "leveraging social media": Tracey asked Terence if he knew how to use LinkedIn and other social platforms to generate deal flow—without alerting his employers to what he was doing (buying a business). Terence admitted he had no clue, and Tracey assured him this was something his coach would show him how to do. She then suggested Terence check his employment contract to ensure he'd have no non-compete provisions if he were to leave to run his own show. Terence had, in fact, already checked on this earlier that day with his buddy Lawrence, who was an employment attorney. Lawrence's son played for the opposing baseball team, so Lawrence wasn't in the best of moods when Terence asked for this favor, but Lawrence had agreed to quickly read the contract through and had given Terence the all clear. *Great to know Tracey's on the ball to think of that*, Terence thought.

The third method Tracey mentioned was to create a network of what she called "deal intermediaries": CPAs, wealth managers and attorneys who were local to the area where Terence would look for deals. Having such a network, she said, is "the holy-grail of deal flow." Terence loved networking and knew a lot of business professionals. This would be his go-to strategy, he thought, although the other methods also seemed very powerful.

Once Tracey had finished, Terance asked her about the terms of joining Protégé. The price she quoted struck him as very reasonable. It was a 12-month contract commitment, and there would be four 90-minute coaching sessions per week, together with a vast library of training, tools and other resources. *An absolute no brainer*, thought Terence. He opted for the monthly plan, which although more expensive, meant he could start immediately. Tracey ran his credit card for the deposit and within 60 seconds, all his login information was available. He would start his live coaching on Monday along with the other Protégés in the program.

Tracey welcomed him to the program and ended the call. Terence's acquisition budget had taken a small hit, but he was now professionally in the game. Carl and his coaches would hold his hand, watch his back and work with him to close deals.

Moments after he closed his computer, his family walked in through the front door loaded down with shopping bags. "Productive trip?" he quipped with a smile. Once everyone had unloaded their treasures and begun settling in for the evening, went into the kitchen to help prepare dinner. Tonight was movie night, and it was Lily's turn to choose. *Hope it's not some soppy rom-com,* he thought.

Chapter 10

The Annuity Deal

Jacqueline had the most enjoyable weekend she'd had in a long time. Most of it she spent with her family and friends, but she also went on a date. Well, it wasn't quite a "date," it was more just dinner with a mutual friend who had recently gotten divorced. Jack Beech owned a commercial HVAC business and was your classic owner-investor. He also chaired the local chamber of commerce chapter that Jacqueline had been a member of for the last five years. Jack had always had a "thing" for Jacqueline, and he was fairly easy on the eye, so Jacqueline wasn't entirely surprised when he called to invite her out for dinner.

The conversation at the restaurant marched in rapid succession through children, grandchildren, the chamber of commerce agenda for the year and the complete absence of dating for both of them.

Jacqueline asked Jack outright whether he'd ever considered selling his business. "Never," he quickly responded. He was lucky. His two sons, Max Beech and Paddy Beech, ran the day-to-day. Max was the sales guy and "could sell snow to the eskimos," Jack proudly declared. Paddy was the ops guy and had the logistical talent of an Army general who directed his plumbing and electrical troops with maximum efficiency. As a result, Beech HVAC Inc. was a thriving business. Almost $20 million in revenues and $3 million in profit.

"I always wanted to hand the business down to my boys like my father did with me 25 years ago," Jack said over the meal's main course. "They're the third generation. Both own 40% of the business today, and I kept the other 20%, so I don't work in the business anymore. I just go in one or two mornings a week for a few hours to help them out, but the boys are doing great pretty much without me, and I just really love seeing them both thrive."

"How did they fund the purchase of the 80%?" asked Jacqueline. "I mean, only if you don't mind me asking," Jacqueline hurriedly added. "I ask only because I'm about to put my business up for sale, so I'm collating all the information and advice I can get."

"Ah-ha!" exclaimed Jack with a big smile. "So that's why you agreed to dinner. It wasn't my charming wit and good looks; it was for my business advice." Jacqueline blushed and took a big gulp of the wonderful Barolo in front of her.

"Don't worry," Jack assured. "Let's make a deal: I'll walk you through our process, then you agree to have dinner again with me next weekend, but this time it'll be a proper date. What do you say?"

Jacqueline was really blushing now. She hadn't even looked at another man since her dear Bill's passing, but she would be lying if she said she didn't enjoy the attention and flirting.

"Okay. Deal."

Jack flashed a satisfied smile, then made good on his part of the deal by recounting to Jacqueline how his sons' majority acquisition of the business had come about.

"I remember sitting down with the boys on our fishing trip to Alaska last summer. They said I looked tired and asked whether they could both step up and run things on a day-to-day basis. It was an idea I had already entertained in my own mind, so it didn't take much convincing for me to agree.

"They were ready and capable of operating the whole thing themselves, but they wanted to retain me as a minority partner so I could still stay connected to the business and our customers.

"So, after returning home, we called in our CPA, who worked up a comprehensive valuation of the business. There were actually three ranges, depending on who the buyer would be:

"The first was a leveraged buyout, which meant my sons acquiring the business. That valuation was $14.3 million to $16.7 million.

"Then there was a financial buyer, which meant a private equity fund or a family office. That would be $16.3 million to $19.2 million. This option was a non-starter for me, as the buyer would have complete control, and it wouldn't have allowed the boys to have any meaningful ownership.

"Lastly, a trade buyer. That would be $18.3 million to $21.5 million. But clearly a trade buyer would've looked for all sorts of ways to cut costs to justify the higher valuation. Maybe the boys would've survived the deal, but maybe not—not to mention the employees.

So, we settled on a leveraged buyout. At first I agreed to a discounted deal for the boys at a $12 million valuation. That was a 4X multiple—a tad low for my size of profit, but the valuation wasn't the issue. The real issue was there wasn't a bank that would fund the deal without a minimum $3 million equity check. I could've just lent the boys the money, but in their minds that was too big of an ask. Also, I would've lost almost half of the money in taxes.

So, I agreed instead to a seller financing deal with a higher valuation at $15 million for the whole business, reduced to $12 million to reflect the 80% buy-out and paid over 10 years. That means they pay me $1.2 million per year. At the end of every month, they wire me $100,000. It's more money than I would ever need, and we solved the problem of the banks wanting their blood samples to even look at the deal.

"The process was also very fast—like two weeks, tops. We hired an independent CPA to verify the books for them, and our own attorney drafted the stock purchase agreement. I didn't have to go through the arduous process a bank will require to vet the business like a forensic pathologist."

Wow, thought Jacqueline. She knew people did that sort of thing in real estate (it's how her late dear husband Bill made his money), but she had no idea you could do this in business.

Sensing her surprise, Jack added, "Actually, creative financing in business acquisitions is more common than you'd think. We just rarely talk about it as sellers. I know of at least four others from the chamber of commerce who've done similar deals. Sometimes they take a small closing payment to have some fun, but the majority of the deal is paid over time."

"How do you protect yourself in all this?" asked Jacqueline.

"Well, I trust my boys, as you can imagine, but my attorney did subject them to the same conditions as any other buyer. I have a lien over the assets and stock in the business, and they also signed up to a performance guarantee, so I get to see weekly financial reports and can see revenues, margins and cash flow. I also still have access to the bank account. If the numbers dip consistently below those marks, I get to take the business back and keep all the cash they've already paid me. Now, please understand, I'd never actually do that. I love those guys, but I wanted them to stay focused on maintaining my legacy and keeping the business strong and healthy. I also get the business back if they miss a payment by more than 14 days, which has never happened. They always pay me 'on the nose."

Jacqueline's head was spinning with all this new information. They wrapped up dinner, Jack paid the check (Jacqueline didn't mind as he was making $100,000 per month after all!), and the two of them made plans for dinner next Saturday at the new local Thai restaurant that was receiving rave reviews.

On her return drive home, Jacqueline went over again the highlights of the evening's conversation. She was more hopeful than ever about the feasibility of selling her business, and now she had something else to look forward to as well: her next (or first?) date with Jack.

Chapter 11

Welcome to Protégé

Terence woke up early on Monday and hit the Peloton. Before showering at 7 a.m., he checked messages (for the first time since Saturday night) and his phone blew up. He was inundated with requests for NDAs, buy-box profiles, asset and liability statements—even a resume request from one broker upstate. "Resume? I'm not applying for a damned job," he grunted aloud. "Why are these guys so prickly?"

One broker from a reputable franchise did, however, sound quite pleasant and considerate in the message he left. *Well*, Terence thought, *maybe they're not all bad.*

Terence had spent part of Sunday onboarding and orienting himself to the Dealmaker Protégé program. He had at that point abandoned the podcast episodes. The community portal had tons of training videos, models, tools and other endless resources—more than enough to keep him occupied throughout the journey ahead.

He also reviewed the calls for this week inside the community.

Monday: Carl was leading a strategy session on off-market deal origination with deal intermediaries, and some of them Carl knew well would be joining the call. *This is perfect timing*, thought Terence. *That's my number one task this week.* Terence looked at the accountability chart, where he was bottom of the list at 0%. In contrast, Dan, Isaac, Clive, Mona, Brittany, Jim and David were all 80% or higher. *Some of these people are killing it*, he thought. *I love the competitive edge here.* The quarter sprint was about to end, so Terence decided to push hard next week when the new quarter started. He also saw the names of Protégés who were closing multiple deals and were showcased on the website holding their deal tombstones. Terence laughed. *That's what they do on Wall Street. Nice touch.*

Tuesday: Advanced track. Roll-ups and big-boy pants deals. *Clearly not ready for that yet*, Terence thought.

Thursday: Red light, green light deal reviews. Carl and his coaches would review anonymous student deals. They'd look at the numbers, valuation and growth options and vet the deal completely, either recommending the student drop it like third-period French (a red light deal) or giving it a pass for closing with a complete playbook on how to get it done (a green light deal). *This stuff is freaking awesome*, thought Terence.

He decided to aim to get at least one deal opportunity this week so he could submit it for vetting.

Friday: Q&A. Office hours with Carl. This was where Protégés could ask Carl any and all questions, even rookie questions. Terence realized he was truly a rookie, but he also knew he had lots of skills and life experiences he could use.

It was going to be a great first week in the program.

He decided to sit on all the broker emails until just before lunch. He planned to work from home this morning, attend the Protégé call at 10 a.m. Central time, then deal with all the brokers before going downtown to an account review lunch with Starbucks to be held in his office. The guys were flying in overnight from Seattle. *I don't envy that redeye*, he thought with a smile.

At precisely 10 a.m. Terence logged into the Zoom. Within a few minutes there were another 200 or so hungry dealmakers on the call. Carl was in his Florida house. (From what Terence could gather, he's co-located between the UK countryside and the Florida space coast.) Carl began the meeting by quickly going around the Zoom "room" saying hello to each of the attendees who had their cameras on.

When he came to Terence, surprisingly Carl somehow knew Terence was from Chicago. *Maybe Tracey told him,* Terence speculated. Carl went on to mention that he had studied at the University of Chicago Booth School of Business back in the day when it was just the GSB (Graduate School of Business). He had lived in a "badass apartment" at the corner of Lasalle and Kinsey near the Merchandise Mart, right on the river. Terence knew the exact building: It was 200 meters away from his corporate office just across the river.

Ten minutes later Carl had welcomed and briefly chatted with everyone He then launched into a few ongoing deal stories that Terence found fascinating. *What I love about this guy*, thought Terence, *is that he's not just coaching; he's actually doing deals every single day.* Carl was acquiring at least one business a month—and not just small fry. Some were cranking out $2 million and more in profit. He was buying a CPA firm, ecommerce businesses, online coaching businesses and engineering deals. He owned a private equity firm called KOD and was also investing in student deals. *What an interesting fellow*, Terence thought.

Next, Carl went into deal origination strategies for generating off-market deal flow. Terence found the direct approach and social media strategies very interesting, but the "build a deal intermediary network" part of the training was really powerful. Carl also called on several of the more senior and tenured Protégés present to share their own experiences.

It sounded like wealth managers and CPAs were the best people to network with since both groups would have serious vested interest in the successful outcome of a transaction. The CPA would get fees for handling due diligence, and the wealth manager working for the seller would potentially have funds to invest in the markets and make commissions. *This is genius*, Terence thought.

The call ended, and Terence drove downtown to his lunch meeting with Starbucks. Jane Packer, the SVP of corporate marketing and branding for Starbucks, was extremely picky during the meeting. She didn't like any of the marketing promos presented to her, and the PR strategy about the new fall drinks menu went down like a fart in an elevator.

All this just made Terence want to go even faster with the business acquisition project. He was only a few days in and had already (1) nailed his mindset and created at least ten hours a week of surplus time to attack the work, (2) defined his buy box, and (3) decided he would supplement his consideration of broker deals by leveraging his network to find wealth managers, CPAs and even attorneys to connect with about deals.

He would stay off LinkedIn for now. More than 50 of his corporate colleagues were connected to him there, and he would need a VA to handle the direct approaches. He would message Tracey about that. She did say she would help.

He went through the motions the rest of the day. As he walked out of the office, his lawyer friend Lawrence from Saturday literally bumped into him in the foyer. They again traded opinions about the little league game, then decided to sneak into the local Irish pub down the street for a drink before they would each hit the road out to the suburbs. Lawrence lived about five minutes farther north in a gated community. He was a partner in a local firm and made $500,000 per year. *Nice bank*, thought Terence wistfully.

The Irish pub where they sat at the bar was one of the only pubs in Chicago that served real Irish Guinness. Most Guiness is brewed inside the United States, so it has a weird, tangy and bitter taste to it because the water is different to what is used at the original brewery in Dublin. But some U.S. pubs actually bring it over in a carefully controlled way so it tastes just like it does at the Temple Bar, Dublin's crazily busy downtown drinking mecca.

As the two professional friends sipped on their smooth, silky-velvet pints, Terence told Lawrence his plans.

"I'm looking to leave the corporate rat race. I know I'm not going to evolve in the corporate world, and I want to venture out on my own. But I want to buy an existing, small firm here in the city rather than start a business from scratch." Terence went on to share Carl's "buy a car; don't build a car" analogy.

"That's smart," said Lawrence. He was a practicing employment lawyer, but he knew something about mergers and acquisitions from his time at law school.

"Where will you find the deals to vet?" asked Lawrence.

"I'm going to play with some business brokers and also build out a deal intermediary network of local business attorneys, CPA firms and wealth managers in town. My mentor tells me that apparently most business owners talk to these people first before they ever go to a business broker to list their business for sale."

"Well, I can definitely help you with that. I can connect you to my own wealth manager. Also, my partner, Brittany, runs the business law practice at our firm, and she knows all the CPAs in town, especially the ones who have lots of business clients. Let me get home, eat dinner and help Janet put the kids to bed, then I will fire off a bunch of email introductions. I can also share contact phone numbers with you as well."

"I really appreciate that," Terence said. "Let me get the beers, and if I close a deal from one of your networks, I'm putting $500 behind the bar here and we can meet every week until it runs out!"

The friends laughed and said goodbye, then each sped off north to the suburbs.

Chapter 12

Jacqueline Calls the Brokers

After spending a fun Sunday with the grandchildren, Jacqueline called Jeremy (her CPA) first thing Monday morning and walked him through the deal structure Jack had described with his HVAC business.

"Yes, that's called an annuity deal," Jeremy explained. "It's essentially a long, seller-financing deal with recapture provisions upon default. If you know, like and trust the buyer, this can be a way to get more money, pay less tax and complete the process end to end very quickly."

Jacqueline definitely wanted at least $100,000 at closing, maybe as much as $250,000, but she was slowly beginning to see that finding an individual willing to embrace her legacy and the culture of the business would be the perfect exit for her. She vowed to herself that if she found that perfect person, she would get creative on the deal terms.

"Let's keep all our options open, though," Jeremy added. "There's lots of fish out there."

"Now, there is something I want to suggest to you. I'm more than happy to represent you on this deal, whoever the buyer is, but if you want to consider trade buyers, I highly recommend you talk to a business broker. Those guys are in the business of selling businesses to other businesses. I have two names in particular for you. One is James Brock, who I don't actually know well but I met last week at a conference. He's here in town—a one-man shop but seemed knowledgeable. There's also Beau Harding. He's more into big-ticket deals and a really nice and super sharp guy. I'd like you to chat with them both, today if possible, then we could meet for lunch tomorrow and map out the entire process. Deal?"

"Yes, it's a deal," said Jacqueline. This was the second "deal" she had made in three days, and they both involved food. *At least when I'm retired, I can spend more time working out*, she thought.

Jacqueline spent the day meeting with her employees, including a two-hour one-on-one with Phillip and an hour handling admin with her assistant.

As the employees started leaving the office after 5 p.m., Jacqueline locked her office door, pulled out her notepad and got ready to dial James Brock and Beau Hastings.

James went to voicemail, but Beau picked up after three rings.

"Hello, Beau, it's Jacqueline Turley at JAT PR. My CPA, Jeremy, gave me your details."

"Yes, thanks for calling," said Beau. "Jeremy told me to expect your call. How can I help you?"

"Well, I'm looking to sell my business, and Jeremy wants me to speak to a broker to see if that's the best option of representation for me and the business. Is this something you can help me with?"

"Well, I'm flattered by the approach, and please don't take this badly, but your business is just too small for us. We typically look at deals greater than $10 million in asking price, and although I haven't seen your numbers, Jeremy did say it wouldn't be a $10 million or higher acquisition. We aren't really a business brokerage, we're a boutique corporate finance firm. We don't just list a business for sale on our website. We work with the seller to create a buyer list, sometimes 100 or more companies, then proactively market to them and create a competitive process."

Jacqueline thought this was fascinating but felt disappointed that the deal wouldn't be big enough to entertain Beau. She then remembered the magic question: "What would have to be true?" It was a clever pre-framing technique she had learned at a mindset seminar five years ago.

"Beau, let me ask you a question. What would have to be true for you to take my business and sell it for $10 million?"

Beau laughed. "I would have to look at your numbers first, but I'd be looking for at least $1.5 million in profit. That would be a 7X profit multiple, which is a stretch in the current market, but you never know."

"Well," Jacqueline responded, "my profit is approximately half of that, so I'm guessing the business is worth $5 million."

"Unfortunately not. I'll let your CPA run the numbers and valuation for you, but at that level of profit, you'd be looking at a 4X multiple, so something in the $3 million range—subject to a much deeper analysis, you understand. Also, our minimum retainer is $15,000 per month along with a $400,000 success fee. So, assuming a six-month process end to end, it would cost you, let's see . . .

about $490,000 minimum, and from a $3 million deal that's not good value for you."

Beau didn't have any referrals for a lower-ticket broker, but he wished Jacqueline all the best. "If you don't sell and you end up scaling to at least $1.5 million in profit," he added, "give me a call back."

Jacqueline ended the call and immediately heard a ping on her voicemail. It was a message from James.

She called back and James picked up immediately.

"Thanks for giving me the opportunity to sell your business, Jacqueline."

Woah, thought Jacqueline. *Steady on there.*

"Well, I am looking at broker representation, and my CPA, Jeremy, connected us. Mind if I ask you some questions?"

"Sure, fire away," replied James.

"First, what's the minimum size of business you'll consider selling?"

"We take anything," said James. "Big, small, you name it. We've got you."

"Ok, great. And what's your process?"

"Process?" said James, sounding confused by the question. "What do you mean?"

"Could you walk me through your system for selling businesses?" Jacqueline was starting to become annoyed.

"Umm, okay. Well, we put a valuation on your business—on the high side, right? Buyers will always knock you down on price, so we start high and see where we go."

"We then create a confidential information memorandum, then list your business on our website alongside the many other businesses we have to sell."

"Do you focus exclusively on PR firms?" Jacqueline interjected.

"Hell no," James replied. "We sell everything. Gas stations, websites, pool routes, pet rental businesses, even retail. You name it. We sell it. Makes no difference to us. A buck's a buck."

"Okay, I have two more questions. First, how do you research the market to determine the buyers to target?"

"Humph," James grunted. "Naw, we don't do that. Waste of time. We just list you on our site, and buyers come look at our listings. We'll list you for a year, plenty of time to get a few interested parties."

A year! Jacqueline was really starting to get angry. This guy was arrogant, lazy and not filling her with any confidence.

"Okay, what about your fees?"

"Simple, we charge $10,000 per month, then a 10% success fee."

Wow, that seems high, Jaqueline thought. *So my profit is $800k and change.*

She probed further. "What multiple would you expect me to see from buyers?"

"You're in PR, right? At least an 8X multiple, maybe more. There was a $10 billion merger last year I read about in the Wall Street Journal. I think that deal was around 12X, so probably 8X to 10X, I would say."

"That high? The feedback I've had so far has been to expect something in the 4X range."

"Really? What do they know? Let's shoot for the moon here, Jacqueline. Let's push the envelope on this one. I can see a big exit for you here. Are we good? Ready to roll on this?"

"Not quite," said Jacqueline. "Send me a proposal, and I'll talk it over with my CPA." She hated being called "Jackie."

"Really?" James said, his voice exuding mock injury. "C'mon, let's just rock and roll. I'll tell you what: Let's take the first $10,000 monthly payment now on a card and kick this off. No point waiting, right?"

"No, this is the biggest business decision of my life. I need to make sure I'm working with the right partners." Jacqueline was desperately trying to get off the phone. This guy was creepy and came across like a used car salesman.

"Just send me a proposal," she insisted. "I will text you my email. Goodbye, James. Thank you for your time." Jacqueline's finger had been hovering over the end call button for at least 30 seconds but it seemed like an eternity. She finally let it drop.

She drove home feeling extremely deflated.

Beau was a great broker or "boutique corporate financier" (if she remembered the phrase correctly), but her business wasn't big enough for him to take the listing.

And James was a slime ball. No way would she ever do business with him.

"So, some brokers are great, but some are terrible," she said out loud.

Just like the drivers on her route home. Some were pleasant and safe. Others are reckless and dangerous. It was the perfect metaphor.

Why don't I just let Jeremy sell my business, she thought? *I've known him for years. He knows my business inside out, and surely he has a network?*

Sitting in her driveway, Jacqueline texted Jeremy to confirm the lunch meeting tomorrow. This was going to be a very important meeting.

Chapter 13

Terence Hits the Deal Origination Machine

Terence decided to work from home again. He woke at 5 a.m., declined the Peloton today and worked like a banshee from 5:30 until 11:00 to clear the decks for the rest of the day. After 11:00, he was off the corporate clock. No meetings, and apart from answering his phone and checking his Slack and email, he could focus the rest of the day on deal origination. He had just 48 hours left to submit a deal for this week's Protégé Red-Light, Green-Light call, and he was adamant to make it happen.

He started by calling Bill Frisk, the cocky broker from the weekend.

"Got your proof of funds, pal?" Bill asked within the first 10 seconds of the call.

"No. I can't provide you with proof of funds until I see the full financials. All I have in the one sheet is five numbers. It's impossible for me to evaluate the business and put a value on it from that."

"Ok, pal, so what do you need?"

What I most need is for him to stop calling me "pal," Terence thought, but he bit his tongue. He had his notes in front of him and had watched the deal-vetting training from Protégé late last night.

"I need a number of things to know where I stand on this deal." Terence then began listing them off . . .

"Last three years of financial accounts,

"Corresponding tax returns,

"Interim financial statements for the current year to date, including a very recent balance sheet"

"A copy of the business plan (if there is one), including forecasts for the next three years,"

"Details of the current shareholding, organization chart, customer and employee lists . . ."

At that point Bill cut him off. "Woah, pal, calm down. Most of that is for due diligence. You won't get employee and customer lists anytime soon, but I can get you the full CIM (which has most of the information you need), and we have all the financials you mentioned."

"But let me ask you," he continued, "how are you going to fund this deal? The seller wants $1,500,000, and you know that's a steal, right?"

"Well, I don't know that, yet. But assuming that's the case, I'll probably get an SBA loan. I have an excellent FICO score and enough money for the down payment." Carl had walked the Protégé group through the SBA loan program on a call a few weeks ago (before Terence had joined), and Terence had come across the recording.

"Okay, pal. But before I share all this with you, I need a bank statement showing at least $150,000 for the 10% downpayment, and I also need to know the name of the bank you'll use for the 80% SBA financing. Get those to me today, and I can share the numbers with you. Then, you can talk to the seller. We can set up a meeting or call before the end of this week."

"Why do you need my bank statements?" Terence challenged. "I'm not comfortable sharing those."

"We need to know you have the dough, pal. I'm not wasting my client's time with tire kickers. I get you don't want to fund the entire deal in cash, but if you're going down the SBA route, I'm only asking for what the bank will ask. This isn't moving forward until you get me that information. Your call, pal."

Slightly annoyed, Terence promised nonetheless to get him the information by the end of the day.

Broker call two was with Martin Crowther. Another henchman. Same drill. Needed proof of funds or at least the name of the bank for the SBA loan and proof of the down payment. Regardless, Terence didn't like this particular business. Revenue was declining, clients were leaving and the husband and wife owners were going through a bitter divorce. It seemed one of them was using the business as the big negotiation chip against the other. Carl had said in a recent Q&A session (again, Terene had watched the recording), "walk away fast from divorce deals. They aren't worth the time and effort. Move onto a different deal."

Broker call three was with Leanne Deakins. This one was a great call. Leanne was pleasant, friendly and provided tons of information. Strangely enough, she didn't want any financial information from Terence before she would email the financial pack and CIM and offer up a seller call.

"How long has the business been listed?" asked Terence.

"Nine months," replied Leanne. "There was a lot of interest at the start, but all the prospective buyers thought the business was overvalued, and the seller has only recently agreed (albeit reluctantly) to reduce the price by 40%."

"Why is the owner looking to sell?"

"He's actually looking to retire. He's a bit burned out and doesn't believe any of his current team can run the business."

"Why don't you meet him?" she then offered, to Terence's surprise. "I can set up a call this afternoon."

Great, thought Terence. *Gives me a few hours to run through the numbers. Maybe this is the deal I can present on the Red-Light, Green-Light call.*

Leanne had texted the seller during the call, and he was free at 5 p.m. for a Zoom. The business was in Dayton, Ohio, and Terence would go there as a next step if the initial call went well.

They ended the call with the plan that Leanne would join Terence and the seller later on Zoom.

Following Carl's guidance, Terence had asked basically the same questions on every call. He looked at his notepad.

Broker one – prickly with barriers; listing time, 3 weeks.

Broker two – prickly with barriers; listing time, 2 months.

Broker three – very pleasant with no barriers; listing time, 9 months.

This was exactly what Carl had predicted. Brokers get nicer the longer the deal has been listed.

Perhaps I should only look at broker deals that are at least nine months old, Terence observed wryly.

He downloaded his bank statement from his phone, air dropped the PDF to his computer and redacted the routing and account numbers. The account was in his name and registered to his home address. He sat on just over $275,000; however, his wife Julie had approved only $100,000 max to be used for the acquisition. Bill the prickly broker didn't need to know that though, did he?

Under an SBA 7a loan, the deal structure would be …

$150,000 buyer deposit

$150,000 seller note

$1,200,000 SBA 7a loan payable over 10-years

This was all assuming the business was worth $1,500,000. There would also be loan fees and other closing costs. The seller would receive 90% of the total deal at closing, so $1,350,000.

Terence balked at the 10X multiple of profit, but he badly wanted to get some deals in so he could vet them and use the Red-Light, Green-Light deal review process in Protégé.

He sent the bank statement to prickly Bill.

Next, he needed to deal with the SBA 7a loan program. He had already researched and found that Live Stem Bank was one of the nation's primary lenders under the SBA program. He had emailed a woman at the bank called Lisa Trammel requesting an introductory call (he got the details from the website), and he had pinged the Protégé Circle community for any recommendations for recommended SBA lenders.

In their responses, none of the Protégés cited a particular bank. However, at least five of them were recommending Anthony Marks. Anthony was an SBA financing broker whom Carl had personally vetted and made available to the community. It seemed like lots of dealmakers were using Anthony to broker the funds for them and handle the process. Anthony charged a fee (split between lender and buyer), but it was contingent, that is, paid only at closing.

Terence found Anthony in the Protégé rolodex and made a note of his email and phone number. He then emailed Anthony, again asking for an introductory call. He was reading the information on Anthony's website when his computer pinged loudly.

It was an email from Bill. "Thanks for the bank statement pal. Who's the bank you are using for the SBA loan? Need to know before I release numbers. Thanks, Bill."

Jeez. This guy is relentless, Terence thought.

He spent the next hour on corporate stuff. Took a few calls, reviewed the final contract for a new big retail client, cleared his emails and Slack messages and then scanned the recent comments in the Protégé Circle community.

He had 30 minutes left before his first seller call with Leanne (broker three). Both SBA emails pinged into his inbox within five minutes of each other. Lisa (Live Stem Bank) and Anthony (SBA loan broker) were each free to have Zoom calls later in the week.

Terence replied to Bill's email.

"Hi Bill. I'm talking to both Lisa Trammel at Live Stem Bank and also Anthony Marks, an SBA loan broker recommended to me by my business acquisitions mentor."

Bill replied in under two minutes. "That's great, thanks. So, you have a mentor? That's great, pal. Is he partnering with you on the deal?"

Terence ignored the email but was pleased ten minutes later when he received another email from Bill with a link to a Google Drive, which appeared to contain all the information he had asked for, absent customer and employee lists.

Fifteen minutes to go to the seller's call. Terence made a coffee, took a final skim of the financials from Leanne and made a list of all his questions.

Chapter 14

Jacqueline Meets Jeremy for Lunch

Despite having had a restful sleep, Jacqueline felt anxious. It was the fear of the unknown. She knew business, and she knew PR, but she was embarking on something so critical and important to her life, her business and her family that her lack of insight into business acquisitions was a major issue.

It took her back to her first time being pregnant. The same kinds of feelings. Anxiety, terror, worry, just not knowing what was going to happen. After the first one, it became easier with the others. She knew the drill. But with selling her business, her life's work, this was going to be the only time she would do it.

She knew many entrepreneurs in her chamber of commerce chapter who had sold a business at a young age, then gone on to either start a new venture or buy an existing one. She didn't know all the details, but she imagined the second, third and other times you go through the process would be far easier. Just like childbirth.

She took a shower, ate breakfast and decided to go to a yoga class. Dressed in her Under Armour outfit and Nike 270 sneakers, she breezed into the studio. Her blonde hair was wrapped up in a bun and she caught some envious stares from the other ladies in the class. Jacqueline was a doll. She looked amazing for 60.

She dropped her mat in the center of the room and started stretching before class. Mindfulness was the goal today although Jacqueline had enjoyed all the other amazing benefits of yoga as well over the years. Muscle tone, flexibility, low stress and low blood pressure.

After plenty of low lunges, cobra poses and some painful downward dog moves, the class ended, and she decided to just hit the office in her yoga outfit. It made her feel clean and fresh. No need to power dress for the day. She had her weekly financial review meeting and lunch with Jeremy, her CPA.

She went to the office, checked in with her assistant, spoke briefly with Jeremy about a client pitch he had that afternoon and quickly reviewed the financial KPIs (key performance indicators) that were part of the weekly financial dashboard.

Revenues were up 6.7% year to date. Margins were starting to expand, and cash flow for the previous month hit $100,000 for the first time in the business's history. *I'm sure selling my baby at the right time*, she mused.

The restaurant was only 300 yards from the office, so she left a few minutes early to enjoy the beautiful fall weather Chicago is famous for.

She walked into the restaurant and found Jeremy waiting for her in a booth to the side of the main dining area. This was a great place. Dark oak tables and rich brown leather chairs, the perfect spot to talk business. In fact, she had closed several existing clients in this very booth before she transitioned the business development to Phillip.

"Hi, Jacqueline," Jeremy said, greeting her in an unusually perky, upbeat tone. He was normally a dour person, but he did great work as her CPA. He also received the weekly financial dashboards.

"Are we celebrating today, Jacqueline?" He smiled. "You guys hit $100,000 in cash flow for the first time ever, as I understand it."

"Yes," she said with a smile, as the waiter arrived at the table. Still feeling the burn of yoga, Jacqueline was agreeable to a nice, zesty prosecco. It took almost 30 seconds for the first pour of bubbles to settle to the middle of the glass. Once the waitress finished the pour and excused herself, Jeremy began sipping on his bottle of Peroni, and they quickly scanned the rest of the numbers. All was good with the business.

"So, how were the broker calls?" Jeremy asked.

"Mixed. Beau was great, however the business isn't large enough for him. I think he would probably do it, but the minimum fees would be too extreme for me.

"James, however, was terrible. Made me feel very uncomfortable and, honestly, I don't think he knows what he's doing. He just wanted to close me and have me start paying the retainer. So, back to square one, I'm afraid."

"Well, that's a shame. Let me make some calls and find you some other options."

"No," Jacqueline replied sternly. "I want *you* to handle this for me, Jeremy. I know you, like you and trust you. You understand the business inside and out, are a part of the team, and I truly feel you have my back. You're the perfect advisor to handle this for me. Will you do it?"

"Yes, I will, of course. The data room is already complete. I can create the CIM and one sheet in the next 24 hours and create a target buyer list of financial and trade buyers. I'll also create some interest from individuals by circulating the one sheet across my network. And I don't need a retainer for this project. I'll just charge you a success fee. How does 5% of the total deal value sound?"

"Yes, that works. Thank you. Are you sure you don't need a retainer?"

"No, it's not necessary. We already bill you for the accounting work we do and for my fractional CFO duties, and I have all the data we need since Lucy did such a great job of populating the data room."

"Okay, then. Thanks. One more question for you: Do I tell all the employees? I've only told three people: Phillip, Lucy and my assistant, Barbara. The rest don't know."

"No," Jeremy said, "I wouldn't tell them yet. Once you've signed an LOI, the buyer you select may want to speak to more of the key people in the business—particularly the senior account managers and the lead designer, brand manager and marketing manager. But, we'll cross that bridge later in the process."

They ordered pasta and focaccia but declined coffee and dessert. When the meeting ended, Jeremy promised to be back in touch within a few days with a list of potential buyers.

Chapter 15

Terence's First Seller Call

Terence was staring at his deal notes for the upcoming Zoom with Leanne (broker three) and her seller.

Revenue = $7,200,000
SDE = $800,000
Margin = 11%
Asking price = $2,400,000
Multiple = 3X

Since this deal had been discounted by 40%, Terence figured the original ask was around the 5X multiple range.
Interesting, though, were the profit numbers. Terence was staring at three in particular.

Net operating income (from the tax return) = $100,000
EBITDA (including add backs) = $500,000
SDE = $800,000

Terence's head was pounding. He felt totally out of his depth and decided he wouldn't get into the numbers on this call. Instead, he'd follow Carl's advice and build the relationship first, then ask business questions. The numbers could wait until he felt more comfortable talking about them.

Terence logged into the Zoom, and within a few minutes both Leanne and her selling client, Roger, joined the call. Leanne looked radiant in a black turtleneck sweater, but Roger had his camera off, which Terence thought strange.

Introductions were made. Both Terence and Leanne were upbeat. Roger, however, practically grunted his answers and made zero attempt to build a relationship.
This isn't how it's supposed to be, thought Terence.
He had attempted to make a tenuous connection with Roger by joking around when Roger's love for sailing was brought up in the conversation. Terence himself actually hated the water. "I can't take up sailing," Terence said at one point, "because I'm pretty sure the fish wouldn't want me getting seasick in their ocean." This attempt to inject some humor had done nothing to build rapport.

Leanne sensed the tension and gave a brief summary of the business, which Roger added to with frequent interruptions, sometimes to the point of rudeness. There was clearly no love lost between these two. *I wonder why*, thought Terence.

The business was a PR firm called Ret Med Services Inc. that also handled marketing and advertising for its clients, most of which were regional, midwestern businesses typically in the $20 million to $100 million revenue range. There was a big focus on assisted living and private medical facilities.

Terence then posed the five primary questions he had learned from the Protégé coaching.

Terence: "Why are you selling the business, Roger?"

Roger: "I want to retire. I'm 64. I've owned this business for 20 years, and my children aren't interested in taking over. My team doesn't know which day it is most of the time, and the business has lost its vibe. It used to be jumping, but lately it's grown stale. We're still profitable, but we haven't grown revenues in the past three years. In fact, last year our revenues dipped 15%. I just don't think I have the passion and energy to keep going, and my employees know it."

Terence: "Who operates the business?"

Roger: "I do, full time. I have a controller, sales team and three team leaders who run our three major lines of business: PR, advertising and marketing. We actually acquired a very small digital marketing agency two years ago, and I had hoped the owner would step up and be the CEO of the combined business, but he left after his earn-out. There's no solid number two in the business who can operate it in my absence, so if you buy it, you'll have to operate the business yourself or bring in a CEO to do it for you. Nobody on my team is capable of running this business."

Terence wrote down the term "earn out" and promised himself to look it up later. He then proceeded to his last three questions.

Terence: "What's your business development strategy to win new customers?"

Roger: "It's funny, isn't it? We actually don't do any marketing for ourselves, believe it or not, yet we do marketing for our clients. All of our business comes from repeat customers and word-of-mouth referrals. We lost a big client last year when it was acquired by a much larger business that had their own internal PR team. Honestly, I've just not felt comfortable growing the business much beyond its current level. It provides me with a good living, and I didn't want to rock the boat too much by growing quickly and creating chaos. I'm really just a PR guy at heart. I wouldn't call myself a CEO by any stretch."

Terence's hand was burning with all the notes he was making. Roger was really starting to open up.

Terence: "Let's talk about your market and competition. Who are your competitors, and how do you beat them?"

Roger: "Hmm, that's a good question. We win when we focus on our core market, regional health businesses. We try to often be the lowest cost provider, and that helps us win, especially in the assisted living market. Those guys are very price sensitive. We stay in our lane. We often get asked to bid for work out of state, but I don't like traveling, and the clients will only deal with me. My sales team are more like account managers. I'm the one who has to go out and win the new business, and since I hate doing that, it's why we haven't really grown over the past few years. Our three biggest competitors are Win PR, Vision Brand and Total Marketing Solutions. They're all much bigger than us, and often, due to our smaller size, we can be more nimble and agile, especially when clients want to quickly pivot on a campaign or marketing strategy. I'd be willing to say our reaction times are the best in the industry. Our average client tenure is more than four years."

Terence: "Where are you in the process? Do you have offers on the table?"

"Let me answer that one for you," Leanne interjected, jumping into the conversation. "We were under LOI a few months back, but the buyer couldn't qualify for financing. We do have interest from one of the largest clients to acquire the business and create an internal PR team, but they don't want the advertising and marketing parts of the business. PR is approximately 60% of the revenue and 80% of the profit, so if we did do that deal, Roger would most likely shut the other teams down; however, he'd prefer an outright sale. So, nothing really pending at this stage."

"That's great," Terence said. "Thank you both for your time. I'll likely have follow up questions and will want to run through the numbers with you in some detail later, Leanne, but I have enough for now as a preliminary assessment. One last question, aside from the financial aspects of the deal, is there anything else really important to you, Roger, that I should be aware of at this time?"

For nearly a minute there was eerie silence. Then Roger turned his camera on for the first time. He looked pale, drawn and disheveled. Terence had worked in PR his entire career and had met thousands of people but never someone who looked so miserable.

"I really like that question, Terence. Thank you for asking. I would say I'm looking for a fair price for the business, but the qualities of the buyer really matter to me. I want an operator. Not one of these financial buyers that are only looking at the cash flow. I want someone who's going to give a crap. Inject some energy into this business and shake the tree. I've taken it as far as I can. It's time to hand over the baton.

"Now let me ask you, Terence, why do you want to buy this business, and what's your background?"

Not sure I do, thought Terence, but he gave Roger a two minute summary of his background and achievements.

Leanne moved in for the kill. "Do you have financing available for this deal, Terence? If not, I can help with that. I'm connected to lots of local banks in the SBA program and also several angel investors if you need an equity partner for the down payment."

"Thank you, Leanne. But I have my own contacts, and I also have cash for the down payment. However, if my financing partners don't pan out, I'll give you a call."

The three wrapped up the meeting and promised to stay in touch regarding next steps.

Chapter 16

Terence Receives Three More Deals

It had been a great day for Terence. He'd learned so much by simply taking action. What he had realized throughout the day was that you can read books, listen to podcasts, watch coaching videos and all that stuff, but where you really learn is when you take action and get out onto the field of play.

The whole family was home, and Joshua had baseball practice, so Terence wrapped up in his office, closed the door and got ready for the short trip to practice. Julie was making his favorite dinner tonight: Italian sausage pasta bake. He could smell the garlic, onions and sweet Italian sausage sauteing in the pan. He suddenly realized that he hadn't eaten lunch, he'd been so engrossed in his dealmaking day.

He grabbed a packet of trail mix and inhaled it in the car. Practice and dinner were both great and he slept soundly that night, his head still spinning with all the new information he was learning and the action he was taking.

The following morning, he hit the Peloton hard. He wanted to sweat. After getting dressed and eating breakfast, he whizzed downtown early to the office.

By 10 a.m. he had again completed all his primary daily corporate tasks. He had meetings scheduled for 2 p.m. to 5 p.m., so he logged into his private email account and spent the next four hours until then focused on dealmaking.

Lawrence had followed through. There were email introductions with a bunch of attorneys, wealth managers and CPAs. At least two of each. Terence opened his new dealmaking rolodex Google sheet and entered the names and contact details of them all.

Bill Frisk called. "How's it going pal?" he boomed into the phone. "Are you doing anything with this deal? We have an offer on the table. Snooze you lose. I can hold the seller off until the end of the week. Do you want a meeting with him?"

"Yes," replied Terence, but he told Bill it would have to be in a few days. He had a lot of other stuff to do and hadn't really looked at the numbers yet.

"Well, don't sit on this for too long, pal. If I don't hear from you by Friday, I'm going to assume you're not interested. Cool?"

That worked.

Terence looked at his action sheet in Google. Six new people to call that Lawrence had introduced him to. All six had responded asking Terence to call them at his convenience.

He had listed them in numerical order in his sheet.

1. Max Spenman. MLS Wealth Management
2. Boris Ryan, CPA. All Plus Accounting
3. Diedre Glenn. Lee, Ravers and Glenn Attorneys at Law
4. Jeremy Brown, CPA. Jeremy Brown and Associates, LLC
5. Michael Rees. Tudor Wealth Management
6. Laura Cole. Attorney at Law.

He was about to call Max; however, that's when he saw on his bookshelf a large rubber dice he had been given at a recent charity fundraiser. He reached over, picked it up and threw it hard against the external wall of his office. It bounced and finally rolled to a stop just under his desk.

"4"

Well, he's first then. Let's call Jeremy Brown.

Terence placed the call. A secretary answered.

"Jeremy Brown, please."

"I'm sorry, he's on another call at the moment. Can I ask who's calling?"

"Yes, it's Terence Turner. I was referred to Jeremy by an attorney friend."

"I see," the secretary answered politely. "Actually, Jeremy has just become free. Let me put you through."

"Hello, Terence. Nice to meet you. Lawrence tells me you're a friend and looking for a CPA. How can I help?"

"Well, actually," said Terence. "I'm not looking for a CPA just yet. I'm actually looking for a business to buy, and, yes, once I find one I'll be looking for a CPA to help me buy the business and then manage all the financials and taxes afterwards."

"Great. What type of business are you looking to buy?"

"Ideally a PR agency in Chicago or close by. I work for a very large PR firm here in Chicago and want to go out on my own."

"Wow," Jeremy suddenly said, then started laughing.

Terence was instantly irritated. Why was this guy making fun of him?

"Did I say something funny, Jeremy?"

"No, not at all. Maybe this is fate, I'm not sure, but I have a PR agency client here in Chicago who's looking to sell and asked me literally just yesterday to manage the process. I was actually just creating a buyer list to present to her tomorrow."

Now Terence started laughing too. Yes, this was all rather spooky.

"What can you tell me about her business?"

"It's very solid. JAT PR LLC. Owned by Jacqueline Turley. Looking to retire. Solid team. Let me send you an NDA, then I can give you the CIM and the data pack. If it's up your street, I can set up a call or meeting. She's here in the downtown area."

"What are the high-level numbers?" asked Terence.

Jeremy listed out the figures.

"Revenue $3,460,200
SDE (seller's discretionary earnings) $814,500
Net working capital $912,000
Cash on hand $540,000
Non-current liabilities $137,000"

"Okay, so that's definitely in my sweet spot. How long has it been on the market?"

"It's not actually on the market as of yet, so consider this an off-market deal. Some may refer to it as a pocket listing. I'm not a business broker, so I won't be listing it on a website, but once Jacqueline approves the potential buyer list, I'll be reaching out to generate interest."

"And one more thing, Terence. I can't advise you on this deal, as I work for the seller. I'm the external CPA for the firm and also serve as a fractional CFO supporting the internal controller, who is very good, by the way. So, you'll need your own CPA for this deal. But if you do buy it, I'd be delighted to continue working for you."

"Okay, I understand," assured him. "Does Jacqueline operate the business?"

"No, she's already semi-retired now, really. Spends about 10 to 15 hours a week there. She has a general manager called Phillip who runs the business day to day but doesn't want to acquire it. Again, he's solid, so he'd be a great advocate for you. Both Phillip and the controller know the business is going to be sold and are onboard."

"Sounds great. I love the sound of this business. I'm very early in my process, though, as I've only looked at a few deals. Go ahead and send me the NDA, and then let's chat again in a few days."

Terence was blown away by the call. This method of generating deals was so much simpler and nicer. Build a relationship network of deal intermediaries and connect with them. "They all have dealflow," Carl had said. He was right.

Screw the brokers for now. What a pain in the butt most of them are.

Terence used the dice to make the rest of the calls. All of them had deals and would be sending NDAs. The deal via Jeremy sounded like the best fit, though. Profitable (not all of the deals were). Owner-investor not owner-operator (only Jacqueline's business was in this category). And local (a few other deals were also in Chicago).

Terence wrapped up his calls and was about to leave for the day when he saw the email from Jeremy. It contained a one-sheet and an NDA.

He DocuSigned the NDA without actually reading it, saved the one sheet to his Google drive and quickly replied to the email.

He glanced at the one sheet before leaving the office.

Award winning Chicago PR Firm
20 years old
Loyal customer base and excellent management team
Semi-retired owner looking to retire
Revenue $3,460,200
SDE (seller's discretionary earnings) $814,500
Net working capital $912,000
Cash on hand $540,000
Non-current liabilities $137,000
Asking price: Open to offers

This was the first deal Terence had looked at that didn't list an asking price. *Very strange*, he thought. He had already mastered the mental math, and at $800,000 and change in SDE it would likely be a 4X multiple, so the deal would be something in the $3,200,000 range with some adjustments for the surplus cash and non-current liabilities.

Probably a three-million-dollar deal, he thought. He would need an investor for sure if he went down the SBA route. He could raise $200,000 of equity capital, combine that with his own $100,000 and make the $300,000 down payment. The bank would kick in the $2,400,000 via a SBA 7a loan, and the seller would have a $300,000 note. He was proud of the fact he could mentally work this out in under 30 seconds even though he'd been a dealmaker for less than a week.

He would definitely be sharing this information with Live Stem Bank and Anthony Marks, the SBA loan broker. He had Zoom calls with each of them separately tomorrow morning. He would be working from home again.

He left the office and drove home. It was the youth theater tonight with his wife and son. His daughter was in the orchestra playing the piano. Mamma Mia. *Should be fun,* he thought as he whizzed through Linkin Park on his way home.

Chapter 17

The Buyer List

This time, Jeremy went to Jacqueline's office to present the buyer list. Jacqueline had Phillip, her GM, and Lucy, her financial controller, join the meeting.

Jeremy was a bit surprised when he saw all three of them sitting around the small table in the corner of Jacqueline's office.

"Good morning, Jacqueline," smiled Jeremy.

"Good morning, Jeremy. I've asked Phillip and Lucy to join us today."

"Great," he said. He opened his briefcase and pulled out three documents: the one sheet, the full CIM and the buyer list.

Lucy started skimming the one sheet and CIM, especially the numbers. Satisfied, she put the documents on the table, and Jeremy started walking through the buyer list.

"I've done some research on who I believe would be prospective buyers of JAT. I have essentially three groups.

"The first are trade buyers," Jeremy said, then began listing them off:

"Total PR LLC. Los Angeles. Annual revenue = $43,000,000. They're acquiring outside of California.

"Laser Business Services Inc. New York. Annual revenue = $13,500,000. This will be their first acquisition.

"Creative PR Inc. Chicago. Annual revenue = $133,000,000. This may be too large a buyer, but they're local, so it's worth putting them on the list. Acquired two other smaller businesses last year, one in Detroit and another in Dayton.

Hype Machine Ltd. London. Annual revenue = $18,200,000 (converted). They just landed a large bakery client in Chicago and are looking for a regional PR firm to support it.

Narrative PR Inc. Boston. Annual revenue isn't known. No financials available in my database on these guys. Look great on their website, but they may be too small.

Chaos Communications LLC. Dallas. Annual revenue = $8,900,000. They were just acquired by a small private equity firm and are looking for acquisitions.

Kron Business Media Inc. Scottsdale. Annual revenue = $13,600,000. I know their CFO; we went to college together. He said he'd love to buy a business in the midwest.

Message Masters LLC. Miami. A start-up but heavily VC backed. They have a $20 million M&A warchest. It's a buy and build strategy.

"Media Mavens Inc. Chicago. Annual revenue = $3,900,000. They're basically the same size as JAT. Maybe it will be too small unless they can raise capital."

The last one also happened to be the arch enemy of JAT. *Absolutely no way*, thought Jacqueline. *I'd rather swim with crocodiles through a sea of nuclear waste than dance with those crooks.*

"The second group," Jeremy explained, "are financial buyers."

All the ones Jeremy presented were either family offices, private equity firms or other investment consortiums who had a history of targeting PR, media, advertising or marketing agencies. All had at least $50 million of assets under management. Jeremy rattled off the list:

Masters Capital LLC. Dallas.
Whisper Capital Management Inc. Boston.
Tony Investments LLP. New York.
Ciotto Ventures Inc. San Francisco.
MAV Capital LLC. Huntsville
MAT Financial LLC. Atlanta
Boom Capital Management LLC. Baltimore
Viera Ventures LLC. Florida

Lastly, there were the individual buyers. Apart from Terence, whom Jeremy had spoken to via Lawrence, the other hits on this list came from a LinkedIn post Jeremy had sent out yesterday to his 13,500-strong network. He'd also posted in a Chicago-based M&A LinkedIn group and on the local Chamber of Commerce Facebook page.

Terence Turner. Senior Account Manager, Creative PR, Inc.
Michael Reeves. Entrepreneur
Laura Moody. Dealmaker
Peter Swann. Angel Investor
Dan Gordon. Consultant
Lewis Toms. CFO, Solid Media LLC
Tom Bressler. Retired CMO
Sean Evans. SVP Sales. Hollow Media Inc.
Tania Scott. CFO. Smith Pine Communications LLC
Belinda Watson. Attorney at Law. BW Legal LLP

    In all, there were 27 different options. The only one Jacqueline immediately struck off the list was the arch enemy, Media Mavens, but she approved all other 26.
    She was confused about Creative PR, Inc., though. It was a business she knew well, but she couldn't place Terence Turner, who'd been listed as an individual buyer. "Creative PR is a duplicate, right? It's in the trade buyer group but it's also in the individual bucket with this Terence Turner. So we really have only 25?"
    "So . . . not exactly," replied Jeremy. "What's interesting here is that I had put Creative PR on the list, but when I actually spoke to Terence, it turns out he's looking to acquire a business just like yours for himself. So, he wouldn't be acting on behalf of his employer."
    Wow. What a coincidence. This really intrigued Jacqueline. The biggest PR game in town was on the buyer list, and one of its senior employees wanted to buy her business.
    Jacqueline would look back at this moment in years to come as the moment it felt like a warm, cozy blanket had wrapped itself around her. She suddenly felt . . . calm. Comforted. Confident. She didn't know exactly why. Perhaps it was just the thought of a corporate exec in the same town wanting to buy *her* business. Was Terence the buyer she was looking for? The "safe trusted pair of hands" that would love and nurture her business to another level and care for her clients and employees like she'd herself done? *I have to meet this guy*, she thought.
    Jeremy then explained the next steps. He would make contact with each of the 26, send the one sheet, and if the potential buyer showed interest, he'd send an NDA, then the CIM and data pack.

The list would get pared down significantly in the coming weeks to potentially four to six, and Jacqueline and the team would make management presentations to each potential buyer on the short list.

Jacqueline scooped up the documents from the table, then ushered Jeremy, Phillip and Lucy out of her office.

Once everyone had gone, she picked up her iPhone and first went to Facebook and searched for Terence Turner. In an instant, there he was.

"Senior Account Manager, Creative PR, Inc." She recognized him from somewhere. It wasn't in the PR world, however. JAT and Creative had never locked horns or crossed paths. They dealt with Nike and Starbucks. She had small accounts.

But she knew him from somewhere.

She started scrolling through his Facebook feed and, boom, there it was. He was a baseball dad. He had checked in at Horner Park, where lots of little league baseball games were played. Jacqueline regularly went there to watch her grandson, and it would appear he played for the same club as Terence's son (but in a younger team). *What a small world*, she thought.

She sent Terence a friend request, closed down the app and went out to a lunch appointment with her attorney, Herb. Time to put him in the loop on this deal. Things were starting to move.

Chapter 18

Terence's RLGL Submission

Terence couldn't stop thinking about JAT. He had researched the business via its website and scouted its beautiful and elegant owner, Jacqueline Turley on LinkedIN. She looked familiar but he couldn't place her. They had never crossed paths in the PR world or at any networking functions, but he felt he knew this lady. He had seen her before. He started preparing his Red Light, Green Light submission.

Then something happened that hit him right between the eyes. His Facebook app buzzed on his iPhone.

Friend request . . .

Jacqueline Turley

Woahhhhhhhh

Really?

This was spooky. He was literally just thinking about her, and now she sends him a friend request.

He pondered for a moment but wasn't sure if he should accept it.

Maybe Jeremy told her about me. Maybe that's it.

He thought of sending Jacqueline a message but decided against it. *Let Jeremy make the intro*, he thought. Besides, he needed to put together his deal submission for the Protégé call tomorrow, and he also had corporate work to do.

Terence followed the one-sheet training and put the numbers Leanne had provided into the model template he had been given in Protégé. It was simple and took him only about 30 minutes.

He entered in the three years' of financial data.

In the profit line, it wasn't referred to as SDE. Instead it was called adjusted EBITDA.

Carl had explained that they needed to calculate the normalized profit. Simply stated, that's what the profit would be if the owner weren't in the business. This included something called add-backs, which included the owner's salary (over and above what it would cost to replace).

In this particular deal, the owner was taking $400,000 per year out of the business (in salary, benefits and bonuses), and the cost of a replacement operator (either Terence or someone he would most likely hire) would be $100,000. So that was a $300,000 add-back because the profit would go up by that amount.

In the broker CIM, there were other add-backs, including bad debts written off and one-off marketing spend. Carl had explained that they shouldn't allow both of those as add-backs. All businesses have bad debts that get written off—it's just part and parcel of owning a business. Marketing spend in the prior two years had generated the revenues and profits that were driving the valuation, so, again, these were not allowed.

The Protégé model also calculated a three-year average of profit so that in a case where the profits were increasing, they wouldn't just be paying for a recent banner year. Likewise, if profits were declining, they should only take the last number for the valuation. But they should also pay careful attention to what was going on in the business to cause the rise or fall in profits and consider whether this would be likely to reverse under their ownership.

The three-year, average adjusted EBITDA, in this case, was $617,000. This was lower than the $800,000 current-year SDE number Leanne had provided in the one sheet.

Next, the model calculated the enterprise value, or EV. This is the value of the business, not the equity or stock value.

Terence used a 3X multiple for the valuation.

EV = 3 x $617,000 = $1,851,000

Next, the model calculated the equity value. This was the value of the shares or stock in the business.

"It's like real estate," Carl would say. "Just because your house is valued at $500,000, that's not necessarily the value of the equity. If you have a $300,000 mortgage, then the equity is only $200,000. It's exactly the same in a business acquisition."

Roger's business was carrying approximately $150,000 in debt between taxes payable and a bank loan. There was no real estate in the deal (the premises were leased for $135,000 per year). However, there was $1,000,000 cash in the bank and approximately $1,600,000 working capital in the business. Carl had said to always acquire a business with no less than two months of working capital in the business, with at least 50% of that in cash.

The annual revenues here were $7,200,000, so two months of working capital would be ...

$7,200,000 x 2 / 12 = $1,200,000, including a minimum of $600,000 in cash

That meant there was $400,000 of additional working capital that either the seller could take out at closing or that would just get added to the purchase price. Terence liked the idea of inheriting all that working capital, so he decided to add it to the purchase price.

Therefore, the 100% equity value would be ...

Enterprise value = $1,851,000
Less debt to inherit = ($150,000)
Add surplus working capital = $400,000
100% equity valuation = $2,101,000

The model also calculated various debt coverage ratios depending on multiple deal structures and financing solutions. All of them worked. Terence decided on the SBA 7a loan structure.

It would be an even $2,000,000 offer:

$200,000 as a buyer deposit (Terence would split this with an investor)
$1,600,000 as an SBA 7a loan. At about 9%, this would cost the business $243,000 per year in interest and capital repayments over a 10-year term.
$200,000 as a seller note

The debt service cover ratio on the SBA loan would be $617,000 (average adjusted EBITDA) divided by the $243,000 debt service, which was 2.76X. Carl had recommended a minimum of 1.50X, so there was lots of headroom in this deal.

Terence sent in the one sheet and seller notes to the coaching team and looked forward to pitching the deal on the call tomorrow.

As soon as he submitted the deal, he saw an email come into his personal inbox from Jeremy, the CPA for JAT.

"Good news, Terence. Jacqueline says she would be happy to meet about the business. Please sign this NDA, and I will send you the full CIM and financial pack."

Terence felt he would quickly become a master of vetting deals, meeting sellers and making offers. He already had one seller call under his belt, and he felt it went well, despite a rocky start. He wanted to have at least three more, then he would meet with Jacqueline.

He agreed to a Monday morning meeting at Jeremy's office. Jacqueline hadn't told most of her employees yet, so it needed to be off-site, and only she would be attending, together with Jeremy. If the meeting went well, he could visit the office and meet the GM and controller in a subsequent meeting. Both of those people knew about the sale, it appeared.

With the meeting confirmed, Terence went back onto his Facebook app and confidently accepted Jacqueline's friend request.

He then wrapped up his corporate work and spent the evening relaxing with the family.

As he was climbing into bed, he reached for his phone to sit it on his wireless charger and noticed a Facebook message. He opened it and saw the message was from Jacqueline Turley.

"Hi, Terence. You may not remember, but we met last year at the annual BBQ for the Windy City Mavericks. Your son and my grandson play for the same club but at different ages. Jeremy has indicated your interest in acquiring my business, and I'm looking forward to meeting you on Monday. Regards, Jacqueline."

Chapter 19

Impromptu Meetings

Saturday morning, Terence and Jacqueline had very different plans. Saturday mornings were crazy in the Turner household. Baseball ruled. Terence had his son ready for the game, and they set off early to hit Dunkin Donuts on the way. It was a baseball ritual before each game.

Jacqueline was up early and reading the latest Jack Reacher novel in her summer room. Although it was well into the fall, the weather was unseasonably warm, so she loved using the weekend to catch up on her reading. It was her favorite hobby.

Jack Reacher was kicking butt somewhere in Florida saving the local town once again from the bad guys. As she was skipping through the chapters, her phone rang. It was her daughter Tina. She was preparing to start her shift as a midwife at the Cook County Medical Centre. She sounded distressed.

"Hey, mom, I really need your help. As you know Brian is away with the boys this weekend, and my friend Jenna was taking Jerrad to his baseball game with her own son Randy. Unfortunately, both Jenna and Randy are really sick and staying home. Jerrad doesn't want to miss the game, and it's too late to cancel my shift. Are you able to take him for me, then have him hang with you for the rest of the day? He can even sleep over if that works for you."

"I can do the baseball game, no problem," Jacqueline assured her, "and take care of him until the early evening, but I actually have . . . erm . . . a date tonight."

"Wow," said Tina. "Mom, that's amazing. Good for you. When were you going to tell me?"

"Well, it kind of slipped my mind."

"Hey mom, don't worry. I finish at 6 p.m., so let me scoop Jarred up then, and I can drop you off for your date so you don't have to drive. You can have a relaxing evening and let it take its course."

"Tina." Jacqueline dropped the tone of her voice decisively on the second syllable of her daughter's name, in mock seriousness. "It's not *that* kind of date!" She was blushing like a rosy red apple. "He's a business acquaintance, and, yes, he does have a crush on me, but I'm after his brain not his body."

"You just keep telling yourself that, Mom," Tina said with a smile and a chuckle. "But that's great. I'll meet you at the baseball field in 40 minutes, drop Jerrad off with you and then pick him up again around 6:30 tonight."

"Sounds good; I'll see you soon, dear."

Jacqueline dressed in a hoodie, Lululemon yoga pants and her prized Chicago Cubs baseball hat. She and her dear husband Bill were season pass holders, but she hadn't set foot inside Wrigley Field since he passed.

She drove her Range Rover Velar to the baseball field, arriving five minutes early. Shortly after, Tina and Jarred drove into the parking lot and got out. They all embraced.

"Thanks for doing this, Mom."

"Don't worry. I was only reading. I actually had nothing else planned until tonight."

"Yes, your *date*. What other secrets are you keeping from me?"

"Nothing," Jacqueline said defensively. She was blushing again.

They kissed like mothers and daughters do, then Tina left and Jacqueline walked Jerrad to the baseball field for the game.

As they were chatting about where they might go for lunch after the game, Jacqueline suddenly froze. Not twenty yards ahead of her and coming in her general direction was Terence Turner, in the flesh. He was walking away from the field, where his son's game must have finished prior to Jerrad's. Moments later Terence looked up, squinted for a few seconds and then smiled.

"Hello, Jacqueline," he said, approaching. "You know, I actually can't remember our meeting last year at the BBQ. I probably had had too many beers, but I recognize you from your Facebook profile picture. You're wearing that same hat in what looks like Wrigley Field behind home plate."

"Yes, it's where my late husband, Bill and I had our season passes."

"Oh, I see," said Terence. "I'm sorry for your loss."

There was an awkward silence for a few seconds, then both started to talk at once. Stopping, they both chuckled. "You first," Terence said, with a gentlemanly wave of his hand.

"I was just going to say that I guess we'll see each other on Monday," Jacqueline said.

"Yes, I look forward to it."

They shook hands warmly and said goodbye. Terence and Joshua continued on to their car, while Jacqueline handed Jerrad off to the coach, then sat down in the front row of seats to watch the game.

What are the chances of such an impromptu meeting, she thought? She loved the fact that Terence took his son to baseball and that he must have been a Cubs fan. Otherwise, how would he have known it was Wrigley Field?

Jerrad's team lost 4-1, and he was unusually grumpy on the walk back to her car.

"What do you want for lunch, my darling?" Jacqueline queried.

"Panera Bread, please, Grandma."

They drove about a mile to a nearby plaza, then went in to order and eat. Jerrad had the half tuna melt and Jacqueline the caesar salad.

"Who was that man, Grandma?" Jerrad asked in between bites of his sandwich.

"A business associate of mine." Jerrad was only seven but had a bright and inquisitive mind.

"Does he work for your business?"

"No, sweetie, he actually wants to buy my business."

"Wow, really? He must be really rich then."

"Hopefully!" Jacqueline laughed. They finished lunch and went back to her house.

As planned, that evening Tina picked her mother and Jarred up around 6:30 p.m. and then dropped Jacqueline off at the new Thai place.

She was ten minutes early, so she sat at the bar waiting for Jack to arrive.

He came right on time. He was a stickler for punctuality.

Coming up to the bar, he kissed her gently on the left cheek. "You smell nice," he said.

Jack looked different from their last meeting. He was in nice jeans, those funky blue shoes with the white soles Elon Musk wears, a crisp white shirt and a blue Ralph Lauren blazer. Freshly shaven and with his gray hair slicked back, he looked great. *Way younger than 65 years*, Jacqueline thought.

Jacqueline herself was dressed in leather pants, black boots and a figure-hugging sweater. Her hair was down, and her makeup was tasteful. It was apparent from the look on his face that Jack was quite taken by her appearance.

The evening went wonderfully. The food was mind-blowingly good, and Jacqueline lost count of the number of glasses of wine they both drank. Both were thoroughly enjoying the other's company.

As the plates were being cleared, Jack asked about the business. "Are you definitely going to sell?" he asked.

"Yes," Jacqueline answered. "My CPA is going to manage the process for me, and he gave me a long buyer list earlier this week containing trade buyers, financial buyers and also some individuals who've expressed an interest."

"Sounds like a good start. Have you met any of the prospective buyers yet?"

"Not yet. It's still early days. There are 26 on the current list, and we've already whittled that down to 16 based on interest. Jeremy is continuing to vet them, but I expect I'll meet at least six or seven of them next week. In fact, the first three meetings are all on Monday."

"Ah, tell me about them; I'd love to hear."

"Sure," replied Jacqueline, who found Jack's enthusiasm and genuine interest in the process rather endearing. "The first is a large PR firm out of Los Angeles. They're in town on other business and will stop by. There's also a private equity firm from Baltimore doing a professional services roll up and an individual from a large PR firm here in Chicago who's looking to buy."

"Interesting. Is he buying for his employer or for himself?"

"Himself. He's a senior account manager for the largest PR agency here in the city. They're huge. Jeremy tells me this fellow's frustrated with corporate politics and wants his own firm."

"He sounds like a solid option for you. I mean, he can bring some of his clients across—maybe some of his colleagues as well."

"Yes, I've thought about that," Jacqueline said. "But his accounts are apparently all major corporations."

"And what's wrong with that? You're in a people business. Often, smaller agencies are better because you're more nimble and agile and would be much more responsive."

"Good point. Well he's the final meeting of the three on Monday, and I actually bumped into him this morning at the baseball field."

"Woah. What? You know him already?"

"No, not really. His son plays in the same little league baseball club as my grandson. We did meet last year, but it was just a coincidence we saw each other today. Tina needed me to take Jarred to a game, and this fellow was there with his son."

At that moment, Jacqueline froze. The second time that day.

And for the second time that day, she saw Terence.

He was standing at the restaurant's check-in desk with a woman who appeared to be his wife. And in a further twist of irony, he was wearing practically the same outfit as Jack. Blue blazer, white shirt and jeans, but with Chelsea boots instead of Elon Musk shoes. The hostess began walking them to their table, and as they walked past Jacqueline and Jack, Terence froze like a rabbit in the headlights.

"Jacqueline! We have to stop meeting like this."

Both burst into laughter.

This time, Jacqueline rose from her seat and gave him a hug. She never did that and didn't quite know why she did it this time.

Jacqueline introduced Terence to Jack, and then Terence introduced his wife Julie to both of them. They chatted politely about the food for a minute. "Definitely have the chicken and truffle dumplings and the pad thai noodles. They're incredible," Jacqueline said, and Jack nodded like an obedient puppy.

After taking their leave, Terence and Julie proceeded to their own table and sat down. "Who was that, my love? Should I be worried?" she asked with a grin.

"*That*, my love, is Jacqueline Turley. She owns a PR firm here in the city called JAT. I'm meeting her on Monday about potentially buying her business."

The Turleys had been crazy busy during the week (in addition to having her hands full with the kids, Julie worked a part-time schedule as a dentist), so this was Julie's first time to hear of Terence's upcoming meeting with Jacqueline.

Terence spent most of the meal updating Julie on his acquisition project. He talked about all the calls he'd had, the new connections he'd made and what was on the docket for next week.

"Does Creative PR know what you're doing?" she asked.

"Not really. The boss called me yesterday and said he'd noticed I've been distant since I lost the Nike account and had it replaced by Universal, so he seems to know I'm not exactly happy." (Terence had to fly out again next week to Los Angeles—something he wasn't looking forward to.)

"Clearly, though, I can't quit my job until I own a business and it's generating cash flow for us. We have a good financial foundation right now, but I don't want to put it at risk by disrupting our income. I'm looking at multiple deals right now, and I'll make sure the business I buy has enough free cash flow for us, after debt service, so there's no dent in our income. In fact, with my skills in business development, I expect we'll be generating a lot more income for the family within two to three years."

"That all sounds great, dear. Where are you finding these deals?"

"Well, JAT came from her CPA. He knows my attorney buddy, Lawrence, and he connected us. All the other deals in my funnel are from brokers, and these people, for the most part, are arrogant and aggressive. They seem to be geared for selling businesses to competitors rather than individuals like me."

"So, JAT's your favorite so far?"

"Too early to say. I've only had one real seller meeting. I'm meeting in-person with Jacqueline Monday afternoon to get under the hood of her business, but I have three seller Zoom calls that morning before I meet with her. I'm going to take a personal day on Monday to smash out all these meetings. I should have a good sense of the perfect business by the end of the day, since by that stage I'll have interacted directly with five of them."

The evening was wearing on by then, so they wrapped up dinner (the chicken and truffle dumplings had proven to be outstanding, just as Jacqueline predicted), paid the check and caught an Uber home.

Chapter 20

The Big Meeting

On Monday morning, Terence hit the Peloton, showered, dressed, ate breakfast and then spent an hour clearing the messages from his corporate life. Although he was on a personal vacation day (he had four seller meetings today), he wanted to make sure the wheels would still be turning in his absence.

His meeting with Jacqueline wasn't scheduled until 4 p.m. Prior to that, he had three back-to-back meetings between 9 a.m. and noon, all on Zoom. Although he felt a little nervous for the first one, by the time he finished the third meeting, he'd begun to really enjoy them, and his confidence had shot up 10 times compared to what it had been before.

After lunch, Terence went back over his notes from the morning's meetings:

Deal 1

Spook Media LLC
Gary, IN
Revenues = $5,350,000
SDE = $387,000
Ask = $2,000,000
Multiple = 5.2X
Pros: Retiring business owner. Friendly broker. Listed for 11 months. Open to a creative deal.
Cons: Out of state, overvalued, only 30% of revenue from PR. Seller not really motivated.

Deal 2

Staple Communications Inc.
Detroit, MI
Revenues = $2,593,000
SDE = $146,000
Ask = $650,000
Multiple = 4.5X
Pros: 100% PR-focused. Solid number two to run operations.
Cons: Out of state, overvalued. No recurring revenue, all project-based.

Deal 3

Whitecloud Services LLC
Chicago, IL
Revenues = $1,560,200
SDE = $302,400
Ask = $900,000
Multiple = 3X
Pros: Recurring revenue, ideal bolt-on acquisition to a larger deal. Strong focus on online women's retail (high-growth market).
Cons: Seller "is" the business. No real team, not enough free cash flow to quit the W2.

It turned out that two of these three brokers were, like Bill Frisk the "pal" guy, overly aggressive nutjobs, but the broker on deal one was super professional and actually took the time to try to sell him on the acquisition, which Terence appreciated. The broker had thoroughly researched Terence and sold him hard to the owner.

Why can't all brokers be like that? he wondered.

He concluded, however, that deal one was a no-go. Just too many negatives to outweigh the positives. Deal two ticked a lot of boxes; he would offer on that one, perhaps next week. Deal three was too small and too owner-dependent, but he had watched Carl run a training for bolt-on acquisitions. Once you've acquired your platform business, you can then bolt on or tuck in smaller deals and use your existing team and infrastructure to support it. Deal three would be one of those, surmised Terence, but he needed to close his first deal before entertaining any sort of offer for deal three.

Terence dressed conservatively for the 4 p.m. in-person meeting. He was actually wearing the same jeans from Saturday night (he hoped Jacqueline wouldn't notice) but had on a blue shirt and gray blazer this time. A black pair of Cole Hans completed the ensemble.

As he walked down Michigan Avenue to the meeting, he snuck into a sports retailer and purchased a Chicago Cubs hat to wear to the meeting. He felt after the two impromptu meetings on Saturday with Jacqueline that rapport was building between the two of them, and he recalled her love of the Cubs with her late husband. Walking into the meeting sporting a Cubs hat, he decided, would be a nice touch.

At the reception desk of Jeremy Brown & Associates, Terence gave his name, then saw Jacqueline through the glass walls of the conference room. When she saw Terence, she started laughing. He walked into the room (Jeremy was wrapping up a call in his office, ironically with another potential buyer), and both Terence and Jacqueline embraced (again) like old friends. Jacqueline was blown away by the Cubs hat. He clearly wasn't wearing the hat for warmth (it was near 70 degrees outside) or for style (he looked odd with it on). He was wearing it as a gesture to her.

Amazing.

"Nice hat, Terence," laughed Jacqueline.

"Yeah, I thought you'd like it. Go Cubs!"

The two chatted for a few minutes about the food on Saturday night (the dumplings and noodles received an inordinate amount of praise) until Jeremy walked in.

"Good afternoon to you both. I see you already know each other?"

"Well, not really," replied Jacqueline, "but the universe seems to have this idea that we should keep meeting. We bumped into each other twice on Saturday alone, but we haven't spoken about the business at all yet. I didn't want to do that without you being here."

Jeremy put a pile of documents on the table. The CIM, financial accounts, a summary of the KPI financial dashboards from the prior 24-months and also a stack of tax returns, in case Terence needed them.

"I'm actually not going to dive into the numbers in this meeting," Terence clarified, "but thank you for bringing all of this. We can connect on the numbers later. I really just wanted to meet Jacqueline, but in a formal capacity this time, and get to understand the business and whether it's a fit for my requirements."

"Why don't you paint that picture for us first, Terence?"

Sure. I'm 40 and have been in PR ever since college. I'm a senior account manager for Creative PR, Inc. We typically work with Fortune 500 accounts. I look after Starbucks, Publix, Universal Studios, Apple's iCloud business and several smaller accounts.

My biggest account used to be Nike, but it was taken away from me recently, and that flicked a switch in my brain. I want to be a partner at the firm and actually left my last employer because there wasn't a partnership track there for me. I'm sensing the same thing at Creative PR. I make great money but not to the levels where I can retire early or do crazy things.

I've always wanted to be my own boss, and, quite frankly, the thought of starting a business from scratch terrifies me. I've been learning all about business acquisitions and decided that acquiring a cash flowing, successful small business close to home and going in as an owner-investor versus an owner-operator would appeal more to my skills.

"I'm great with numbers, vision, strategy and big-ticket selling. I don't handle the weeds too well, so I definitely want to buy a business that has an operations team that can continue the day-to-day."

"Where are you in the process?" asked Jeremy.

"Well, very early, to be honest. I have approximately 15 deals in my pipeline at the moment. None are at an advanced stage; however, I'm close to submitting an offer on one. This is the only off-market deal I'm looking at right now. The rest are broker deals; however, I'm going to be adding more off-market deals to my funnel in the coming weeks."

Jacqueline frowned when she heard this. She felt less "special." She'd thought Terence was her perfect buyer and had scouted only her business. But, to be fair, Jeremy had set up almost ten other meetings for her to talk to prospective buyers; however she really liked Terence. It wasn't the hat (although that was a lovely gesture). He just seemed perfect as the new owner of this business. *Let's wait and see*, she thought.

Terence then added, "But this is my favorite business on paper at this point. It's a bullseye hit in my buy box."

Terence walked over to the whiteboard in the conference room and wrote out his buy box in bright red marker.

Business: PR agency but can also include marketing and advertising services

Location: Chicago, wider Illinois, Michigan and Ohio
Size: $3 million to $5 million in revenue
Profit: $450,000 to $750,000 (15% margin)
Role: Owner-investor but needs a solid GM in place to drive operations day-to-day

Jacqueline smiled. Yes, her business was a bullseye hit.

Jacqueline confirmed this verbally and then said something that really resonated with Terence.

Look, Terence, let me level with you. I'm going to be talking with and meeting lots of potential acquirers over the coming days and weeks. Some are competitors of ours. Others are financial buyers, and there are others, like you, from the PR industry that want their own business. I do want a fair deal, but the future of the business and my life's work is very important to me. I feel like my business is my legacy, and I want to protect that. Also, my employees are like my family. I need to ensure they'll be protected through this, and with my endorsement of the right buyer, they'll run through brick walls for that person.

With that in mind, I do like you and would love to tell you more about my business. We have a management presentation prepared, and I can walk you through it. I can conference call my GM, Phillip, and controller, Lucy, if needed; however, Jeremy here isn't just my CPA, he also serves as my fractional CFO, so he can answer any financial questions you might have.

"If you still want to move forward after today, I'd then like you to meet Phillip and Lucy."

Terence expressed his agreement with her plan, so Jacqueline walked him through the management presentation, with Jeremy interjecting several times regarding the financial aspects.

She covered the history of the business, the sales cycle, the operating model and how the various teams (PR, advertising and marketing) delivered projects to clients. She also went through the organizational chart in some detail and walked Terence through how it had been built, who was accountable for what results and how those results were measured and reported weekly. She logged into her business intelligence dashboard at one point and pulled up real time statistics on the new business pipeline, marketing return on ad spend metrics, even the productivity metrics for her team.

This is an excellent business, thought Terence. It was by far the best opportunity he'd seen so far. But the absence of an asking price still felt odd.

"Thank you, Jacqueline. That was most helpful. Do you mind if I ask you some clarifying questions, please?"

"Sure, go ahead," Jacqueline said with a nod.

"First, and excuse my ignorance, but I don't see an asking price. All the other broker deals I'm looking at have clearly defined valuations. I have to say some of them are overpriced, but I'm learning quickly that some brokers do that."

Jeremy interjected. "We do have a valuation range in mind, but we aren't prepared to share that at such an early stage. I'd recommend you continue to vet the business and once you're ready, make an offer. Then we can get into valuation and deal structure options with you. So, what I'm really saying is that we're soliciting offers, and we're going to set a deadline of two weeks from today for all offers. Then Jacqueline will make a decision, and I'm sure she'll take my counsel on this."

"Okay, that's fair," Terence replied.

He went through all of his clarifying questions, covering margins, length of sales cycle, and so forth. Jacqueline also went into the new business pipeline in more depth and even dropped names of some businesses close to mandates. Terence actually knew one of the businesses on the list. It was Smile Exotic Inc., the dental practice chain his wife worked for. Terence also knew its head of marketing very well.

"My wife works there as a dentist," said Terence, "and I'm great friends with Toni the marketing director. Want me to put in a good word for you? Regardless of what happens here, I'd be happy to do that. JAT seems the perfect fit for those guys."

The rapport was going deeper and the relationship was getting stronger. Terence was really playing full out.

He wrapped up with a great question at the end.

"If you weren't selling and you had unlimited resources, what would you do in the next five years with this business?"

Jacqueline was floored by the brilliance of the question. She suddenly felt a surge of excited energy flow through her body.

Well, I'd definitely go much deeper into the medical sector. It's very strong here in Illinois, and I know a lot of the mid-market providers don't have great PR partners.

I'd also open offices in Ohio and Michigan. We're constantly receiving requests for proposals from both states, but I've been narrow minded and have kept my business firmly entrenched here in Chicago.

And I'd explore multiple joint ventures and perhaps acquire a small marketing agency. That's the weakest link in our chain. Filling that gap would allow us to win more marketing projects, then pull those clients over into our advertising and PR, where we're much stronger and the margins are much higher.

Jacqueline was speaking with a great deal of energy, so much so that Terence began to worry if it was a good idea to have asked the question. Her body language had changed, as if she'd caught on fire. Then, just as suddenly, she closed her eyes, sat back in her chair and sighed wearily, her mind over-taxed by the attempt to sort out the many strategic, tactical and operational elements needed to pull all these plans off.

After a few more moments lost in deep reflection, she composed herself, then resumed speaking.

"Terence, let me first say 'thank you' for asking that question. Attempting to answer it has actually confirmed in my mind just now, in a very strong way, my absolute desire to sell this business and retire. The business certainly has great potential to grow, but the task is much more than I want to take on at this point in my life. If you do buy the business, though, I would love to stay connected and give you any advice you might want moving forward, over and above any formal handover period."

Terence smiled. He definitely liked the thought of keeping Jacqueline around in some capacity.

Can I keep her as a minority shareholder? he thought to himself. *How would that work?* That was a question for Carl on the Protégé Q&A call later in the week.

They wrapped up the meeting. It had lasted almost two hours—much longer than the Zoom call from the first seller call.

Everyone said their goodbyes, and Terence promised to get back to them with next steps.

There hadn't been a single question on how he was going to fund this deal. *Refreshing*, he thought as he skipped out of the lobby and into the sunshine. He vowed to himself, following the success of this meeting, not to pursue any more broker deals beyond the ones currently in his pipeline.

He loved this business and dreamed of owning it. However, he also thought about what Carl would remind them on every Protégé call, "It's a numbers game. Don't get deal heat." He was definitely falling in love with this business. *Time to find other options in case Jacqueline sells to someone else*, Terence told himself.

Chapter 21

More Seller Meetings

Jacqueline and Jeremy met with ten other potential buyers besides Terence, making a short list of eleven.

Five were trade buyers.
Three were financial buyers.
Three were individuals, including Terence.

The three financial buyers had in common that they each wanted to buy 70% of the business, retain Jacqueline for two years, then acquire her remaining 30%. One wanted her to work full time (which was a deal breaker), but another, Jolene Vardy of Masters Capital LLC of Dallas, wanted just a 10-hour-per-week commitment, which was roughly what Jacqueline was doing today. Master's investment thesis was to do a roll-up of smaller professional services businesses throughout the country, targeting PR, advertising, marketing, recruitment, legal and CPA firms. It had been steadily acquiring legal, financial and recruitment businesses. However, it had identified a big demand from its customers for PR, advertising and marketing. JAT appealed to them since it did all three and would, therefore, be a good test-case acquisition.

Jacqueline didn't really buy into the strategy, but she really liked Jolene. Jolene was a 25-year CFO and private equity partner who had come from the pharmaceutical industry. Jacqueline's role would be to effectively sell her business into this roll-up, then be the spokesperson for other retiring sellers. That part did actually appeal to her, which meant Masters was still high on her list.

Terence's question about future growth plans had created lots of conflict within Jacqueline. Yes, it confirmed she wasn't the leader to make all of that happen, but staying loosely connected and supporting a new owner who would execute on that vision was very appealing to her.

The trade buyers didn't really interest her. None of them could care less about her culture, her brand or her operation. They each had their own and would be spreading it into her business as soon as the deal was closed. Jacqueline found all three trade buyers focused only on the numbers—nothing else mattered. A shame.

The guys from LA wanted to essentially create a Chicago office and promised to keep the entire team intact and move offices to a much larger space to scale it 3X to 4X over the next few years. They had a lot of accounts in Chicago, but clearly the culture would change drastically and her brand, JAT, would disappear basically overnight.

From all the meetings, only Masters Capital and Terence felt good to her. The rest were of no interest; however, Jeremy warned her about dismissing anyone until offers had come in, since those offers could be leveraged in negotiations with her preferred buyers.

Jeremy and Lucy worked with all of the prospective buyers on the numbers, and several promised to submit offers before the deadline, just over a week from now.

For his part, Terence met with six more business owners after meeting with Jacqueline. Some had come from direct approaches his new VA had originated for him. Others came from leftover broker leads and some from his favorite deal flow method, the deal intermediary network.

Lawrence himself had originated a deal for him, but it was losing money, so Terence dropped it.

Shortly after the meeting with Jacqueline, Terence stopped by his wife's dental practice and, as he had promised, put in a good word with Toni about JAT. He even told her in confidence (they were friends, after all) that he would be making an offer later that week to acquire the business.

While he was there, Toni gave him a lead from a frustrated PR firm owner who had pitched for the dental business. He called the business owner and got the summary numbers. They were terrible, however. He sighed and remembered Carl's advice: "It's a numbers game." Well, these numbers were shit. He moved on.

All in all, he had met or had Zoom calls with ten different businesses, and it was time to start making offers.

There were two things, however, that he needed to do first.

One, he needed to start talking to financiers. His initial calls with Live Stem and the SBA broker, Anthony Marks, had gone well, but he wanted expressions of interest on both before he made offers. He guessed that any sellers would want proof of funds before signing an LOI, potentially even a term sheet.

Second, Carl was running a training on the next Protégé call about seller psychology and how it impacted both the valuation of a business and the potential deal structures and terms you could offer.

Once he had checked both these items off his to-do list, he'd be ready to make all his offers.

Chapter 22

Terence Values JAT

Terence had attended a training from Carl called the four pillars of valuation. It was fascinating. Terence always thought valuation came down purely to the numbers (which was one pillar), but there were three other pillars as well: seller psychology, the deal structure and the transfer of value across the four segments of business goodwill—namely, customer goodwill, employee goodwill, social goodwill (brand, culture, reputation, etc.) and, finally, structural goodwill (systems, processes, KPIs and owner dependency).

Carl had provided the worksheet to run the analysis, and following a review of the CIM and his notes from the seller meeting, Terence decided to do the work.

JAT PR LLC

Pillar	Rating	Score
Customer	Strong (6)	5
Employee	Strong (6)	5
Structural	Strong (6)	3
Social	Strong (6)	3

18/24

DEALMAKER WEALTH

75%

Terence went through the checklists of the four pillars.

JAT was above average on customer and employee goodwill. There was low customer concentration but not much recurring revenue. Most work appeared to be project based, which was a shame but something Terence could fix very quickly. All the clients at Creative were recurring monthly fees with larger fees for specific bulky projects.

Although Terence hadn't met any of the employees, they also seemed above average. *Typical for a smaller firm*, he thought.

What really impressed Terence was the structural goodwill. All systems and processes were documented, the owner didn't operate the business and there were 24 months of KPIs that showed the business was performing well. All key metrics were measured and managed.

Social goodwill was also above average, which was strange for a PR firm. The outside reputation was good, but the internal culture lacked energy, sort of like the current owner. Terence smiled. *These guys won't know what's hit them if I buy it and put my mark on it.* He hoped the majority of the employees would stay and embrace some of the high-energy changes he would quickly make.

All in all, JAT was a solid business. An 18 out of 24 goodwill score, or 75%. So, not quite best-in-class, but above average. The business would probably land in the middle of the multiple ranges for the sector.

Next, Terence plugged the numbers into the Protégé model Carl had provided.

Income Statement	2022	2021	2020
Revenue	3,460,200	3,172,882	2,873,882
Y/Y Growth	9.1%	10.4%	3.5%
Cost of Goods Sold	(200,584)	(329,980)	(235,658)
Gross Profit	3,259,616	2,842,902	2,638,224
Gross Margin, %	94.2%	89.6%	91.8%
SG&A Expenses	(2,659,218)	(2,337,424)	(2,214,667)
EBITDA	600,398	505,478	423,556
Add backs	214,102	198,332	176,382
SDE	814,500	703,810	599,938
Less Take Backs	(120,000)	(120,000)	(120,000)
Adjusted EBITDA	**694,500**	**583,810**	**479,938**
Margin, %	20.1%	18.4%	16.7%

The business was consistently growing close to 10% per year, and margins were solid for the industry.

Terence took the SDE numbers that Jeremy had provided and reduced them by $120,000, which would be his replacement cost as the new CEO owner. He would keep Phillip in the business as the day-to-day GM, but he loved the profit numbers.

The adjusted EBITDA for the last financial year was $694,000 and profit had been growing consistently over the last few years.

NAICS	NAICS Industry Sector	2013	2014	2015	2016	2017	2018	2019	2020	2021	2022
23	Construction	4.0	3.4	3.6	3.3	3.7	4.0	3.5	3.2	4.0	3.5
31-33	Manufacturing	7.2	5.8	6.1	6.5	5.8	7.0	5.1	5.0	4.5	4.2
42	Wholesale Trade	4.8	6.2	6.9	6.4	5.6	4.7	4.9	4.7	4.9	4.5
44-45	Retail Trade	3.1	3.4	3.5	3.5	3.6	3.8	4.0	5.1	3.6	3.0
48-49	Transportation and Warehousing	3.2	3.2	3.5	4.2	3.6	3.2	3.5	4.3	3.9	3.0
51	Information	8.6	10.0	6.9	10.7	13.6	14.7	9.3	18.5	17.4	7.0
52	Finance and Insurance	3.7	6.2	7.8	9.8	13.4	12.1	9.2	8.3	6.2	4.2
53	Real Estate, Rental, and Leasing	2.4	4.5	2.9	3.8	4.2	6.1	4.0	7.7	4.1	3.3
54	Professional, Scientific, and Technical Services	4.6	5.5	8.1	5.5	5.7	4.7	4.7	4.7	3.9	3.6	→ 3.6X
56	Administrative, Support, Waste Mgmt., and Remediation Svcs.	2.6	2.8	3.0	3.8	3.7	3.4	5.0	4.1	3.3	2.9
61	Educational Services	2.7	3.5	3.6	4.1	3.1	4.1	3.8	1.9	9.0	3.3
62	Health Care and Social Assistance	4.6	4.2	3.2	4.2	3.8	4.6	3.8	3.5	4.1	3.5
71	Arts, Entertainment, and Recreation	3.1	3.6	3.3	4.3	3.3	3.5	3.8	4.1	2.9	2.4
72	Accommodation and Food Services	1.8	2.2	2.4	2.4	2.8	2.8	3.3	2.6	2.3	2.4
81	Other Services	2.6	2.4	2.8	2.6	3.1	2.9	3.5	3.4	3.2	3.0
	All Sectors	3.3	3.9	3.8	3.9	4.1	4.1	4.2	4.2	3.7	3.4

Note: Each data point in this chart is based on a minimum of 10 transaction multiples. If there are not enough transaction multiples for a particular year or quarter, the data are not included.

NAICS	NAICS Industry Sector	2013	2014	2015	2016	2017	2018	2019	2020	2021	2022
23	Construction	9%	11%	11%	12%	9%	10%	11%	13%	10%	13%
31-33	Manufacturing	8%	10%	9%	7%	10%	9%	8%	10%	10%	13%
42	Wholesale Trade	6%	8%	6%	9%	8%	7%	8%	6%	10%	10%
44-45	Retail Trade	10%	9%	8%	10%	9%	8%	11%	8%	10%	13%
48-49	Transportation and Warehousing	15%	13%	17%	18%	19%	14%	13%	12%	14%	19%
51	Information	0%	5%	6%	1%	4%	2%	9%	6%	1%	10%
52	Finance and Insurance	26%	21%	19%	24%	27%	24%	29%	15%	20%	38%
53	Real Estate, Rental, and Leasing	25%	17%	16%	17%	15%	14%	25%	13%	13%	19%
54	Professional, Scientific, and Technical Services	10%	10%	8%	14%	14%	14%	17%	15%	17%	22%	→ 22%
56	Administrative, Support, Waste Mgmt., and Remediation Svcs.	18%	16%	15%	15%	17%	15%	14%	12%	16%	22%
61	Educational Services	10%	15%	8%	16%	18%	17%	14%	11%	13%	23%
62	Health Care and Social Assistance	10%	12%	15%	11%	12%	12%	17%	12%	13%	14%
71	Arts, Entertainment, and Recreation	18%	19%	10%	12%	17%	7%	18%	0%	23%	18%
72	Accommodation and Food Services	15%	13%	12%	14%	13%	13%	12%	11%	13%	14%
81	Other Services	13%	14%	14%	15%	13%	15%	11%	10%	15%	19%
	All Sectors	12%	11%	11%	12%	11%	12%	11%	11%	12%	15%

Note: Each data point in this chart is based on a minimum of 10 transaction multiples. If there are not enough transaction multiples for a particular year or quarter, the data are not included.

Terence consulted his deal database that tracked the average multiples (based on profit size) for a range of industries, listed by NAICS code.

3.6X was the multiple for this business, and Terence was also encouraged to see that the EBITDA profit margin was in line with industry averages for the niche.

Next, Terence had to adjust for working capital and any liabilities that were going to be inherited. Jeremy had indicated that Jacqueline would pay off the

$137,000 of non-current liabilities from the closing payment. This was a bank loan.

The net working capital was $912,000, of which $540,000 was cash. The rest was AR.

Terence calculated the ratios.

Net working capital (NWC) = $912,000 / $3,460,200 = 26.3%

He also calculated that it was 96 days, so more than the 60 days (or two months of revenue that Carl recommends).

The surplus was the additional 36 days.

Surplus NWC = 36 / 365 X $3,460,200 = $341,280

Terence added this to the valuation. He didn't want Jacqueline taking the surplus out, as he needed it for growth, so he would have to add it to the enterprise value.

Income Statement	3-Yr Average
Adjusted EBITDA	694,500
Margin, %	20.1%
3-Yr Average	586,083
Multiple	3.6
Enterprise Value (EV)	2,109,898
Add Surplus Working Capital	341,280
Less Inherited Debt	0
100% Equity Value	2,451,178

The valuation came back at just over $2,400,000.

That would involve a $240,000 equity down payment for the SBA, so he would need an investing partner, as that level of investment would clear out virtually all his liquid capital.

Lawrence is pretty rich, Terence thought. *Maybe he'd come in on the deal with me. Or maybe even Carl, if I pitch the deal to him on Red-Light, Green-Light this week?* Terence had seen several Protégés invest in student deals as well, so he was hopeful he would get the additional $140,000 from someone.

Terence then pondered the idea of seller psychology. Carl had mentioned that a distressed seller would have a lower-than-average valuation (and now Terence knew the average valuation was about $2,400,000). Although he knew Jacqueline was looking to sell, she wasn't overly distressed, and especially with other potential buyers in the mix, he knew he couldn't discount the valuation from that perspective.

Finally, he looked at the deal structures. $2,400,000 would be for an SBA deal. But, what about an annuity deal? He knew the valuation would have to increase (since the seller would be taking all the risk), but by how much?

Terence decided to use one of his 911 allotted one-to-one coaching calls. He submitted the request and was promptly scheduled to chat with coach Wayne in two hours.

On the call, Wayne went through the deal with Terence and explained Carl's algorithm on the annuity deal. Carl had analyzed hundreds of deals, looking at how much cash was paid at close versus how much was in seller finance or earn outs. Some of those deals were his; some were from the hundreds of deals closed by Protégé students.

The math looked like this:

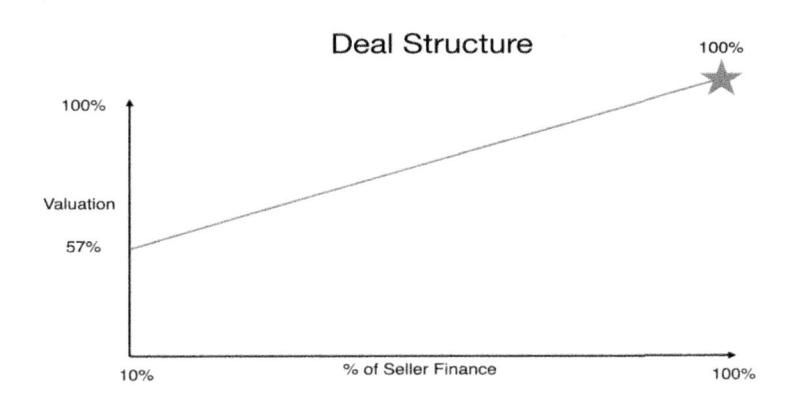

Deal Structure

(Graph: Valuation on y-axis ranging from 57% to 100%, % of Seller Finance on x-axis ranging from 10% to 100%, with a line from (10%, 57%) to (100%, 100%))

Carl had calculated that if an SBA deal was presented, it reflected 57% of the valuation for a 100% seller finance deal structure.

Terence quickly did the math for an annuity deal.

$2,400,000 / 57% = $4,21,000

Wowzers! thought Terence. *That's more than four million dollars. But Jacqueline is taking all the risk, right?*

The final step was to calculate the most important number of all: the debt-service cover-ratio, or DSCR. Carl would reject all deals where this was less than 1.50.

The DSCR was essentially cash flow generated by the business (adjusted and recasted EBITDA) divided by the amount of debt service the deal needed to pay for itself principal and interest).

Terence calculated it for the two deal structures.

Carl's model on the SBA payment structure calculated the following . . .

SBA 7a Calculator	
Purchase Price	2,400,000
SBA Fees @ 3%	72,000
Closing Costs	30,000
Total	2,502,000
Buyer Equity @ 10%	250,200
SBA 7a Loan @ 80%	2,001,600
Seller Note @ 10%	250,200
Interest Rate	8.0%
Annual Repayment	219,419
Term	10 Years

The DSCR was now easy.

DSCR = $694,500 (current adjusted EBITDA) / $219,419 = 3.17

So, way north of 1.50. *Bingo!*

Now, Terence was curious if the 10-year annuity deal would work. He wouldn't offer interest to the seller, since the valuation would be almost double that via the SBA analysis, therefore …

$4,210,000 over 10-years = $421,000 per year
DSCR = $694,500 / $421,000 = 1.65

This was much closer to the 1.50 minimum but still cleared the hurdle, and with his plans to grow the business, the DSCR would increase in both deal structures. Terence was delighted.

Chapter 23

Terence Prepares JAT for the RLGL Call

Curious as to whether Carl and his coaches would like the JAT deal, Terence was determined to get it presented to the Red-Light, Green-Light call this week. He had only 24 hours to hit the submission deadline.

He completed the deal submission model and, once he had inputted more detail from the balance sheet, came up with virtually the same valuation numbers—to within $50,000.

Terence's one-sheet, which Carl and his coaches would review on the deal.

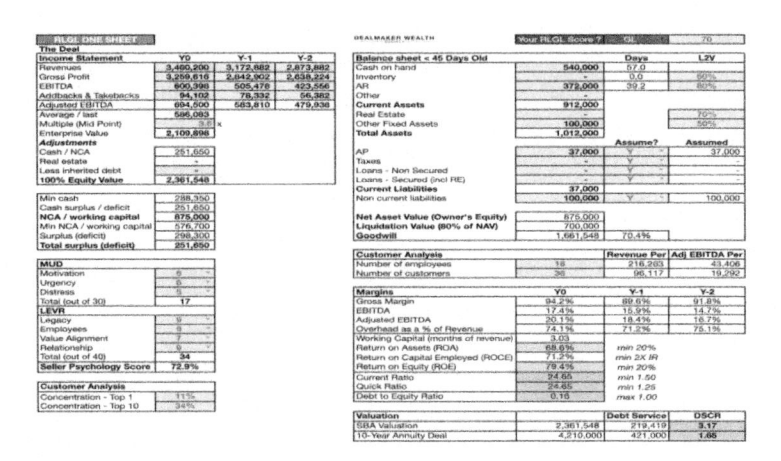

(For a copy of this model for your own deals, please visit
http://www.creativedealmakerbook.com)

The model also calculated the various business and financial ratios and computed the seller psychology scores.

The MUD score reflects three elements of seller psychology:

Motivation
Urgency
Distress

Jacqueline scored 17 out of 30, so average. She was motivated to sell but not distressed.

The LEVR score tracks the following:

Requirement for legacy
Employee protection requirements
Values alignment
Level of rapport and relationship

    Jacqueline scored very high on this measure, 34 out of 40, so combined with the MUD score, she had a 72.9% seller psychology score, which is high. This would allow Terence to acquire the business on sensible terms.
    Terence submitted the deal and in surprisingly short order received confirmation via email that it had been accepted for presentation. He was stoked. Now, he needed to wait 24 hours to have Carl grill him on the deal.
    "I can't wait," Terence said to himself.

Chapter 24

Jeremy and Jacqueline Set the JAT Valuation Range

Jacqueline was happy to have completed the seller meetings and was now simply waiting for the offers. Terence had said in a follow-up meeting that he'd be submitting an offer within a week. He was just vetting the deal and would be meeting with the bank and pitching to investors in a group deal community he was part of.

In preparation, Jeremy brought in a college buddy, Matthew Parris, who was a Certified Tax Planner. Jacqueline joined him and Jeremy on a Zoom call.

"I wish you'd notified me earlier," Matthew said in a lightly scolding but friendly tone. "If I'd known six months ago, I could've put measures in place to minimize tax liability on this deal. There are a few things we can still do, however, and I appreciate you bringing me into this deal."

Matthew then went down a very deep rabbit hole on tax efficiency strategies, none of which would yield too much in savings at this late stage.

"The best I think we can do on this will be about 25% in taxes, provided you sell the equity and not the assets. The buyer may want to do an asset deal, since they'd get a step-up in tax basis and will probably not want to inherit any liabilities.

"If it's a trade buyer, definitely expect an asset sale. If it's an individual, he or she will probably want to do a stock or equity purchase, as it makes it easier for external financing. Financial buyers will typically do either."

Okay, so definitely a stock deal, Jacqueline thought. *Now all I need to do is convince the right buyer to follow suit.* Matthew then laid down the likely taxation on an asset deal. Based on Jacqueline's and JAT's particular circumstances, it was brutal: 40%. *Ouch!*

Jeremy laid out the valuation ranges he had come up with. He too (although independently) had performed some transfer-of-value analysis. He scored JAT slightly higher than Terence had.

JAT PR LLC

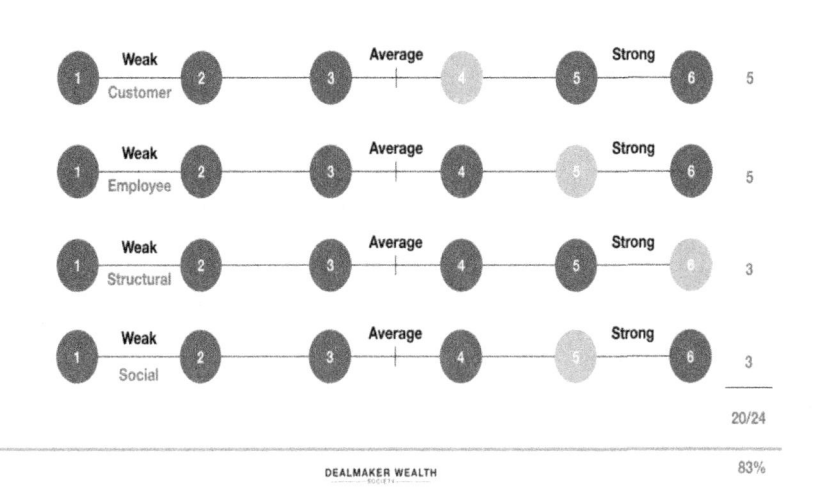

Category	Weak	Average	Strong	Score
Customer	1 — 2	3 — 4	5 — 6	5
Employee	1 — 2	3 — 4	5 — 6	5
Structural	1 — 2	3 — 4	5 — 6	3
Social	1 — 2	3 — 4	5 — 6	3

20/24

DEALMAKER WEALTH — 83%

"At 83%, Jacqueline, your business is best-in-class. Although this is a subjective analysis, I'm confident that with the buyers in the mix, we can command a premium multiple of your adjusted or recasted EBITDA.

"My deal database predicts a multiple of 3.6X as an average PR business with the full range of values from 1.8X to 5.2X, so I'm going to price the business at a 5X multiple of your 2022 recasted EBITDA.

"I'm then going to vary that for the three different buyer groups. Individual buyers are generally at the mercy of the capital markets, namely, the SBA 7a loan program, and with interest rates at 8% I can't see the banks supporting a 5X multiple. Trade buyers and financial buyers will have no problem supporting that valuation. Trade buyers may go to 5.5X or even 6X based on the cross-selling opportunities they can realize and, of course, the financial synergies from combining your business with their own."

Jeremy's Multiples

Average for market = 3.6X

Best-in-class business = 5X
Trade buyer = 6X
Financial buyer = 5.3X
Individual = 4.5X

2022 recasted EBITDA = $694,500
2023 forecasted EBITDA = $987,300
Average = $840,900

Jeremy stated that he would use an average of both last year and the current year forecast, although the year was only part way through.

Valuations		EV
2022 R/EBITDA	694,500	-
2023 R/EBITDA Forecast	987,300	-
Average	840,900	-
Multiples		
Trade Buyer	6.0X	5,045,400
Financial Buyer	5.3X	4,456,770
Individual	4.5X	3,784,050
Market Average	3.6X	3,027,240
Best in Class	5.0X	4,204,500

Using this two-year average and applying the different buyer-case multiples generated a valuation range between $3,027,240 and $5,045,400, with the buyer-agnostic, best-in-class valuation being about $4,200,000.

Jeremy was confident he could command and receive a valuation north of $4,000,000.

He presented this information to Jacqueline, who cracked a wide smile. "You really think the business is worth $4,000,000?"

"Yes, I do. I'm very confident with the growth you're experiencing. $1,000,000 in profit next year is definitely achievable, and it's just a 4X multiple of that. Yes, I can deliver $4,000,000. Now, $5,000,000 may be a stretch, but let's wait for the offers and deal structures to come in, and then we can decide who's the best buyer with the best deal terms for you."

Jacqueline left the meeting in high spirits and went to meet some friends for coffee. On the walk to the coffee shop, she marveled at the science behind all this. It reminded her of her late husband's real estate career. Although a developer, he would price real estate in the same way: look at market comparables and have different price ranges based on who the end buyer was.

There're so many parallels between business and real estate, she mused. *If only Bill were here to help guide me through this.*

She looked up at the sky and thought of Bill fondly. At the same time, her phone buzzed, revealing a text message from Jack. *Spooky*, she thought. *Maybe Jack is the new Bill.* She pondered that thought in multiple ways. They were getting closer, and she really liked him. Jack was, she could tell, enamored by her. *Maybe he can be a confidante in business, then a confidante in life, afterwards?*

Intrigued by the thought, she was grinning like a Cheshire cat when she walked into the coffee shop and greeted her girlfriends.

Chapter 25

Carl's RLGL Review of JAT

Carl started the Red Light, Green Light (RLGL) review call in the usual way. He went around the room quickly greeting all the attendees with their cameras on. This was about 50 of the approximately 170 people on the call. He gave a big shout out to Terence and mentioned his deal as one of the four being reviewed that day.

"Terence from Chicago has submitted a badass PR agency for consideration." Terence smiled. *I think he may like it.* This gave Terence a big boost in confidence.

His last deal review pitch bombed. Carl and his coaches hated it and rightly so. It received an average RL 68 score.

Carl, his coaching team and the fellow Protégés voted on each deal put up for consideration in a RLGL review. The rating system was as follows:

A green light (GL) meant "proceed with the deal," using the instructions to close provided in the review call. A numerical value was given along with the green light designation: the higher the score, the better the deal. For example, a GL100 would be, essentially, the best deal you've ever seen, what Carl called a "golden buzzer" deal (a phrase he had borrowed from the popular TV show, *America's Got Talen*t). Carl had only ever handed out three "golden buzzer" scores in the past four years of the program. All three of those deals closed, and Carl actually partnered on (i.e., invested in) two of them. (All, by the way, later yielded huge returns for investors.) A GL10, on the other hand, would be the lowest score a deal could get and still be a green light: effectively, a narrow pass, so "proceed but with caution."

Conversely, an RL100 would be the *worst* deal ever. Carl likes to tell the story of the "pet rental business" someone pitched in the past. (Think about that one for a moment.) An RL10, on the other hand, would be a narrow fail; that is, the deal could potentially pay off, but there would likely need to be some major pivots.

The point of this weekly exercise was not only to give Protégés clarity on their deals (and exactly how to close them if it was a GL) but to provide a safe space for them to pitch the deals before the inevitable pitches to sellers, financiers and professional advisors. Excellent training wheels.

Terence's deal was third up out of four that day. Deal one was a marketing agency pitched by Erin. Solid deal and received a GL72 score. Deal two was a home services business pitched by Jesus. Nice business but too owner-dependent. Terence was eyeballing the transfer of value scores during the pitch and qualifying questions. That deal got an RL68, so drop it with no regrets.

Terence was now up. He had 20 minutes to pitch the deal and answer the clarifying questions. Exuding an enthusiastic confidence, he ran through the numbers, the two valuations (SBA deal and annuity deal) and spoke about the growth opportunities (leveraging his extensive network of clients) and perhaps one or two bolt-on acquisitions in the future. He also presented an exit strategy to a larger trade buyer once the business had grown substantially. He even mentioned two or three particular trade buyers who he predicted would want this business (at scale) and laid out a plan to build it to that exact recipe so all three would salivate about owning the business.

Some questions came in around non-competes, as Terence was employed by a large competitor. "We aren't playing in the same market," he responded, pointing out that his non-compete was extremely loose. (Lawrence had reviewed it for him yesterday and wasn't worried at all.)

Carl went back to Terence's earlier RLGL submission. It had bombed as a stand alone. However, Carl had a suggestion.

"That deal would work really well as a bolt-on to this business," he said. "Although I didn't like it as a stand-alone, I can see how combining operations would work as a combo deal. But, close this new deal first, then bolt the other one into it."

That caused some major buzz in the group. The scores came flooding in. GL92 was the average, so not quite a golden buzzer, but almost.

This result surprised even Terence, and gave him a strong assurance that JAT was, indeed, his deal. He decided to submit the offer that very day and vowed to do whatever it would take to eventually close the deal.

Chapter 26

Terence Makes His Offer for JAT

As Terence sat down to draft the offer for JAT, he went back over the basic guidelines he had learned from Carl and his team about making offers. Carl had said it was best, for example, to first always send out a written offer. Jeremy had, in fact, asked for all offers for JAT to be put in writing, so that worked out well.

In the normal course of events, once an offer (which typically addresses just the price, terms and retained owner involvement) is accepted, then the parties will proceed to negotiate a letter of intent (LOI). The LOI addresses additional issues such as the amount of working capital that will remain, due diligence requirements, closing and legal timelines, representation and warranties and a bunch of other stuff. Carl emphasized not to put LOI's in initially. Instead, reach agreement on the major points first (i.e, in terms of the offer), then negotiate the details immediately after once a relationship has been established between a willing buyer and willing seller.

One of the best trainings Carl had done on drafting offers was in regard to the two-offer structure. In it he explained that the two-million-year old human brain was designed to make binary decisions. Black or white. Yes or no.

So then, if you make a single offer to buy a business, the seller is going to either say "yes" or "no" to that offer. When the answer is "no," a counter-offer usually (but not always) follows.

On the other hand, Carl explained that if you present *two* offers side by side (in the same letter or offer presentation), the seller's brain will tend to gravitate "yes" to one of them (i.e., rather than rejecting them both), making you much more likely to secure a "yes."

It's like asking someone if they want a glass of wine. They'll say either "yes" or "no." But if you ask them whether they'd like a glass of red wine or white wine, they'll say one or the other of these options (rather than "neither") more than 90% of the time. (Try this with your spouse or a friend.)

Following Carl's advice, Terence drafted the two offer structures, one involving an annuity deal and the other an SBA deal. He was clear to sell the benefits of the annuity deal over the SBA offer, namely, faster time to close, less tax, higher valuation and extremely light-touch due diligence outside of any external financing involvement. Both structures were included in his offer letter:

Jacqueline Turley
1651 S Wabash Office #3
Chicago
IL
60637

Dear Jacqueline,

Further to our conversations and your kind provision of financial information, I have pleasure in enclosing two offers to acquire 100% of the equity JAT PR LLC.

Offer One

Total valuation = $2,400,000
Closing payment = $2,160,000
Seller note = $240,000 paid 24-months from closing
Total offer = $2,400,000

Offer one is a smaller valuation; however, the cash at close is the majority of the total offer.

Closing is anticipated to take between 12 and 16 weeks depending on the bank's due diligence process, legal process, internal credit review process and verification by the SBA.

Offer Two

Total valuation = $4,160,000
Closing payment = $0
Seller note = $4,160,000, payable in 120 monthly payments of $34,667, starting 30-days post-closing.
Total offer = $4,160,000

  Offer two is a much larger valuation; however, there is no cash component at close. You will retain a full lien on both the assets and equity in JAT PR LLC, and I can provide a service guarantee on both trailing EBITDA levels and cash held on deposit in the business bank account.
  Closing is anticipated to take a maximum of 10 days. I will undertake a very small amount of legal due diligence. The majority of the diligence will be carried out after closing.

There are significant benefits to you from offer two, namely:

1. The total consideration is higher
2. Your total tax liability will be lower (as a % of the total offer) since the payments are spread out over 10 years
3. The amount of due diligence we need to complete pre-close is 95% less than what would be required with offer one
4. Closing is much faster
5. You get to stay connected to the business

  The dual offer contained in this letter is valid for 72 hours, and we look forward to learning of your preferred option.
  Upon your acceptance of this offer, we would move to a full LOI within 48 hours to incorporate working capital requirements and any retained involvement from your side.

Sincerely,

Terence Turner

Terence signed the letter, downloaded a PDF from his Google docs and emailed the offer to Jeremy along with the following email preface:

To: Jeremy Brown
From: Terence Turner
Subject Line: Offer for the purchase of JAT PR LLC

Dear Jeremy
As discussed, I attach an offer letter for the above.
I look forward to hearing back in due course.

Sincerely,
Terence Turner

    Now, for the wait. Terence knew Jacqueline and Jeremy were soliciting other offers. How long would he have to wait for feedback? The suspense was going to kill him.
    Carl had cautioned his Protégés several times:
    Don't get deal heat!
    Dealmaking is a numbers game!
    Make multiple offers on deals!
    Terence knew he'd have to make offers on other deals, so he decided that tomorrow he would block out three to four hours and make offers on the other seven deals he liked and for which he had completed the valuation—although he didn't like any of them as much as JAT PR.

Chapter 27

Terence Reviews All His Other Deals

The next day, Terence prepared to submit offers on his other seven deals, using the same two-offer structure. He really liked the annuity deal concept, but he also needed to discuss the SBA aspects of his offers with both Live Stem and Anthony Marks. Those calls were set up for that afternoon.

In preparation for the banking calls, Terence completed the deal priority matrix Carl had developed for the Protégé students. Carl said he used this tool whenever he liked lots of businesses in the same niche and wanted confirmation of the best deal that fit his particular buy box. Specifically, the matrix plotted out the *attractiveness* and *relatedness* of each deal.

Attractiveness was related to the financial performance of the business: the valuation (vs. market), the profit margin and current growth rates. Also, Carl would capture future growth and exit potential in this metric.

Relatedness would map the fit of the deal to the student's buy box. Was this deal in the student's lane? Could the student add value to the business easily? Did the student have a network he or she could plug into the business to make it fly? Did it have inherent KPIs, systems and processes to hit the growth button instantly, or did the business need optimizing and fixing first?

Terence populated the model sheet and stared at the output:

Attractiveness - Relatedness Matrix

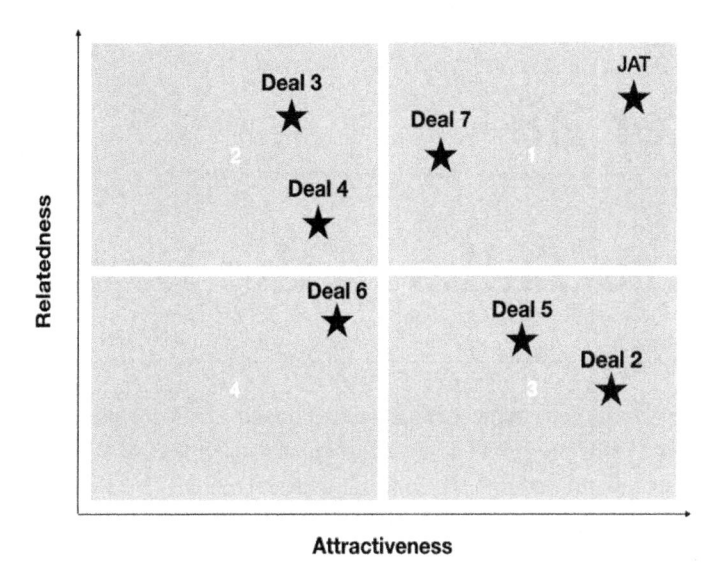

```
                                              JAT
              Deal 3                           ★
               ★         Deal 7
                          ★
         2                       1
              Deal 4
               ★
Relatedness
              Deal 6
               ★         Deal 5
                          ★
                                 Deal 2
         4               3        ★

                    Attractiveness
```

DEALMAKER WEALTH
SOCIETY

    JAT was clearly the stand-out deal. He also really liked deals 3, 7 and 5, and the matrix was a great affirmation that his favorite deals ranked the highest.

    Carl always recommended starting with offers on deals in quadrant 1: highly attractive and related. Then move to quadrant 2, given that relatedness is more important than attractiveness since the former is about value-add and the power to move the needle in the business. Quadrant 3 featured highly attractive deals that were not highly related, so Carl suggested that when considering those deals, partner with people who have the value-add skill sets and experiences.

    Quadrant 4 deals were always a no-go for Carl.

    With this in mind, Terence scrapped deal 6 and only sent offers for the ones in the other three quadrants.

    He would wait for feedback from them all, but he yearned for JAT PR LLC to accept his offer.

    Having sent the deals out, Terence went to make himself a coffee. He had 30 minutes before his back-to-back banking calls.

Chapter 28

Terence Talks to the Banks

Terence was nervous at the start of his first banking call. It was with Lisa Trammel from Live Stem Bank, one of the largest banks under the SBA 7a loan program. Lisa managed the self-sponsored team, which essentially meant she dealt with buyers who had or had access to the down payment.

Which, in fact, Terence had. He needed between $250,000 and $375,000 to close the various deals in his pipeline. He had $100,000 of his own capital, and following his RLGL pitch of JAT PR, several other Protégés had messaged him offering equity partnership terms, both on that deal or anything else he was going to close in the PR space. People liked him and his clearly bullseye buy box and massive amounts of value-add.

Lisa was pleased to hear that Terence had the capital pledged. With that requirement met, she walked Terence through the process of closing a deal via SBA.

She recommended the 7a loan structure, as there was no real estate in the deal. She then took Terence's valuation and provided him with an outline of the terms. A full term sheet would be issued once the bank could underwrite the deal, and Terence would have to open up the data room for the full range of financial information that would be required.

For now, Lisa fired off an email to Terence to give him an "expression of interest." He knew Jeremy would need this to take his offer seriously, if, indeed, Jacqueline wanted to go down the SBA route.

To: Terence Turner
From: Lisa Trammel (Live Stem Bank)
Subject Line: Expression of interest
Dear Terence:

It was a pleasure to speak with you. This letter confirms our interest in JAT PR LLC and the other deals in your pipeline. We look forward to receiving your signed LOI and access to the data room so we can conduct preliminary due diligence.

Upon access, we anticipate the issuance of a term sheet and closing timeline within 14 days, provided there are no significant issues with the business or deal.

Sincerely,

Lisa

Lisa Trammel CFA
Head of Self-Sponsored Team, SBA Loans
Live Stem Bank

  Based on his initial conversation with Lisa, the bank would support up to a $2,700,000 valuation and would also add $300,000 of additional working capital (via a separate loan) to give Terence the fuel for explosive growth. Jeremy and Jacqueline didn't need to know these details, but it gave him some negotiation room if indeed Jacqueline opted for the SBA deal.
  Lisa also mentioned the $5,000,000 SBA cap and said she would be excited to work with Terence on financing bolt-on acquisitions.
  "The program was created for buyers like you," Lisa had said to Terence.
  Damn straight it is, thought Terence.
  The second call was just as positive. Anthony Marks was a financing broker and had a platform of over 100 banks, credit unions and other debt lenders all under the SBA program.
  He offered to beat terms offered by the main banks; however, he took a 2% closing fee. Still, he was offering to do all the legwork.
  Two great banking calls and two home runs. Terence was on a roll.
  All he needed now was feedback on his deals.
  He closed his laptop and went into the nook for dinner. Julie had ordered in. Mexican. The burritos and tacos from Moe's smelled amazing. Terence lunged into a burrito, and the spicy red sauce exploded down his white shirt. The children

burst into laughter, and Julie just closed her eyes and shook her head—while desperately trying also not to laugh.

The family played the Exploding Kittens card game for a while after dinner. Then, once the children had been tucked into bed, Julie and Terence retired early for some adult time.

Chapter 29

Jacqueline and Jeremy Review the Offers

Over the previous week, Jacqueline (sometimes accompanied by Phillip and Lucy) had given ten management presentations. Seven of the ten had follow-up meetings to clarify information, and five offers had come in that had either proof of funds or expressions of interest from financiers. There was also an offer from another individual that didn't have any proof of funds, so this one was initially rejected but held in reserve, in case none of the other offers moved forward.

One of the five offers being considered was from Terence.

One was from Laser Business Services Inc. New York. Annual revenue = $13,500,000. A trade buyer, this would be their first acquisition.

One was from Hype Machine Ltd. London. Annual revenue = $18,200,000 (converted). Also a trade buyer, they had just landed a large bakery client in Chicago and were looking for a regional PR firm to support it.

The last two offers were from financial buyers: Masters Capital LLC in Dallas and Whisper Capital Management Inc. in Boston. Both had more than $250 million in assets under management so clearly had the funds.

The two trade buyers and two financial buyers had each only made a single offer. Terence had done something unusual by making two offers side by side in the same letter. Although Jeremy thought this odd, he actually loved it and saw it as a master dealmaking move. Giving the seller multiple options was impressive, and since he knew Jacqueline really liked Terence, it would provide a punch to the offer, although it was the lowest offer of all.

Jeremy had called a meeting in his office with Jacqueline to review the offers.

As she walked in, head to toe again in Lululemon, he was laying out the offer summary document on the boardroom table.

"Good news," said Jeremy. "We have five offers. I want to run through them all with you so we can decide which of these we want to take seriously and consider next steps. We don't necessarily need to pick a preferred buyer today, but hopefully the top two or three—then we can clarify any terms on the offers and begin negotiating."

Jacqueline studied the summary. All the multiples were calculated based on Jeremy's $840,900 average recasted EBITDA number; however, it wasn't clear which profit number each potential buyer had used. That would be investigated as part of next steps with the offers that were both interesting and credible.

Offers for JAT PR LLC

Buyer	Offer	% Purchased	Valuation	Multiple	Closing Payment	Seller Note
Terence SBA	2,400,000	100%	2,400,000	2.85	2,160,000	240,000
Terence Annuity	4,160,000	100%	4,160,000	4.95	0	4,160,000
Laser Business Services	4,700,000	100%	4,700,000	5.59	2,800,000	1,900,000
Hype Machine	3,550,000	100%	3,550,000	4.22	3,550,000	0
Masters Capital	2,825,000	70%	4,035,714	4.80	2,200,000	625,000
Whisper Capital	3,200,000	60%	5,333,333	6.34	1,600,000	1,600,000

Jacqueline's first question was why Terence had made two offers simultaneously. "Simple," said Jeremy, "he's trying to give you the two extremes."

Jeremy reminded her of one of their first conversations in which he had explained that buyers would typically discount offers with all (or the majority of) cash at closing. Conversely, if the seller was willing to take some risk and roll payments over an extended period of time, the valuation would increase.

Jacqueline nodded that she understood, then for her own sake ignored Terence's offers for the time being. He was clearly the perfect buyer for the business, but she wanted to understand the other offers for now.

She started with the two trade buyers. She really didn't like Laser Business Solutions even though it was a really solid multiple. They would gut the business, and her brand, culture and legacy would disappear as soon as the contract was signed. She much preferred Hype Machine as a trade buyer although the valuation was lower than Jeremy had expected.

Of the two financial buyers, she most liked Whisper Capital. They would be hands off for the most part and would share control with Jacqueline until they exercized their option to buy out the remaining 40% of equity. Whisper wanted to buy only 60% for now and do a buy-and-build. The CEO had asked Jacqueline to stay on for three years, not as CEO but as an ambassador to convince other small PR firms to sell to them. This was something that Jacqueline was quite interested in.

Jacqueline wasn't a big fan of the Masters Capital offer. It wanted full control of the business (even though Jacqueline would retain 30%), there was no future buyout option and Jacqueline would have no voting rights, no board seat and nothing by way of control. Also, the valuation was far below that of Whisper.

So, they were down to three solid options. One trade buyer: Hype. One financial buyer: Whisper. And Terence.

Jacqueline asked for Jeremy's opinion on the two offers from Terence.

"The advantage of the SBA deal is you are getting 90% of the cash at close, although the valuation is low. The annuity offer is a great valuation (for an individual), but there's no cash component at close.

"I think what you really need to decide, Jacqueline, is who do you really want to own this business. Then we can use the other offers to negotiate the very best terms for you.

Jacqueline wasn't sure. She liked all three offers. Being that it was Friday afternoon and she was tired, she decided that she wanted to ponder all this over the weekend and come back to Jeremy Monday morning. They arranged a 10 a.m. Zoom for Monday and ended the meeting.

Jacqueline had a date that evening with Jack to go to a charity fundraiser. She would probe him for advice. Surely, he would have some insight . . .

Chapter 30

Charity Fundraiser with Jack

Jacqueline looked radiant in a black dress. Her hair was in a perfectly tight bun atop her head, and she wore her new Jimmy Choo slingbacks for the very first time.

Jack wore a tuxedo with a gray waistcoat and matching tie.

Tonight was the annual Butterfly Ball, to support the Chicago Academy of Science. Jack had purchased a full table of eight and had invited three other couples. Jacqueline sat down with doctors, scientists and the current assistant coach of the Chicago White Sox.

After coffee, Jacqueline and Jack retired to comfortable chairs at the perimeter and sipped a fine Caymus Cabernet together. Jack had sensed all evening that Jacqueline wanted to talk, and it was obvious it was about the sale of her business. Jacqueline updated Jack on the offers she had received and confided in him that she was having difficulty making a choice.

"What does your *heart* want? What's it saying to you? Jack asked, leaning over on the armrest of her chair and looking directly into her eyes.

"I just want what's best for the business," she replied. "I want a fair price, of course, but I also want the business to be in safe hands once I've exited."

Jack had gone through an exit process himself, but in his case he had always known he would be selling to his two sons. Clearly, there was no similar family succession plan in Jacqueline's case. Nonetheless, Jacked talked through what he saw to be the pros and cons of each of Jacqueline's top three potential buyers based on her descriptions of them.

"I'm going to sleep on this," she said.

Jack rode in the Uber with Jacqueline to make sure she got home safely.

He was dying to go into the house. Jacqueline thought about it, but it was too soon for that. She cut him off at the pass.

"Jack, I know you want to come in for "coffee," but I just have too much on my mind right now to enjoy myself. I tell you what, let's have another date next Friday, and we'll see what happens then. I should have a deal agreed on by that time."

Jack, looking slightly despondent, agreed and took the same Uber back to his house close by.

Jacqueline went into her house alone, got undressed and changed into her sweats. She was too amped up by deal noise to go straight to sleep. She made green tea and went into her study.

Just as she switched on the light, her laptop pinged and she noticed she had been copied into an email, actually by mistake.

From: Lyle Parsons (CEO, Hype Machine)
To: Terry Silver
CC: Martin Samuels, James White, Jacqueline Turley

Gents,

We went to offer on JAT today. Great business and we went hard on the offer. We will strip it back significantly through due diligence, just like we did on the Brand Now deal last year. Remember, we ended up saving 40% on the closing payment just by wearing the seller down with data requests.

Her advisor isn't cut out for these types of negotiations anyway, so I think we can get the price down massively on this one.

Martin / James: get ready for battle.

Justin: we aren't going to need anywhere close to the $3,550,000 at closing. I'm tasking you with paying a maximum of $1,500,000 upfront.

Let's rage!!

Lyle

Jacqueline read the email in horror, three times.

Clearly, Lyle had rushed the email and instead of adding Justin (whoever that was), he had typed "J" into his email and accidentally clicked on "Jacqueline." They had exchanged pleasant emails after the management presentation a few weeks ago.

Clearly, these guys were trying to take her for a ride. She quickly forwarded the email to Jeremy, then texted him to go read it.

She didn't sleep well that night. What if Whisper Capital was just like this? Even Terence. She trusted Terence; they had met multiple times now, and she had a warm, fuzzy feeling about him. She had also made calls to some of her other PR friends in the city and always got solid recommendations about him from those who knew him.

Saturday morning, she was exhausted. Her daughter was on shift again at the hospital without a babysitter, and she was taking Jerrad to baseball again. Would she see Terence there? She hoped so. She just wanted that feeling of certainty with him.

A few hours later, her daughter dropped off Jerrad, and Jacqueline drove him to the baseball field.

As they walked up to the gathering of other children, coaches and parents, Terence came from behind and tapped her on the shoulder.

"Good morning," he said.

She turned and grinned a mile wide. "I thought I might see you here," she said.

They talked about baseball for a few minutes, then Terence asked, "Did you receive my offer?"

"Yes, we did. I'd say it's between you and another interested party. I'm meeting Jeremy Monday morning to make a final decision."

Pleased to hear this, Terence used one of Carl's classic questions.

"Let me ask you a question. What would have to be true for you to sell me your business?"

She blushed. Here Terence was using a line she herself had learned from a seminar years ago and had posed to others from time to time since. Now the tables were being turned on her. She was stymied. The words just couldn't come out, primarily as she didn't know what to say.

She finally muttered something about needing to understand the difference between the two offers so she could determine which would make more sense to her, but she knew it was a rather prosaic response.

Undeterred, Terence followed up with another question. "May I ask who the other buyer is?"

"I can't give you the name at this point, but I'll tell you it's a private equity firm wanting to do a roll-up of multiple PR businesses in the midwest. I like them and their strategy, but I'll be honest with you, Terence. I can really see you owning my business, and I think the team may prefer you—with your energy and ideas versus being just a division of a much larger entity."

Terence wasn't ready to mention to her at this point that he would be doing a roll-up as well. He had attended the advanced track Protégé training on Tuesday and was blown away by Carl's training on the subject.

Jacqueline promised that Jeremy would get back to Terence sometime on Monday about next steps.

They shook hands warmly and went their separate ways. Jarred was staying overnight, and she had promised him Five Guys and a Harry Potter movie (he was a big fan).

Jacqueline and Terence both had restless Sundays, but for slightly different reasons. Jacqueline was weighing the decision, whereas Terence just wanted to be put out of his misery.

He had made several offers, and deals had been agreed on for two other businesses (deals 4 and 5 in his matrix). Deal 4 would be a perfect bolt-on acquisition locally, and 5 would add presence in Indiana, which was a growth market. But he really wanted JAT badly.

He would wait until Tuesday before issuing LOIs on the deals. One needed SBA financing, the other had opted for the annuity deal, but it was smaller, and he would have to handle a lot of the work himself. If he acquired JAT, it would perfectly bolt into JAT, and his new team could handle most of the work.

Chapter 31

Jacqueline Makes Her Decision

On Monday, Jacqueline logged into the Zoom for the decision meeting. She and Jeremy spent the first five minutes talking about the Hype email. They easily agreed that, clearly, they shouldn't continue discussions with that firm.

It was now a straight shoot-out between Terence and Whisper.

Jacqueline liked Whisper and loved the offer. But Terence was her preferred buyer, and because she wanted a closing payment, his offer was too low.

"What do you think, Jeremy?" she asked.

"Well, I think Terence is the best buyer; Whisper is the best offer."

"I'm not sure my employees here would love being part of a private-equity-owned conglomerate. We love our vibe and culture. I think Terence should own the business but not on the terms he sent. I don't really want to do the annuity deal. I prefer the large cash at close. Can we get him to improve his offer?"

"Yes, we can try," Jeremy confirmed. His offer will ultimately be underwritten by the SBA and the partner bank. I do think there's some upside in the deal potentially."

Jeremy and Jacqueline worked on a counter: $3,000,000, with $2,700,000 at close. Accept and the business would be his.

Jeremy had some concerns whether the SBA would go to that level, but following a beer with one of his banking buddies over the weekend, he knew they would go higher than $2,400,000. Perhaps $3,000,000 would be achievable, considering that the cash flow in the business was growing.

Jeremy placed the call to Terence, but it went to his voicemail. Moments later, Jeremy received a text back from Terence saying he was in a meeting but would call back in ten minutes.

As soon as Terence sent the text, he excused himself from the meeting (Publix quarterly branding review meeting), ostensibly to hit the restroom. Once out of the Creative PR conference room, he walked to his office and closed the door behind him, sat down at his desk, and returned the call.

Hi Terence. Jacqueline has reviewed all offers and believes you're the best person to buy the business. However, your offer is too low. Jacqueline doesn't want to go down the annuity route but would agree to do this via the SBA option for a $3,000,000 valuation with 90% (or $2,700,000) payable at closing.

Terence agreed to get back to them later that day, but his heart sank. He knew the SBA wouldn't go that high. Lisa had maxed out at a $2,700,000 valuation although she had committed to $300,000 of working capital. The term sheet had landed in his email late Friday.

He quickly placed a call to her.

"Lisa, it's Terence. JAT countered at $3,000,000 with $2,700,000 at close. I know that's outside your range, but can you confirm this deal works for you if I take $100,000 of the working capital and add it to the deal? I can easily scale this thing on $200,000 of additional capital, especially since Jacqueline is leaving all the cash and AR in the business. I can even use the $200,000 to bolt in a smaller business, and with synergies and cross-selling, I'd generate more than that within the first 60-days."

Lisa was noncommittal. "Let me get back to you," was the most she would say.

He didn't hear back the rest of the day. On his drive home, he hit Jeremy's name on his Tesla screen and called his cell.

"Hi, it's Terence. I spoke to my bank earlier, and I'm waiting to hear back from them, but I can tell you we can't do $3,000,000. I think I may be able to bridge the gap, though, and I'd be happy to only buy 90% of the business, leaving Jacqueline with 10% retained equity so she can have a second bite of the cherry in the future."

"Okay," Jeremy replied coolly. "Once you get feedback from the bank, please resubmit your best and final offer."

They ended the call.

All day, Jeremy had dodged calls from both Hype and Whisper seeking feedback on their offers. He had rejected Hype. Kyle knew why. He had spotted his fatal mistake in the email after one of the other recipients alerted him to it. *Damned email*, he fumed.

Whisper had indicated this was an opening offer and there was potentially more cash available at close and a smaller seller note. He asked them to resubmit a best and final, and Jacqueline would make a final decision.

Chapter 32

Best and Final

Jacqueline slept in on Tuesday morning, showered, dressed and drove downtown to her office. She walked in at 10:30 a.m. to find an email from Jeremy.

Both Terence and Whisper had made their best-and-final offers. Jeremy had summarized them on a new, shorter, one sheet.

Best & Final Offers for JAT PR LLC

Buyer	Offer	% Purchased	Valuation	Multiple	Closing Payment	Seller Note
Terence SBA	2,800,000	90%	3,111,111	3.70	2,520,000	280,000
Whisper Capital	3,200,000	60%	5,333,333	6.34	2,000,000	1,200,000

"Please call me at your convenience to discuss," he said in the email. He had promised to get back to both parties today.

She smiled at the sheet. Terence was actually offering more than the $3,000,000 valuation. She could retain 10% and loved his strategy of bolt-on acquisitions. Perhaps she would get another check in the future, but at the very least she would enjoy some distributions, so she could bank her after-tax closing payment and not have to dip into it for her living expenses.

Terence was actually paying the higher closing amount as well. She liked Terence and liked the deal.

She called Jeremy and said just one word.

"Terence."

He laughed and promised to get back to both parties.

Jeremy called Terence first. The latter fist-pumped the air at the news and promised to send the updated term sheet from Live Stem and also submit an LOI within the next 48 hours.

Whisper took the rejection in stride. Jeremy promised to keep the offer on the sidelines if the preferred buyer option fell through.

"No worries," the Whisper CFO affirmed. "We're a buyer on those terms, so get back to me if the other deal aborts."

Chapter 33

The LOI

Terence was elated. He just couldn't believe his luck.

Now, he had to turn his attention to the LOI (letter of intent).

He didn't know how to complete one, so he watched the online Protégé training on the subject and downloaded the template.

From the training video he came to understand that the LOI has several primary objectives and that the closing attorneys would use the LOI as the executive summary of the deal and, therefore, create the various closing documents based on it.

The LOI was to contain the price and terms of the deal, together with any conditions.

Next, it would specify the rules around how much working capital would be left in the business and how the purchase price would be adjusted either for excess working capital at close or, conversely, for a shortfall.

The LOI would also handle any continuing involvement from the seller, including an agreed handover period, any retained equity and for time involvement, consultancy fees. Finally, the LOI would set a timeline to closing, including the target closing date and the length of exclusivity the seller would give the buyer to close the deal. "At least 90-days," Carl had advised. "Longer if you're using SBA financing. That's now typically a four- to five-month process."

Terence edited the template for the JAT deal and proofread it.

He desperately needed an attorney and had arranged to use the business partner of his friend, Lawrence. Brittany Anderson, a solid M&A attorney with lots of small deal experience, had gladly agreed.

Terence emailed his draft of the LOI to Brittany to check over. He knew it was always a good idea as a first-time business buyer to have your attorney review the LOI before you submit.

Brittany called within an hour of receiving Terence's email. She walked him through a few small tweaks then approved its release.

Terence emailed it to Jeremy.

Jeremy read the LOI, saw no issues with it, then forwarded it to Herb Sanders, Jacqueline's M&A attorney.

Attorneys sometimes like to flex their muscles as early as possible in the process, and this appeared to be true in Herb's case. He created a red-line version in which Jeremy felt he was changing minor language "just for the sake of it." The LOI went back and forth between Brittany and Herb several times before it was finally signed by both Jacqueline and Terence several days later.

Terence found this delay highly frustrating. *How complex are the main deal legals going to be*, he mused, *if the attorneys have already started arm wrestling and chest pumping with an LOI?*

He brushed it off and reminded himself that tomorrow the due diligence would start, so progress was being made, even if slower than he would have liked.

He climbed into his Tesla X and left for home. About 20 minutes from his destination, Julie called and said she'd had a tough day at the dental clinic. She had already changed into her sweats and was relaxing with a glass of chardonnay.

"I ordered Mexican food," Julie announced, "and it should be ready in ten minutes. Please, my love, would you swing by and pick it up? It's already paid for."

When Terence arrived at the restaurant, he was told the food was going to be another ten minutes. As Terence and his family were regulars, the owner Santiago ushered him to the bar and within 30 seconds, an ice cold Modelo Negra had been placed in front of him. Terence quickly downed the first half of the bottle, then proceeded to sip the rest. The bartender soon had another one ready, and by the time Terence had finished both bottles, the sack of burritos, salsa and corn chips was ready.

He paid for the beers (including a generous tip for the bartender), then put the sack of food on the passenger seat and set off for the five-minute drive home. The heat of the food sack generated a ring of condensation on the black leather car seat.

When Terence walked into the house he was greeted eagerly by his wife and two children. ("Is it me or the food?" he quipped.) The table was already set and Julie had poured him a glass of the chardonnay. The meal was brief (everyone seemed to have worked up an appetite), and the family members discussed their respective days. Afterwards, the children went to their rooms to do homework.

"Why was your day hard?" asked Terence.

"The usual," Julie replied. "Although I'm now part-time, I'm expected to still see nearly the same number of patients as before. I just don't think I'm able to give my patients the best care, and it's really bothering me. Now that you've also connected JAT into the business to run the marketing campaigns and drive more leads, I fear it's only going to get worse. I'm thinking I may leave. The kids are starting to need me more and more, and as my parents get older I'm going to have to support them more too."

At that time, the Turner family needed both paychecks. With the mortgage note on their splendid home, along with two car payments, private schools and multiple and expensive extracurricular activities, they couldn't afford to drop Julie's paycheck.

"As soon as we close on JAT, I'll make enough money to cover us both," he assured her.

At this, Julie lit up like a Christmas tree, then pulled out her MacBook and opened the family expenses spreadsheet.

Turner Family P&L

Income (after tax)	$
Terence	10258
Julie	4293
Other	3430
Total	17981

Expenses	$
House PITI	5493
Cars	1533
Food	1560
Utilities	1305
School fees	4033
Misc	1575
Total	15499
Savings	2482

DEALMAKER WEALTH

After taxes and all expenses, the Turner family was currently saving $2,482 per month. Without Julie's income, they would be in the red. Acquiring JAT would allow Terence to earn more money, retire his wife and still have monthly cash flow as a family.

Chapter 34

Due Diligence

Terence had signed the LOI for the deal and also had the term sheet for the SBA loan from the bank. The bank was doing its due diligence, but he wanted to do his own as well. Not really do it himself, but quarterback the process.

He attended a coaching call with Carl on the topic of due diligence.

Carl had confirmed that in small deals, there were three primary areas of due diligence, or DD for short.

Financial DD
Commercial DD
Legal DD

The financial DD would cover the tax returns, quality of earnings and an examination of the balance sheet. It would also review bank statements, accounts receivable (AR), accounts payable (AP) and determine the true value of the assets on the balance sheet. As a professional services business, there were few such assets, over and above the AR and some furniture. All the computers and other technology used by employees were leased. Jacqueline also had prepared a three-year financial forecast with Jeremy, and the assumptions on that would be tested and verified.

The commercial DD covered the market and the business's position within it. Yes, Terence could hire a consultant to do that for him, but he wanted to do it himself for two reasons: One, he could save $5,000 in fees, and two, doing it himself would give him a fast start on identifying quick wins for growth. The cornerstone of his commercial DD would be the SWOT analysis.

S - Strengths of the business
W - Weaknesses of the business
O - Opportunities for the business to grow revenue, profit and market share
T - Threats the business currently faces or may face in the future from changing trends in the PR, advertising and marketing niches

    The legal DD would be carried out by his attorney, Brittany. Alongside drafting the stock purchase agreement (the primary contract buyer and seller would sign to transfer the ownership of the business), Brittany would essentially determine (or not) that the business was safe to buy.

    She would check that Jacqueline actually was the owner of the business, check the legal incorporation, vet material contracts and then seek disclosures from Jacqueline based on any issues that Terence needed to know about the business he was buying.

    From that, Jacqueline would be required to sign representation and warranty agreements, effectively providing Terence with a guarantee that he was buying what he thought he was buying. The required streams of due diligence would confirm everything was safe.

    Terence needed someone to do the financial DD. He didn't know anyone, so he called Brittany for help.

    "Hello, Terence. You must be feeling excited about the deal. I've just gotten started on the legal due diligence and the initial draft of the stock purchase agreement."

    "Great. Thank you. I was actually calling for advice and hopefully a recommendation. I know I need to do commercial DD, and I want to do that myself. I also understand that I need to have someone do financial DD, and I need something called a quality of earnings report?"

    "That's correct. Ideally you'd want a CPA (Certified Public Accountant). Do you know anyone or do you need a recommendation?"

    "No, I don't really know anyone. This is my first deal. Who would you recommend?"

    "Peter Hitchen. He's a CPA specializing in SBA acquisitions who could handle the due diligence and deal management for you."

    "Okay, great. Not sure I need the deal management. I like this part of the process and being the quarterback, but he can certainly handle the DD for me."

    "Excellent," said Brittany. "I'll introduce you via email."

    Brittany made the introduction, and several hours later, following a call, Terence hired Peter as his CPA to handle the financial DD.

He now had a full team. Both Brittany and Peter would also liaise with Live Stem, who would be conducting their own due diligence in advance of the financing.

Chapter 35

Four Weeks Later

The deal execution phase went fairly smoothly. Brittany found only minor issues in the legal DD, and the stock purchase agreement was now at an advanced stage. Herb continued to flex his muscles every few days, but Brittany knew how to handle him. They'd worked on several deals together previously.

The financial DD also went fairly well. In fact, the bank had signed off on the financials about a week before Peter submitted his report to Terence.

Peter had questioned some of the add-backs and saw that it had a profit approximately $43,000 lower than what Jacqueline had reported. Also, some of the accounts receivables were beyond 120 days, which he considered bad debt. It was only $26,000, but he wanted Terence to be aware of it.

"Normally, we'd renegotiate the deal based on these items. However, since the bank has already signed off on the deal structure and valuation, I'm not sure it's worth you trying to renegotiate. We're talking about very small tweaks, and sometimes it's not worth harming the buyer-seller relationship for minor items."

"No problem," said Terence. This was still a great deal for him, and if the bank was happy to advance him all the money, he wasn't going to rock the boat.

Chapter 36

Jacqueline Gets Cold Feet

The process was almost complete. All the due diligence had been completed, and both her attorney, Herb, and Terence's attorney, Brittany, were accelerating the final turns on the stock purchase agreement. Even the legal counsel for Live Stem, Kevin Hart, was now involved and was performing a high-level overview of all the legal documents, including the new operating agreement, to reflect Terence and Jacqueline's partnership moving forward.

It was a Friday, and Jacqueline had spent the afternoon in the office with Jeremy reviewing the month's financials as well as reviewing the sales pipeline and key client projects. The business was continuing to accelerate.

Tonight was JAT PR's annual work party. There would be drinks at the bar down the street followed by dinner for all employees and their spouses (or significant other or friend) at the Weber Grill. JAT did the PR for Weber Grill in Chicago so received a significant discount for all meals and events there.

As Jacqueline was wrapping up the meetings, she reflected on the weekend ahead.

Friday night out with her employees. Saturday and Sunday . . . nothing.

Jack was away fishing in Alaska with his two boys. Jacqueline's only local family in Chicago were also on vacation, so there would be no baseball or date nights with Jack. She had literally no plans for the weekend. All her close friends were married and had no plans either, so they might have been available to do something, but she didn't want to be the odd one out on a three-person date.

As she pondered both the solitude and loneliness of the weekend ahead, it made her realize that JAT PR was her family. It had consumed such a major portion of her life, and even one weekend alone was freaking her out. Imagine the rest of her life on her own. Yes, she spent time with her Chicago family and grandkids and would be able to travel to other parts of the country to see her other children and their families, but selling JAT was starting to feel like those painful days when her children went off to college. It was something they needed to do, but it had been painful for her and Bill nonetheless. She'd had little control over her ambitious children's education. But she did have full control over the fate of her business.

For the first time in the process, Jacqueline started to have doubts.

The pre dinner drinks at the local bar were pleasant, and the company dinner out was its usual great success of bonding the team and their families.

As the night was coming to a close and the waiters were clearing up dessert and coffee cups, her senior account manager, Derek Smith, asked for a word in private.

"What's on your mind, Derek?" Jacqueline asked.

"Well, let me get straight to the point. Myself and many on the team have heard rumors that you're selling the business. Everyone, including myself, is nervous, and my two largest clients, Facility Med and Wormley Insurance Services have heard it too—they're also nervous. I can speak for everyone, Jacqueline. We love this business, and we love you. Our clients love us as well. Where are you in the process, and can you tell us who the new owner's going to be?"

Jacqueline was disoriented by the question. She blushed bright red and couldn't look Derek in the eyes.

"Well, erm . . . well, yes, I am in a process. It's got about two weeks to go. I was holding off telling you guys until I was absolutely 100% certain it was going to go through."

"I see," said Derek. "Well, I think you need to address the team Monday morning. Tell them where you're at so we can all feel a lot more comfortable. Is the buyer a much larger company? Because I've seen a lot of mergers and acquisitions in my time, and it rarely ends well for the employees of the acquired business."

"No it's not, Derek. I actually received higher offers from some of our competitors, but I decided to take a lower offer and sell to an individual—someone you'll love and who'll honor the culture of this business and be a safe, trusted pair of hands to take the business to the next level. You'll really like him. He's from the industry, works for a major player in town and I'm sure the business is going to go from strength to strength under his ownership. In fact, I like him so much I've agreed to retain a minority stake, serve on the board and consult for him for the next few years."

"This all sounds great, Jacqueline, thanks for giving me that information. It's your business at the end of the day, but I am sure the team would welcome the positive news and a chance to have a forum to ask you questions."

After a momentary pause, he asked another question: "Do Phillip, Jeremy and Lucy know?"

"Yes, they do. All three have been part of the deal team."

"Well, why didn't Phillip just buy it?"

"I asked him but he didn't want the responsibility right now."

"I can understand that. Well, hopefully you can address the team Monday. That way, I can start reassuring clients about what's happening, or at least the ones that are asking me questions about it."

Jacqueline wrapped up the evening and thanked everyone for attending. Just before the table broke up, she announced there would be an all-hands meeting Monday morning at 10 a.m. for some announcements. Derek gave Jacqueline a wink and sly grin. Philip looked at Jeremy, who looked at Lucy, and all three turned to face Jacqueline with a puzzled look on their faces.

The party broke up and Jacqueline and Jeremy were waiting for an Uber—they lived less than a mile apart. Both would ride to Jacqueline's house, and then Jeremy's wife, Sofia, would collect him from there.

As they climbed into the back of the Uber Black, Jeremy asked what the meeting was about Monday morning.

"Guess," she said.

"Are you going to tell everyone about the sale of the business?" he asked, with a tone of surprise.

"Yes, I am. Derek grabbed me earlier and was asking me about it. The word is out, and not just within the team: Apparently, some of our clients know as well and are asking questions. I don't want the team or client base nervous in any way. I'm going to nip this in the bud Monday morning."

"But what if Terence doesn't close the deal? I know he's far along, but he doesn't have the final SBA sign off at this point, and the bank is still asking Herb lots of questions about the legals."

"I'm confident it'll close," Jacqueline responded. "In fact, I was getting cold feet earlier today, but the conversation with Derek made me realize the business needs to scale, and I'm not the leader to do that. Terence is perfect for the next season in JAT's life. I've known that, but it was reinforced this evening."

The car arrived at Jacqueline's house. She shook hands with Jeremy and wished him goodnight. Then he transferred over into his wife's Audi Q3 mini SUV and they drove off into the night.

Jacqueline made herself a mint tea and stayed up watching the movie *About Time*. It was a fascinating story of a family from the UK where all the men had a superpower that allowed them to travel back to any point in time. Oh, how she yearned to have such a superpower. For starters, she would go back to one of the thousands of amazing times she'd experienced with Bill. Or even her last date with Jack when he stayed over and then cooked her breakfast the next morning. She also thought that if she had this superpower, she could sell JAT and, if it didn't work out, just go back and pick another buyer.

But Jacqueline was 100% convinced this was the right path for her and for the business. She would spend the weekend mapping out the rest of her life and then on Monday announce the sale to her team and her key clients. Once the deal closed in a few weeks, she'd then move on to the next season in her life.

Chapter 37

Terence Gets Cold Feet

At the same time Jacqueline was at JAT's annual party, Terence was drinking Guinness with Lawrence. They were playing the game of splitting the "G." As soon as the Guinness has settled in the glass and turned entirely black, your first slurps of the creamy pint have to be just enough to leave the top of the white frothy head sitting on the shelf made by the "G" in "Guinness" printed on the glass.

Lawrence went first. He took three large gulps then one small one. Putting the glass down on the bar, he frowned when he saw that he had overcompensated. *Darn that last small sip.* He was less than five millimeters below the shelf of the "G."

Terence went next and took three large gulps. He put the glass down and saw that he'd nailed it. The creamy white was oscillating both above and below the "G" shelf. Several seconds later the liquid had stilled entirely, in perfect alignment with the shelf.

"Lucky that," said Lawrence.

"Nah, just call it one of my superpowers," gloated Terence.

Shifting the conversation, Lawrence asked, "Where are you on the closing of JAT?"

"We're fairly close. The legalities are almost done and the bank is almost finished with the underwriting. I had an interesting call with Brittany today, though. Apparently I need to sign a personal guarantee."

"That's right, said Lawrence. "It's common practice for any borrower in an SBA deal who owns more than 19% of the stock."

"Yup. It just freaks me out a little. I mean, I have supreme confidence in my ability to lead and grow the business, but I sure would prefer to sleep at night knowing my house and future weren't at risk if the whole thing implodes for some reason out of my control."

"Sure, I understand your concern. Did Brittany talk to you about surety bonds?"

"She did, but they're too expensive. It's essentially an insurance policy protecting the personal guarantee. What I don't understand is why I need to sign a personal guarantee even though the SBA program has a Federal guarantee for 80% of the total financing?"

"Good point. I'm actually not aware of the SBA ever calling in a personal guarantee. When SBA loans default, which only happens in 8% of the loans they write, the bank makes 'every effort' to recover the money from the borrower. When that doesn't happen (which it never does), the bank calls in the Federal guarantee which covers 80% of the financing, and since some of that will have been paid back and the bank will still have a lien over the business (called a UCC filing), they're able to get all their money back. But surety bonds just give you that piece of mind if you want it. Talk again to Brittany and she'll advise you on what to do."

It was almost 7 p.m. and Terence had to get home. It was games night again in the Turner household—a night for the entire family. Then Saturday night both the children would be sleeping over with friends, and Terence was taking his wife, Julie out for dinner. As for tonight, Julie was cooking tacos (even though it wasn't a Tuesday night, which was usually Taco Tuesday in the Turner house). The family had needed takeout this past Tuesday, as everyone had been so busy and nobody had had time to cook dinner.

As Terence was taking the Uber home (he rarely drove home after Friday drinks), his cell phone buzzed with an unknown caller.

He normally wouldn't have answered in this scenario, but on this occasion, something compelled him to pick up.

"Terence Turner," he spoke into the phone.

"Hi, Terence, it's Jeffrey Miner. I'm the senior recruiter over at Smith and Barrett. Did I catch you at dinner?"

"No, I'm actually in an Uber heading home after drinks. I can talk. What can I do for you, Jeffrey?"

"Well, I have a client who's recruiting a new partner—a major PR company in Chicago. It's a $250,000 package with an equity component that can be paid for over time. It's a no-money-down equity deal.

"Your name is at the top of my list. Rumor has it you lost the Nike account internally due to corporate politics and are considering your future. This is a shoe-in for you, if you want to consider it?"

"Well, I'm certainly flattered by the approach. What else can you tell me?"

"I'll tell you what. Let's meet for coffee tomorrow morning."

Terence was getting excited.

"It will have to be early, and you'll need to come up to me", he replied.

"I have baseball at 11 a.m. with my son. I can meet you at 8:30 at the Starbucks near Lorel Park in Skokie. Do you know it?"

"Yes, that works. I'll text you when I'm near." The two said goodbye and hung up.

Terence made it home, and his head was spinning. *An equity partnership?*

Then again, he'd have an equity partnership in his own business in two weeks, so what was the difference?

During dinner and games night, he was distracted. Julie kept looking at him inquisitively.

After Julie had won the final game of Monopoly Deal, the children went to bed, and husband and wife retired to the den with the last of the fine Caymus Cabernet they'd been enjoying during the evening.

"What's troubling you?" Julie asked gently as she stroked his hair.

"Well, I got a call from a recruiter on my way home in the Uber," he replied. He then recounted the conversation and the plan to meet for coffee in the morning.

"What about acquiring JAT?" She countered. "You can't do both, can you?"

"Absolutely not. It's one or the other, and we're really close on the deal. I just think this has happened for a reason. I'm worried about the personal guarantee, and although I'm very confident I'll do well owning the business, my dream has always been to be a partner in a mega-firm."

"Who's the firm?" asked Julie.

"I don't know yet, but I'm guessing it's Kenton James Ward LLP. They're the oldest, biggest and most prestigious PR and advertising firm in the city. They just had three of their partners retire, or so I read in the Tribune last week, so they're probably bringing in new partner talent to complement the rising stars in the business.

"The same thing happened five years ago. They lost two partners to death within six months. One was replaced externally and another director was promoted from within. That clearly worked well—hence why they would be doing it again."

"Wow, what a conundrum. A $250,000 salary package is certainly attractive—that's nearly double what you make now, and that would allow me to "retire" as we talked about several weeks ago."

"What should I do?" asked Terence.

"Do what makes you happy, my love."

They retired to bed, but Terence hardly slept. He finally got up at 5 a.m. and went on his Peloton to take his mind off the coffee meeting in a few hours.

As he showered and got dressed, he promised himself it would be only a meeting. *Go with a poker face. Just listen to what he has to say. Make no commitments. Receive the information and offer to sit on it over the weekend.*

At 8 a.m., Terence went into the garage and at first was shocked to see a large space where his Tesla should be. *Darn it, I left it in the city.* He searched for Julie's car keys and took her car instead to the meeting.

At 8:20 a.m., his phone buzzed with a text from Jeffrey.

"At the table just inside the front door. What do you want to drink?"

"Tall flat white, 3 shots please," Terence responded.

"Got it, see you soon."

Terence parked a few minutes later and noticed Jeffrey walking back to the table with Terence's drink.

He walked through the door, and they shook hands vigorously. Both were wearing the same Lululemon crew but in different colors. Spooky he thought.

"Nice crew," said Jeffrey.

"And to you," grinned Terence.

They sat down and Jeffrey started the conversation.

"Thanks for taking the time to meet me this morning. We needed to move quickly on this, as my client is looking to make a decision early next week." Jeffrey paused for effect, then announced, "I represent Kenton James Ward LLP."

Terence smiled. He was right.

"They recently retired three partners, are promoting two internally and want to bring a new, outside partner in to freshen things up. Our number one candidate who we've been speaking with for weeks has taken the head of PR role at Google out in California. We just couldn't match the salary package and options package.

"But we actually think you're a better candidate. When we started the search months ago, we weren't aware of you, but several of our sources in the market tell us you're both partner-ready and might be available."

"Well, yes, my plan is to leave Creative as soon as possible."

"Epic!" Jeffrey responded, as if Terence had just accepted a job offer.

"But hold on. I'm actually close to acquiring a business in town. I'm probably less than two weeks away from it, but you certainly have my attention."

"Well then, I suppose it's going to be an interesting decision for you. Let me lay down the terms and the opportunity, and if you think it's an option, I can set you up for a meeting with the current partners Monday morning."

"Okay," replied Terence.

Jeffrey and Terence chatted for the next 30 minutes. It was a compelling opportunity and offer.

Kenton James Ward LLP had the bluest of blue-chip clients. Amazon, Microsoft, Tesla, Walmart, Sephora, Gucci, Land Rover, The New York Times and almost 10% of the Fortune 500.

Terence agreed to the meeting at ten Monday morning at the offices of the firm. He had a legal call scheduled with Brittany at 9:30 and a call with Live Stem at 10:30, both to review the JAT deal, but he could reschedule both of those to the afternoon. He was intrigued by this opportunity and wanted to at least have the meeting.

The two shook hands, and Jeffrey promised to be in touch later with a meeting confirmation.

Terence drove home, collected his son and went to baseball. Then, Julie drove him downtown to pick up his Tesla. Shortly after 1 p.m., Jeffrey texted the confirmation of the meeting.

"They want your resume," he added. *Surely, my LinkedIn profile is enough*, Terence thought, but later in the afternoon, just before taking the children to their respective sleepovers, he emailed Jeffrey his resume as requested. Luckily, he had Jeffrey's email from the business card he had given Terence that morning.

Chapter 38

Date Night

Terence was in a very good mood. He ordered an Uber Black to take him and Julie to dinner. A new steakhouse had opened about five miles away, to rave reviews. It was a four-week wait for a booth on a Saturday night, and they had both been waiting patiently. Outsourcing the children tonight was a big part of the plan.

Riding in style, in a brand new, black Escalade, Terence was grinning as he looked out the window.

"What are you thinking about, my love?" asked Julie.

"I just can't lose either way, can I?" he replied.

"No, not really, but take the interview, then let's discuss it Monday evening," she suggested. "You could also get an update from the bank and your attorney on the personal guarantees, and then you'll have all the information you need to make a decision."

"Perfect," he replied.

They walked into the restaurant, which was lavish. The table cloths were pearly white, and Terrence could smell the oaky leather in the booth as they sat down.

The menu was thick and interesting. They ordered calamari to split for an appetizer and also split the tomahawk entre. $200, but who was worried? He was either going to take a partnership in the most prestigious PR firm in the city of Chicago or become owner of a solid business he could scale to the moon.

Julie normally ate vegetarian, not by moral choice but for health reasons. However, once or twice a year she allowed herself to enjoy some quality red meat.

Terence also ordered a 2016 Barolo, another $150. It was going to be an expensive night.

The calamari was fantastic, but the real highlight was the 30-ounce tomahawk. The server placed it gently on the table then sliced it for them. Cooked to medium-rare perfection, the juices oozed out of the meat and spread slowly across the board, touching the multiple sauce containers. Red wine jus, bernaise and horseradish.

They helped themselves to the delicious meat, the chunky steak fries and the salted asparagus. The food was delightful, and both were full with over a third of the meat still untouched.

"Should we get it to go?" asked Julie.

"Of course. Joshua can have it tomorrow. You know he loves red meat."

They finished the wine, declined dessert (as they were both so full), paid the check, collected the leftovers and Terence hailed an Uber to take them home.

They spent Sunday with their children, and then Julie's parents came for dinner. Terence excused himself around 7 p.m. to prepare in his study for the big meeting tomorrow.

Chapter 39

Jacqueline Addresses the Team

Jacqueline was nervous as she walked into the building at 9:30 a.m. There was a tension in the air; she could feel it.

She walked into her office, placed her Starbucks on the glass desk and switched on her computer. Less than a minute later, Jeremy walked in and closed the door.

"Jacqueline, I need to level with you. I don't think it's a good idea to have this meeting. I just spoke with Brittany, and Terence has canceled his call with her this morning—the one where they were supposed to go over Herb's final turn of the legal documents."

"Why did he do that?" she asked, alarmed.

"I don't know. I hope he isn't having second thoughts."

"Well, I was having second thoughts of my own on Friday, but the conversation with Derek that evening got me back on track. Besides, I've spent all weekend mapping out the rest of my life. I'm really counting on this deal at this point."

Jacqueline had downloaded the old (but still very effective) Tony Robbins "Unleash the Giant Within" and spent all weekend going through it and making plans in multiple areas of her life.

She had decided to spend a lot more time on her health. Including her current yoga schedule, she had joined the local tennis club and signed up for lessons. The first one, in fact, was tonight. She had also had a long conversation with Jack in which they had both decided to "go steady." Indeed, she was planning to move in with him within the next few months and put her own house up for rent. The real estate market in her neighborhood was continuing to rise, and since she didn't need the capital, she had no reason to sell it.

She had also been inspired to learn a new language, Italian. Her and Jack were planning a big Italian vacation to go wine tasting and to take in the Tuscany countryside and ancient buildings, including San Gimignano, the ancient town with the stone turrets.

She was also going to invest some capital in the new health food restaurant of her friend Cassandra. Jacqueline loved the salads, smoothies and acai bowls served there. Casandra needed capital to expand to an online presence and was going to lease a new facility in a cheaper rent district to act as the central kitchen in which to produce both the high-volume items sold in the restaurant and the items that would be part of the pending expansion online. It would also allow her to increase her covers in the restaurant by 50%. The place was rammed every day from open to close.

Cassandra needed $250,000 in working capital, and Jacqueline had negotiated a 25% ownership stake. Jacqueline could also help with the marketing and advertising; it was, after all, her wheelhouse, whereas Cassandra was just a passionate health food chef, not a business person. Jacqueline would be a great asset to the partnership, aside from the capital.

In other words, Jacqueline had an after life, as some exit planners or business brokers call it. A calling. A specific plan of action once the business transition was complete. She was really excited by her new life. Her future.

"I'm selling the business, Jeremy, no matter what. If Terence aborts, we go back to the private equity firm waiting in the wings. Are they keeping in touch?"

"Yes, they are. I spoke to them last week. They just closed on a deal but reiterated their desire to buy JAT if Terence aborts. Besides, his exclusivity period expires in three weeks."

"Well, let's go tell the team what the plan is. They need to know."

Jacqueline, followed by Jeremy, walked into the board room. All the team were present. Since Lucy knew what was coming (she was already part of the inner circle), she volunteered to man the reception desk. She closed the door on her way out of the board room.

Jacqueline cleared her throat.

"Team, I have some news that I wanted to share with you.

"Several weeks ago, I agreed to sell the business to a wonderful, local entrepreneur who'll be a fantastic new owner and leader for this business. He's from the PR industry and works for one of the mega firms here in town.

"I've decided to retire. I considered several offers and decided Terence Turner, from Creative Media Inc, was the best buyer for you guys. We also had a very compelling second option who would also be a great new owner for you. They're waiting in the wings if my preferred buyer can't close the deal.

"Jeremy, Lucy and Phillip have been in the loop from the start, and I also told Derek Friday night.

"The deal is likely to close in the next few weeks, and you'll get to meet Terence.

"Any questions?"

Most of the faces looked shocked.

Lee from accounts asked, "Will Terence let any of us go post-closing?"

"Absolutely not, Lee. Terence has given me his word that all of you will remain in the business."

There was an audible sigh of relief across the room followed by the whispers of several brief side conversations.

Justin from marketing asked, "Is Creative buying the business or just Terence individually?" Justin himself had actually applied for a marketing role at Creative last year and was turned down. In fact, he didn't even make it to the interview stage (which hurt), and it was his goal to eventually work for a mega firm.

"It's Terence individually," replied Jacqueline.

Justin looked glumly at his water bottle placed only a few inches in front of his face. He was now slouching and leaning over the table.

Diane from sales asked, "Are you leaving right away when the sale goes through?"

"Not at all, Diane. I'll work with Terence to fully hand over, and I'm also retaining a minority ownership stake, so I'll be around part-time, helping out where I can."

That response lifted the general mood further.

"Any other questions?"

There were none.

"Okay, guys, it's business as usual. Let's keep the foot to the pedal and continue to grow this amazing business. Terence will be proud of you as a team, and I can't wait for him to meet you all."

The meeting ended, and Jacqueline realized she would now have to tell Terence that her entire staff was aware of the deal. She would also take that opportunity to confirm he was truly going to close.

Chapter 40

Terence Takes the Interview for the Partnership

Terence was no stranger to job interviews. He had sailed through nine during his career and received nine offers. He had taken four of those jobs, so he was, in effect, batting 1000.

He was a master at building relationships, and he knew that at his level successful interviews were more about relationships and character than pure skills and experiences.

Despite his perfect track record, he felt nervous. It was the first time he had interviewed for a partnership. This was, in fact, quite rare in his industry. Normally, firms hired a senior at the director level, and following three to five years of sterling service, those people were invited into a partnership. After five years, if you hadn't been offered a partnership, it was time to panic and move on. That's precisely why Terence had left his last role and moved to Creative PR Inc.

Kenton James Ward LLP was the top firm in Chicago and had offices all over the world. It was easily in the top five creative agencies in the world, probably the top three. With 17,500 employees and over 100 partners, it represented the absolute best in the business world.

Terence strode nervously into the cavernous lobby, the heart of a 65-storey steel and glass cylinder with incredible views of Lake Michigan. It was certainly opulent. He checked in at the ground-floor communal reception desk. Kenton James Ward occupied floors 35 to 41, and their own reception was on floor 37.

The communal reception took his name, called up to the Kenton James Ward reception, confirmed he had an appointment, then took his ID, his picture and finally printed out a pass. The pass would also act as his passage through the security barriers.

He took the pass, placed it in the lanyard and before hanging around his neck, buzzed the security gate and pushed through with his right hip. He headed to one of the 12 elevators ahead of him.

Strangely, the elevators didn't have a call button. Instead the security guard invited him to scan his pass on the LCD screen. He didn't have to remove the lanyard from around his neck, as the screen was chest height, sunk into the marble tiled wall.

Within ten seconds, one of the elevators opened and the guard motioned him to step in. It was pre-programed to take Terence to the 37th floor, which took less than ten more seconds.

He walked out of the elevator and through a large glass door into the Kenton James Ward reception. There was a face recognition camera directly in front of him that in nanoseconds had sent a communication to the reception deck iMac, announcing it was Terence.

Sophisticated stuff, he thought.

"Good morning, Mr Turner," said the attractive young brunette with a smile.

"Good morning. I have an appointment with Leo Tanner and Russell Taylor."

"Yes, sir. It's the first conference room down the hall to your right."

He walked to the glass conference room and saw two middle-aged gentlemen along with a younger assistant all waiting for him.

As he walked in, both Leo and Russell rose to greet him. All three of the men made introductions before the assistant took coffee orders.

Leo and Russell were both partners. Both appeared to be about the same age as Terence.

"Terence, we really appreciate you coming in on such short notice. As you know from our recruiter, we're looking to hire a new partner into the firm, and we're on a deadline."

"Yes, that's what I understand."

"We had made an offer to another external candidate, but, unfortunately—or you might say fortunately for you—he took an executive position at Google.

"I believe you already have our terms. We would like to share our vision of the business with you and discuss the partnership responsibilities."

"Absolutely," replied Terence.

Both Leo and Russell spent the next 30 minutes discussing the history of the firm (Terence had done his research over the weekend, so he knew most of it) but more importantly the vision. The firm was, indeed, the third-largest by revenue and market share but was within striking distance of the number two spot. Revenues were growing at a solid 16% year-to-year, and the company boasted the highest profit margins in the industry for firms in the top 50—more than 33% net operating income.

The two partners walked through all the key accounts and the growth strategies in place to enrich them. Terence would be handed a stable of clients. Most of them were grocery chains, but there was also the large gas station chain Wawa, Disney (which reminded Terence of his last major work trip to Universal in California) and, to top it all off, Microsoft, which Terence was especially delighted to hear.

The partnership would contain equity, much less than one percent, but this was a mega firm. The partnership would cost $600,000, but the firm would advance a fifteen-year, low-interest loan, and the payments would be added to his $250,000 salary package. So, it was, in effect, free equity.

If only Terence weren't in the midst of buying a small business, he would've absolutely jumped at this chance. This was his dream come true. In actuality, he was really torn between this and JAT PR.

The two partners drilled Terence on his work at Creative, enquired as to his notice period (which was only two weeks) and asked when he could start work if he were to accept the position.

"Probably within three weeks," he answered. The two partners smiled. The managing partner had given them a four-week deadline to have their new partner in place.

After another thirty minutes of back-and-forth questions, Leo reached over and handed Terence an offer and contract.

"The full terms and conditions are outlined in this document."

"Thank you. I will absolutely review it later today."

"Terence, can we have your response no later than the end-of-day tomorrow, please? You're top of our shortlist, but if you decide not to take this partnership, we'll need to move on to our other candidates. But know this: The partnership is yours if you want it."

Terence thanked them both and walked out to the reception area, said goodbye to the receptionist, then hit the call button (the down elevators had these). Back at the ground floor, he walked through the main foyer and out onto the sidewalk, blinking in the sunshine.

He had a goofy grin on his face, but what a conundrum . . .

Clearly he couldn't acquire JAT and also take the partnership. He had asked that question in the meeting, and the two partners had replied in unison with a firm "no."

What am I going to do? And more importantly, how am I going to make the decision?

What should the criteria be?

He would certainly need to speak with his wife, Julie. Also, Lawrence, his attorney friend and drinking buddy.

He might also call his dad, Stephen. Stephen Turner was a retired air force pilot who had flown in Vietnam. Not a business guy by any stretch of the imagination, but he had a cool head and could think laterally. He was a master of future-pacing outcomes, so his insight would be valuable. He didn't know about the partnership interview, but he did know about his son's frustrations with Creative and the planned acquisition of JAT.

"Absolutely go for it" Terence's dad had said when he first heard about JAT. He even offered to provide some of the equity capital for the down payment.

Carl, however, had advised against doing that. "Never take capital from friends and family."

So, Terence had raised the capital from inside the Protégé community, specifically, from Len Freemont, David Baskins (who was a former MLB baseball player) and Wes Garrett. All would be minority partners.

Terence decided he would go home, speak to Julie, then canvas Lawrence and his dad later that evening.

Unbeknown to Terence, however, he would have to wait only a few more minutes before making his final decision.

Chapter 41

The Decision

Jacqueline called Terence but got his voicemail. Instead of leaving a message, she shot him a text:

"Hi Terence, can you give me a call as soon as possible. I have some news I want to share with you. Thanks, Jacqueline"

About 30 minutes later, Terence was walking down Michigan avenue, his head still spinning from the interview. He had just decided who would be his advisors for making the impending decision, when he saw the text.

This sounds ominous, he thought. *Maybe she's aborting. Well, that would make my decision much easier.*

He popped in his ear pods and placed the call.

Jacqueline answered after a few rings.

"Hi Terence, how are you?"

"I'm good, thanks, and you?"

"Very well. I just wanted to give you some news. I was out this past Friday night at my annual office party, and one of my senior sales reps confronted me about the sale. He'd heard rumors and told me the news had spread to the rest of the team. Some of my clients apparently know as well. I'm going to be calling some of them this afternoon.

"Most importantly, I wanted you to know that, in view of all this, I went ahead and fully communicated the deal to my entire team. And I gave them your name. I hope you don't mind."

Terence was somewhat startled by this development, but handled it smoothly. "Not at all, thanks for letting me know." Then he added, "What was their reaction?"

"Very positive. There were some of the usual questions you'd expect, but the team is really excited for you to take over the business, and all are thrilled I'm staying part-time and as a minority shareholder."

"That's great. When will I meet them? I guess after closing, right?"

"You're welcome to meet them anytime, Terence, but I completely understand if you want to close the deal first. On that point, where are you in the process? I hear the legalities have stalled. Herb is getting quite frustrated."

"Ah, my apologies, I had an urgent corporate meeting come up this morning, so I had to cancel my meetings with both the bank and my attorney, and I have meetings all this afternoon in the office. I've rescheduled both for tomorrow morning, as I will be working from home."

"So . . . is the plan still to close within two weeks?" Jacqueline pressed.

"Yes, that's still the plan. The bank is close to receiving the SBA loan approval, and I understand Herb and Brittany are almost done arm wrestling on the legal documents. They haven't actually stalled. I just need Brittany to walk me through Herb's latest redline. So, yes, I do believe we are close."

"That's great to hear. Now, Terence, apologies for the directness of my final question, but it's something I need to know."

"Sure. What is it?"

"Can you confirm to me that you intend to go through with this deal? Subject to the bank and the final legal negotiations, I need to know if you're all in?"

"Wow, Jacqueline. Why would you ask me that?" Terence had been growing increasingly uncomfortable with her line of questioning, but until that point had been able to respond with the routine answers one might give when one has the cover of various contingencies, whether explicitly acknowledged or not. At this point, Jacqueline had named off the contingencies one by one and thereby backed Terence into a rhetorical corner. His reflexive, last-ditch reaction was an attempt to deflect the question back upon her.

"I don't know, Terence. I just had a funny feeling earlier that you were getting cold feet. I don't fully know why. My team was getting edgy, and I needed to tell them about the deal. Now that the cat's out of the bag, I need you to follow through with this, or else I need to know if you won't be able to."

Terence stopped and stood absolutely still where he was on the sidewalk. He closed his eyes. To the many other pedestrians passing around him, he might have looked like he was praying or perhaps in a trance. More than ten seconds passed before Jacqueline broke the silence on the line.

"Terence?"

"Yes, sorry, the line dropped there. Can you ask me that again?"

"Of course. I've told my team we're closing in two weeks. Can you confirm to me right now that you're committed to making this happen?"

At that moment, Terence was taken back to a time from his adolescence. He was at high school and being heavily recruited by Purdue to play baseball on a full scholarship. He wanted, however, to stay local and be with his friends. And he also wanted a career in the creative industry. The local university had a better curriculum for that chosen career. He was a good baseball player, but he was never going to be good enough to make it to the MLB, unlike his soon-to-be investing partner, David Barrett, who had played for the Oakland A's.

He recalled the day his father, Stephen, had asked him to make the final call. Just like he knew his dad would do, Terence future-paced the choices. That done, he put his hands in his pockets, looked away and smiled. He rejected Purdue. He knew it was the right choice, and he stood by the decision.

In a split second there on the sidewalk, Terence's imagination ran two parallel tracks. He used the technique his dad had taught him almost two decades ago. Track one was taking the partnership he had just been offered at Kenton James Ward LLP. That track brought the eventual politics and infighting that always happens in large firms. Yes, he would make millions as a partner in the next ten years, but was it worth it?

In parallel, his mind future-paced closing the deal with Jacqueline and acquiring JAT. Owning his own business. Calling the shots. Being the Commander-in-Chief. Growing the business. Acquiring other businesses. Hard work, but very rewarding.

Still with his eyes closed, he thrust his hands into his pockets, looked away and smiled.

"Absolutely, Jacqueline. I'm all in. We *will* get this done."

"That's all I needed to hear. Keep me posted, and see you soon."

Chapter 42

Updating Calls with Legal and the Bank

Terence attended his rescheduled Zoom meeting with Brittany.

Logging into the call, he was surprised to see Brittany didn't have her camera on.

"Hi, Brittany!" He was especially chirpy this morning, now that he'd gotten over his cold feet on the deal and was eager to close.

"Hi, Terence. Apologies I don't have my camera on today. I'm feeling sick and don't look my best but wanted to keep the meeting and update you on the deal."

"No problem. Where are we?"

"Well, I've been back and forward with Herb several times. He was pushing hard for a lien on the business for the seller financing portion of the deal, but as you know, the bank will want that as the priority lien. But we've agreed for Jacqueline to take a second-place lien with no personal guarantee on the money, since she's retaining 10% of the business and will have a seat on the board."

"Great. Anything else contentious?"

"Not really. The representations and warranties are fine, and Jacqueline has agreed to the drag and tag rights."

"Can you explain to me what those are?"

"Sure. 'Drag rights' mean that if you get an offer to sell the business, you can force Jacqueline to sell on the same terms. 'Tag rights' are that in reverse. If you agree to sell your 90%, Jacqueline can take the same terms if she wants to, albeit pro rata to her 10% versus your 90%."

"Okay, great, anything else?"

"Yes, under the new operating agreement between you and Jacqueline, we need a third person to act as an arbiter in case you and Jacqueline can't agree on major decisions. I know you wanted control, but I couldn't move Herb off this point. He's pushing to appoint himself as that third person. He doesn't need equity, but he would be a manager within the LLC."

"Hmm, . . . I'm not happy with that. He's always going to side with Jacqueline, and I want control—it's not like we're 50/50 shareholders."

"Well, this is the only sticking point. Perhaps you need to call Jacqueline and smooth this out. Can you do that now and then call me back? I know the bank wants to close on this within the next seven days. In fact, when is your call with them?"

"In about 10 minutes. Let me call Jacqueline first, then I'll call the bank, then I'll give you an update."

"Okay, got it. Good luck."

Terence called Jacqueline. She was walking from her yoga class and was in the middle of ordering her Starbucks for mobile connection when she saw Terence's name on the caller ID. She suddenly felt anxious. *Why are my emotions all over the place?* In actuality, it was simply because she'd never been through this process before, and since they were so close, she was dreading him getting cold feet, especially now that her team were fully aware of him and where they both were in the sales process.

She took a deep breath and answered the call. She even closed her eyes. *Please no—do not abort, do not abort, do not abort,* she mentally chanted to herself.

"Hi, Terence, how are you?"

"I'm fine, Jacqueline, thanks for asking. You?"

"Sweaty," she laughed nervously. "I just finished my yoga class."

Ouch, thought Terence. He remembered the one and only time his wife Julie dragooned him into attending her class. He ached for almost a week.

"How can I help?" Jacqueline asked.

"It's a quick one. I just got off the legal call with my attorney. Everything has been agreed apart from one item. Herb is pushing for split control with him acting as arbiter, and since I don't know him, I'm concerned you both will effectively have control of the business even though I'll be a 90% owner. That doesn't sit well with me."

"Okay, I understand. I actually wasn't aware of that. You need to understand Herb. He's one of my oldest friends, and he prides himself on being my guardian angel. I'm 100% fine with you having full control. I will let him know so he can amend the document."

"Was there anything else in the legals you have an issue with?" she added.

"No, that was it. Everything else has been agreed on. Once we tie that final point off, we can close, subject to the final closing protocols from the bank. In fact, I have that call next."

"Excellent. I'll call Herb right now. You have your bank call, then please text me when the bank gives you the closing date."

"Will do, and thank you."

As Terence was logging into the Zoom call with Live Stem, Jacqueline was speaking to Herb. She instructed him to drop the dual control issue. Although, predictably, he initially pushed back, he finally conceded and agreed. Herb would email Brittany to that effect.

Terence entered yet another Zoom room and saw three people from Live Stem: Lisa Trammel, Marlyn Day (the assigned closer) and Kevin Hart, Live Stem's legal counsel.

"Hi, everyone," said Terence. "Apologies for rescheduling. Something came up yesterday, and I appreciate your flexibility."

"No problem," replied Lisa.

"Terence, we have good news. We have your PLP number from the SBA, and we're ready to close. We're scheduling a closing date for the middle of next week." That was only six days away.

Oh my God, Terence thought. *I'm going to be a business owner in six days.*

"That's great news," he replied. "Is there anything you need from me at this point?"

"No, we finally got your new life insurance policy, which lists us as the beneficiary, and we have approved your surety bond insurance for the personal guarantee, so we'll get all the documents ready."

"What's the process, please?" Terence asked.

"We're actually doing this old-school," Kevin laughed. "The seller's attorney wants all this to be done in person at his office rather than via Docusign. So, we'll get all the documents ready, vetted by your attorney, and you'll sign them there with her in the presence of the seller's attorney.

"You'll obviously also sign the stock purchase agreement contract.

"We'll place funds into escrow the day before, and as soon as you sign all the contracts, the money will transfer to the seller's attorney. He will take his closing fees, then pay the seller the balance.

"You'll need to have your equity capital placed into the same account the day before as well. We'll not put our funds in there until yours are already there."

"Great, that works. I have mine and my other investors' capital standing by. I'll make arrangements to get that transferred. Please let me know the bank account details of the escrow account. Better still, please provide those to my attorney."

"Will do. Where are you on the stock purchase agreement and the ancillary documents?"

"Almost there. One last point has just been agreed on, so I'm expecting the final contract to be ready later today."

"That's excellent. We look forward to consummating this transaction with you, Terence. It's been a pleasure."

Terence ended the Zoom and called Brittany back. He relayed the closing instructions from the bank and confirmed to her that Jacqueline had waived the dual control issue.

"Yes, I know," she replied. "Herb called me to confirm. In fact, I already have the final contract ready. I'll send it to the bank now."

Terence was grinning like a tickled baby. He was finally home-free.

Nothing could go wrong now, surely. Or could it?

Chapter 43

Government Shutdown

The SBA was born in 1932 under its former name, the Reconstruction Finance Corporation (FRC), by then President Herbert Hoover to reboot the US economy after the Great Depression. It pivoted several times (especially through World War II) until President Dwight D. Eisenhower created the current SBA in 1953. SBA's mission was (and still is) to "aid, counsel, assist and protect, insofar as is possible, the interests of small business concerns." It also is charged with ensuring that small businesses earn a "fair proportion" of government contracts and sales of surplus property.

The SBA assists US small businesses in growth and development, including allowing entrepreneurs (like Terence) to leverage capital to finance business acquisitions.

The SBA, however, doesn't itself have capital. It's more like an insurance policy. Banks under the SBA loan program take customer deposits at nominal interest rates, leverage up that capital in the overnight banking market and then lend that money to entrepreneurs and business owners at much higher rates. The SBA then guarantees the majority of the loan, typically 80%. It's, therefore, Christmas morning for banks and an excellent example of how the government and Wall Street can collaborate for the common good of the small business community.

However, like the National Parks Service, the United States Botanic Garden and the National Library Service for the Blind and Print Disabled, to name just a few, the SBA is a branch of the Federal Government, and when the government shuts down, so do all of these departments, including the SBA.

It was a cold and wet December evening. Late evening. The President's Chief of Staff, Larry Moss and his assistant, Josh Parker, sat in Larry's office, adjacent to the Oval Office. The large, thick, white door was firmly shut. In the room, you could cut the silence with a knife. Josh had sat in negotiations all night with the Speaker of the House of Representatives and his henchmen. The current administration was Democrat. The House was controlled by the Republicans. As has been the case throughout history, the two sides didn't get along. They were still $100,000,000 apart in the annual budget negotiations. These had been ongoing for months. It seemed like the White House and Congress were always negotiating the budget. Bear in mind it took months for all the various government departments, special interest groups and various causes to submit their proposals. Then, it became a game of chess. The dealmaking, horse trading and political games had ended in stalemate.

Congress earlier in the week had approved the final numbers, but now it wanted to trim a further $100,000,000 from the budget. Various continuing resolutions had been approved, but this was it. The White House and Congress had just 43 minutes to agree and sign the budget, or the Federal Government would shut down.

It wasn't the first time. At that point it had happened ten times since the early 1980s. Every time it happened, all Federal employees were furloughed. Currently, there are almost 700,000 of them, including the people who work at the SBA.

Larry and Josh finally looked at each other. Both had been studying memos on unrelated subjects, without either actually reading anything. They were waiting for the President to see them. Senior members of Congress, including Speaker Drexler, would be assembling in a large conference room down the hall.

Precisely five minutes before the meeting, President Gerald Booth opened the door and asked Larry to walk with him to the Situation Room. A rogue terrorist group in the Middle East was provoking a US ally in the region, and the President had to quickly go to the Situation Room for a briefing. Larry had full security clearance to enter alongside the President. It was one of his roles as Chief of Staff.

As the two middle-aged men descended the stairs to the White House Basement, President Booth grabbed Larry by the arm. "What's the latest on the budget negotiations?" he asked.

"Not great," said Larry. "We're still $100,000,000 apart. Congress isn't budging. Perhaps we should?"

"No!" boomed President Booth. We had a deal earlier this week, I'm not budging."

The two men debated the point for a few minutes until the Secret Service opened the Situation Room doors.

As soon as the President entered the room, everyone stood to attention. The briefing lasted only a few minutes. The Directors of the FBI, CIA and NSA gave short, to-the-point briefings, and the Chairman of the Joint Chiefs, Admiral Blair Cole, made his recommendation.

"So ordered," President Booth declared.

Then he and Larry skipped up the stairs to the meeting with Congress.

As they approached the door, they could see the Speaker of the House, Kevin Drexler, his henchmen and most of the West Wing senior staff gathered and waiting for the President to join the meeting.

President Booth stopped Larry from opening the door. He looked Larry directly in the eyes and asked him a question.

"If you give a mouse a cookie, what's he going to want next?"

"A glass of milk," Larry said and smiled.

"Exactly," said the President.

The two men bounded into the room and took their assigned seats, not before everyone had stood to attention. Despite the budget disagreements, it was good to see that respect was still in the White House.

The Speaker started the meeting.

"Mr. President. As you know, we have a budget deal if you cut the last $100,000,000 of spending. The country is hurting, Mr President. As the government, we have to follow suit."

The budget was six trillion dollars. $100,000,000 was what they probably spent on paper clips.

"No, Mr Speaker. We *had* a deal. We aren't cutting more spending."

"Then we're gridlocked, Sir. And let me remind you that in exactly 18 minutes, you'll be responsible for shutting down the Federal Government."

President Booth looked the Speaker directly in the eyes, leaned slightly forward, and with clenched fist pressed down on the massive conference table, slowly uttered just four words:

"Then shut it down."

The President walked out of the meeting, left the West Wing and went to the Residence. The First Lady was at that time on a diplomatic tour of Argentina, and the President's three adult children were off living their lives. An aide poured him a whiskey. A fine Angel's Envy Reserve. He turned on the television and started watching college basketball. His mighty fighting Irish, Notre Dame, were up ten points against Duke. He smiled for the first time that evening. President Booth was a proud Catholic whose family had descended from Ireland and came to Boston in the early 1900s.

The clock struck midnight, and at that moment, the Federal government ran out of money. All 700,000 employees were now furloughed, including all 2,822 SBA employees and the 534 loan officers.

Larry knocked on the door and walked in. The Notre Dame power forward had just shot his fourth consecutive three-point basket in the last five minutes.

"Sir, everyone is still in the room. Let's go back down there and see if we can find a compromise. Can I remind you that we are now officially shut down?"

"I don't care, Larry. We had a deal. I am not negotiating again. We're halfway through our second term. We still have important work to do, and if we blink now—if we yield, if we cave—the speaker will eat our lunch for the next two years, and it's going to make it so much harder for the Veep (the Vice President) to stay in this White House and keep the administration Democratic. May I remind you how much the Republicans will continue to cut taxes if we don't get to stay here?

"I'm holding firm, dammit. The Speaker and Congress can come back to me whenever they've come to their senses. I'm not budging one cent from what was agreed."

The shutdown lasted four weeks. The President won the test of wills, but those 700,000 employees stayed furloughed the entire time, including the SBA.

Once the Government reopened, SBA processing time for 7a loans increased from four weeks to thirteen weeks, to deal with the backlog.

Chapter 44

Pivoting the Deal

About a week after the shutdown, Jacqueline and Jeremy were on Zoom with Jacqueline's attorney, Herb.

It had been eight weeks since the signing of the LOI. The due diligence had been completed, and the last turn of the stock purchase agreement was completed. Closing could have happened imminently, but now the deal faced collapse since the financing was upheld indefinitely by the government shutdown and furlough of all SBA employees.

"How long is this going to take, Herb?" Jacqueline enquired.

"I can't tell you," he replied. "From what the SBA is telling me and what I'm reading in the newspapers, we're in for the long haul. Neither the President nor Congress will budge. This has become a political standoff essentially between the President and the Speaker of the House. All for a mere $100,000,000 out of a $6 trillion federal budget.

"It could take months, and my fear is that when the SBA reopens alongside the rest of the Federal Government, we could be talking many more months of delay. There's probably ten thousand applications lodged with the SBA right now."

Jacqueline was devastated. Her entire life was mapped out starting from the end of the month. She'd been dating Jack for months now, and although he hadn't proposed, she knew it was going to happen as soon as the deal was closed. He had booked a trip for the two of them to visit Rome and Tuscany in a few weeks, and she knew they would be visiting Florence. She had once told him (after too much red wine) that he should propose to her on the Ponte Vecchio, the lovers' bridge in Florence. The trip was happening, but what now?

"Jeremy, we *have* to close this deal in the next few weeks. I have my life to live. I leave for Italy with Jack in three weeks. All our reservations are locked in. I promised Terence a full, one-week handover, then I would be traveling for a few weeks before starting my consultancy agreement of two half-days per week."

Herb chimed in. "I can almost guarantee we aren't closing this deal with the SBA in the next two weeks—not even in the next two months. I'm sorry, but there's nothing we can do about it."

"Can't Terence find the money elsewhere?" she asked.

"Not really. He would need to go raise private equity, and that would cost him at least 50% of the equity in the deal. I'm not sure he would agree to that, and it's so much harder to get cash flow financing for deals outside the SBA."

Jacqueline later asked Jeremy if he would call Terence and discuss all the options. Jeremy agreed to do so.

Chapter 45

The Annuity Purchase Option

Terence had gone to bed the night before the shutdown feeling giddy. His contact at Live Stem had emailed the final closing checklist to him and his attorney. The SBA had already provided the PLP number—the magic number the SBA assigns to your loan once it's been fully approved. From that point, closing is inevitable, often within a week, maximum.

He woke up to the news that the Federal Government had been closed. "Damned politicians," he muttered as he fixed his coffee, not really understanding what this was going to do to his deal.

He was about to get into his Tesla to drive to the office when his attorney called. "Terence, we have a problem."

"What's that, Brittany? I thought you said that all the legal contracts were complete, agreed upon and ready for signing once the bank is ready."

"It's not that. It's the SBA. It's closed due to the Government shutdown."

"What do you mean, 'closed'?"

"It's closed. All SBA employees have been furloughed. I've just been told by Live Stem that it could delay us by two, maybe three months."

"Two to three months?" he boomed. "What the hell?"

"Look, I can't stand another day in my W2," Terence exclaimed. "Why such a long delay? Everything's all ready to go, and I've turned down a *very* lucrative partnership at the most prestigious agency in town. This can't be happening to me."

Terence felt a massive knot forming in his stomach, and he suddenly felt sick. He was fighting the urge to vomit inside his freshly detailed Tesla.

The sensation took Terence back to when he was 15 years old, over 25 years ago. His mother had died suddenly of a heart attack, and the following morning, his dad, Stephen, stumbled into Terrence's bedroom and collapsed in tears, asking Terence (who was an only child) … "What are we going to do, son? What are we going to do?"

The overwhelming uncertainty his father had voiced had, in that exact moment, manifested itself in Terence's stomach. A severe, gut wrenching ache. He felt exactly the same thing in this present moment. The fear of the unknown and the helplessness of having to count on other people to figure this out for him.

"Talk to me, Brittany."

Brittany calmly explained that it was her understanding that the shutdown was going to last for a while and that when the Federal Government (including the SBA) reopened, the backlog would take weeks if not months to clear. "I am working on four other SBA deals at the moment," she said. "One was days away from closing, and all the banks are telling me to plan on sitting tight for at least two months."

"I'm talking to Herb in an hour," she added, "and I'll get back to you with next steps after that call."

Terence slumped into his car and remained in that position for what felt like hours. He couldn't think. He was stunned. He had fallen in love with his future life. Acquiring JAT, acquiring some other businesses, scaling it up then exiting to a large consolidator with bundles of Wall Street cash. *None of this SBA money*, he fumed.

He decided to call the office and say he wasn't feeling well. "Probably the flu," he told his secretary.

He went into his study and, beside himself with worry, logged onto Facebook (he didn't know why).

At that moment, he read a post in the Dealmaker Protégé Facebook group. One of his fellow students was referencing a recent 911 call with a coach that had solved a major last-minute snag in a deal.

Well, time for my own 911 call, he thought.

He opened the circle application on his phone and messaged the Protégé admin to schedule something for him. "I need it to be today, please," he urged.

Less than two hours later, he was on a Zoom with Carl Allen himself. Carl rarely took 911 calls with his Protégés. His coaching team handled them. He did one-to-one calls with his Mastermind students, called the Upper Echelon.

Carl spent the first ten minutes of the call talking about Chicago, his alma mater. Terence interrupted him. "Hey, Carl, like you I love Chicago, but I have a massive problem with my deal."

"I know, Terence, I got your notes."

"Well, we only have 20 minutes left, and I'm not sure you can solve my issue in that time."

"20 minutes?" laughed Carl. "I solved it in 20 seconds. Let me tell you exactly what to do.

"Did you make the two-offer structure like I advised you to do after the RLGL call on this deal months ago?"

"Yes, sir. The seller went for the SBA option, but now that the lousy government has shut down, my attorney has told me it's going to be at least two more months before I can close the deal. I can't wait two months. I can't wait two *weeks*, and I'm very concerned the seller won't wait either. She told me in confidence there was also a financial buyer who was close on the original offers and that they're waiting in the wings."

"Hey man, I got you. Don't panic. I have the solution."

"First, though," Carl continued, "describe your relationship with the seller."

"It's excellent. She loves me. I've seen her four or five times since we signed the LOI. I've even seen her socially. We mapped out her role over lunch, and she's as excited as I am to close this deal, but I can't get her the closing payment. What should I do?"

"Simple," replied Carl. He was a former Wall Street guy. It was like ice ran through his veins. He'd seen it all. Terence was waiting like an expectant father for a glimpse of Carl's magic.

"Go back to your annuity deal offer—it was around $4,000,000 right? Get the deal legals changed but offer to refinance the annuity deal within six months once the SBA reopens and you can close. You have the PLP number, right? That's a guarantee the deal will close with the SBA. Remind me of the numbers, Terence. Apologies, I've looked at over a hundred deals since then."

"Sure," Terence replied, trying to let the significance of what Carl was saying sink in. "The final agreed SBA deal was $2,800,000. The annuity deal was $4,160,000."

"Okay, great, so that's $416,000 per year over 10-years. Around $35,000 per month.

"So, start making the $35,000 payments to her and then as soon as the SBA is back in play, transact on the loan and refinance the annuity deal at the lower SBA amount. Let's say it takes a six-month period maximum: That will be $210,000 in annuity payments, so just deduct that from the closing payment. The

SBA may reduce the loan by that amount, but if not, you just made an additional $210,000, as the business is making those $35,000 per month payments."

Terence was mesmerized by this. The idea was genius. Carl called it the "Annuity-Option" method.

"I love this," Terence said, "but I'm not sure how I can present it."

"Okay, can you invite the seller's broker to this Zoom? I have ten minutes left, let's see if we can get this done in ten minutes."

Terence wasn't convinced he could get Jeremy on the Zoom, so he called him instead.

"Jeremy, it's Terence Turner."

"Terence, I was about to call you. SBA is shut down, Jacqueline is panicking. We need to find a way through this."

"I've got a solution. I'm on a Zoom with my mentor, and he's found a solution that I think will work. Can you join?"

"Sure." Jeremy received the email and had joined the Zoom in less than a minute.

Eight minutes until Carl's next meeting.

Greetings were quickly exchanged, and Carl introduced himself as a private equity investor and business acquisitions coach. He informed Jeremy that he was already familiar with the parameters of the deal and the problem they were up against.

Seven minutes until Carl's next meeting.

"Jeremy," Carl said. "I'd like you to suspend reality for just a minute. What would have to be true to close this deal by the end of the week?"

"I'm not sure. We're looking at two to three months' delay on the closing payment. You mentioned you owned a Private Equity firm. Can you not give Terence the capital?"

"Yes, I can," Carl said, "but we do have a process, so for us to run that and negotiate the operating agreement and terms with Terence would take two to three weeks, if I pushed it. But Terence hasn't asked me for that. We haven't agreed on any equity splits or anything like that.

"I actually have a better solution, one that'll ensure the deal closes this week and that Jacqueline is made whole on the deal, with full guarantees."

Six minutes until Carl's next meeting.

"Okay, I'm listening, Carl. What's your plan?"

"Terence has confirmed to me that he made you guys a two-offer structure."

"Yes, and we went for the SBA option. Jacqueline wanted the cash at closing."

"Well, if she doesn't want to wait to sell the business, why not take the annuity deal now? It's $4,160,000 over 10 years, or roughly $35,000 per month. Let's close the deal now, start making the payments and once the SBA is back in play, Terence will refinance the deal (using the SBA financing) and discharge the annuity loan note."

Jeremy was silent for a few moments. "How fast can that happen?"

"Well, I think we're in the hands of the politicians; however, I don't think the government will stay shut down beyond a month or so—two absolute max. And since Terence already has the SBA PLP loan number ..."

"Yes," Terrence interrupted, "I received that yesterday."

"Well, then, in my experience, closing is inevitable unless something catastrophic happens to the business in the meantime.

"Terence will give Jacqueline a full lien over the assets and equity in the business, together with a performance guarantee so that he can't clear out the bank account or harm the business in any way.

"And although Terence will become the new legal owner, we'll keep Jacqueline on the bank mandate so she can continue to log in."

Wow, thought Jeremy. *This guy knows his stuff. This is clearly not his first rodeo.*

Can you email me this revised structure as soon as possible fellows? "Then, I'll present it to Jacqueline and her attorney. Honestly, I think this is an elegant solution. I think I can sell this."

Three minutes to Carl's next meeting.

"I'm assuming," Jeremy continued, "can we still use the surplus cash in the business to handle Jacqueline's closing costs?"

"I don't see why not," said Carl.

With 60 seconds to spare, Carl logged off the Zoom, leaving Jeremy and Terence in the meeting.

"So, what are the chances of Jacqueline signing off on this?" Terence asked.

"I would say high," Jeremy assured him. "Get me that revised structure, and I'll see what I can do."

Terence had made notes all over his pad. He opened his email and ping, Carl had just pinged him a note with the bullets, from his iPhone. *What a champ,* he thought.

Terence copied and pasted them into a new email, sent them to Jeremy, copied his attorney Brittany and hit "send."

Chapter 46

Jacqueline Takes the Deal

Within five minutes, the email had caused a flurry of activity.

Jeremy immediately forwarded the email to Jacqueline and Herb and suggested a Zoom as soon as possible. One was set up within the hour.

As soon as Brittany read the email, she called Terence.

"This is a brilliant idea," she said, "but I'm not sure they'll go for it. I'll call Herb and prepare him for this. We'll need to change the stock purchase agreement, but that shouldn't take long. I'll start to work with him on this."

Brittany skimmed the current legal documents for the deal and determined what would need to happen to make the changes. About 30 minutes later, she called Herb.

His secretary said he was on a Zoom call and would call back later.

Herb was, indeed, on a Zoom call with Jacqueline and Jeremy.

"I just don't like this, guys," Herb stated.

"But it does solve our deal issue," Jacqueline retorted. "We close the deal now, as agreed. I do the handover. I start receiving $35,000 per month for a maximum of six-months, then the SBA will refinance the annuity loan note and I get the rest of the money, right?"

"Well, yes," said Herb, "but what happens if he tanks the business? Or for whatever reason the SBA doesn't lend him the money? What then? If you really want to do this, we'll need assurances."

"Like what," asked Jeremy?

"Well, first, I need to see confirmation of the loan number under the SBA. That's usually the final step."

"We have that, Herb," Jeremy observed. "I'll forward it to you now."

"Right, okay. Next, does he have all the equity?"

"He does," countered Jeremy. "He used $100,000 of his own capital; he raised the rest from a private investor community."

"Okay, then, his attorney Brittany will need to confirm this, and I'll insist this money is put into escrow, ahead of the refinancing.

"Third, I think we should ensure all your closing costs are covered from the surplus cash and any additional surplus cash is also placed into escrow. How much is this, Jeremy?"

"There's about $350,000 of surplus cash in the business, and we agreed to leave that in the account, under the terms of the deal."

"Well, I'm going to recommend Jacqueline take that as a closing payment. Let's keep his equity in escrow, as he's going to need that 'seasoned' for the SBA.

"I also want to see a proposed lien document and performance guarantee."

"What's a performance guarantee? asked Jacquline.

"Simple," said Herb. "When you borrow money from a bank, the bank places the business under covenants. Think of these as financial rules. If they're broken, fees and premiums will apply, and if they're materially or repeatedly broken, the loan can get called. I say we do the same for Terence, so he has to stay within sensible business constraints."

"Okay, I'm happy with all that," said Jacqueline.

"Me too," added Jeremy.

Herb ended the Zoom, then he called Brittany with the news. "This will work for us, subject to the new adjustments," he said.

Herb then emailed the revised terms back to Brittany, who wanted to call Terence first with the news before forwarding the email. She loved this part of her job: putting buyers or sellers out of their misery. Deals always hit roadblocks, but most could be rescued, though not all. In her experience, resurrecting the deal was the fun part, and for this deal, she wasn't the one who did it. It was Terence and his mentor, Carl Allen.

Brittany agreed to change the stock purchase agreement, then called Terence back with the news that the deal was back on and that he would be the new owner by the end of the week.

Terence paced around his back yard, checking his phone every 60 seconds for a missed call, a text . . . anything. He also scanned his Facebook Messenger as well, just in case Jacqueline wanted to reach out. He knew she wouldn't, but he checked anyway.

He was watching a squirrel run up the tree at the pace of an Olympic sprinter. *That's me scaling JAT*, he thought. Well, if he managed to buy it, that is.

Just as the squirrel hit the tree canopy and disappeared, Brittany called.

Terrence took in a very deep breath, closed his eyes, crossed his fingers, then slid the bar across his iPhone to accept the call.

He tried to play it cool.

"Hi, Brittany, how are you?"

"I'm good, Terence, how are you?"

"Fine, thanks. Do you have any news?"

"Yes, I do, and it's reasonably good news. Jacqueline has agreed to kick this off with an annuity deal structure, with a 180-day refi. However, she wants to use the surplus capital as a much smaller closing payment for now, and this will be netted off the balance of the closing payment when the SBA comes back into play.

"Their only other condition is for you to put your equity capital into escrow for the duration of the annuity term. The SBA will need that anyway for 'seasoning.'"

Terence was elated. He wasn't thrilled with losing the surplus cash, but he could top that up once he closed on the refinancing and then do his first bolt-on acquisition.

All in all, it was still a great deal.

"Let's do it, Brittany," he said.

Brittany said she would tweak the LOI to reflect the new terms and get started on the changes to the stock purchase agreement. "This should all get wrapped up by Friday," she said, "and the deal can close."

Terence ended the call, closed his eyes and let out a great, ear piercing shout of absolute elation.

His neighbor, Jasper, looked over the fence and said, "won the Powerball lottery, Terence?" He was grinning.

"Not exactly," Terence replied "but it's the next best thing."

He rushed into the house, grabbed the bottle of champagne from his giant wine cooler and went in search of Julie.

She was reading her latest Harlen Cobin book. She saw the look on his face, spotted the champagne in his left hand and knew the outcome.

"I did it, babe," he exclaimed.

She beamed the most beautiful smile, jumped out of her chair and embraced him.

"Congratulations, dear. You've worked so hard for this. When will the deal close?"

"Friday at the latest. We're almost there."

Julie was pouring the champagne when Terence saw an incoming text from Carl.

188

"How did the call go? Offer agreed?"

He replied to Carl's text in the affirmative and sincerely thanked him for finding the solution.

Chapter 47

The Closing

The next few days were a whirlwind. Brittany, Jeremy and Herb worked diligently on the final documents, and by 7 p.m. Thursday night, everything was ready.

The legal documents had all been agreed upon and locked.

All the equity was in escrow.

Closing was tomorrow.

Everyone would meet at Herb's downtown law office at 11 a.m., sign all the documents in person, then together enjoy a celebration lunch that was booked at the Capital Grille at 12:30 p.m. Lastly, Jacqueline would walk Terence to the office and introduce him to all the employees.

Terence had already met Phillip and Leanne but was eager to meet with the rest of the team. He would start one-to-one discussions on Monday and also start conversing with key clients. Friday afternoon was devoted to introducing himself and his strategic plan and conveying his hope that everyone would follow him on this new entrepreneurial journey.

He had yet to resign from Creative PR. He would do that via email tomorrow afternoon from his new office at JAT. No point risking anything until he legally owned the business.

At 10:45 a.m. the following day, Terence skipped into Herb's office. Everyone else was gathering by then. He had traded messages with Jacqueline the night before, but as soon as they saw each other, they embraced.

"Thank you for being so creative," said Jacqueline.

"And thank you for being so flexible," Terence replied.

Herb called the meeting to order, as everyone was now in attendance. The documents took less than 30 minutes to review and sign, and the much smaller, closing payment (representing the surplus cash) was released to Jacqueline. Terence was now the 90% owner of JAT PR LLC.

He was thrilled. Jacqueline still owned 10%, and the two of them had just signed a new operating agreement to cement their union as partners. Terence had control of the business, but Jacqueline had a lien over both the equity and assets of the business until the balance of the closing payment was paid.

Lunch was delicious. Terence enjoyed a medium-rare filet steak washed down with a couple of glasses of red wine. After coffee, Terence paid the bill, left a generous tip, and he and Jacqueline strolled the fifteen-minute walk to the offices of JAT. He was thrilled.

He would claim the expense for the lunch back from the JAT bank account later. Oh, the joys of owning a business, he smiled.

They walked into the office, and Jacqueline asked her assistant to call everyone into the conference room. Every employee was present. She had a major announcement, and unless someone was out on an urgent client call, attendance was mandatory.

All 17 employees were watching Jacqueline when she said, "Team, I wanted to introduce you to Terence Turner. As of this morning, he is the new majority-owner of JAT PR. He and I have been in discussions over the past few months, and I signed the contract to transfer majority ownership to him today.

"Phillip and Leanne have been part of the deal. I didn't want to alarm anyone else during the process, but now is the time for you to meet your new owner. I firmly vouch for Terence and know this business will be in excellent hands moving forward. In fact, I'm so impressed with Terence and his plans moving forward, I've agreed to retain a very small percentage of ownership and assist him part-time for the next few years. So, I'm not leaving completely but handing over the baton, so to speak, to Terence."

Terence was blushing terribly. It was a combination of the red wine from lunch and the praise just heaped on him by Jacqueline.

"Hi, everyone. It's a pleasure to be here and I'm thrilled and excited to be the new majority owner of this amazing business. For those of you who don't know me, I'm a corporate PR executive down the street at Creative PR and have always wanted my own business. I looked at a bunch of them and decided JAT was the perfect match for me.

"I would say it's business as usual for now. Phillip will continue to serve as General Manager, and Lucy will continue to keep us all out of trouble as the financial controller." This raised several laughs from the team.

"We will all meet for a working breakfast at 9 a.m. Monday morning, where I'll present to you my five-year vision for the business and some of the small changes Jacqueline and I have agreed to make. Then, I'll meet with each and every one of you one-to-one throughout the day Monday to get to know each of you better."

Half the team clapped. The other half looked shell-shocked. It would be a busy weekend texting each other back and forth.

The meeting broke up and Jacqueline took Terence to her office. Now *his* office.

"Naw, Jacqueline, you can keep your office. I'll sit in the bullpen with the team," he said.

"No way," she responded. "This is the office of the owner. It's yours. You deserve it. I'll occupy one of the spare desks in the bullpen for the small number of hours I'm going to be here."

She shook his hand and went to the door. "I'll send Phillip and Lucy in to see you in ten minutes. Don't you have a resignation email to send?" She grinned wickedly as she spun around and walked out of the office, closing the door behind her.

Chapter 48

Terence Resigns from Creative

  Terence pulled his laptop out of his bag, booted it up and smiled when it automatically latched onto the office Wi-Fi network, remembered from an earlier meeting.
  He wrote the email in less than two minutes.

To: Rudy Jones
From: Terence Turner
Re: Resignation

Dear Rudy

I am resigning from my position as Senior Account Manager at Creative PR Inc., effective immediately.

I have acquired a smaller PR firm in the city. I will be in the office later to collect my personal possessions.

I have enjoyed working with you and the team.

Sincerely,
Terence

Terence hit "send," visited the bathroom and was back in his office waiting for Lucy and Phillip to come see him when his iPhone vibrated loudly in his pocket.

It was Rudy.

Terence quickly answered.

"Hey, Rudy."

"Hey, Terence. Got your email. Not what I wanted to read on a Friday afternoon, but I got it. I'm sorry to lose you but would never stand in your way. What's the business you acquired? Has the deal closed?"

"Yes, this morning. It's a small outfit called JAT PR. About four blocks away."

"Yes, I know them. We looked at the deal when it went on the market, but it was too small for us."

"I think this can be a friendly exit, Terence. I need a full day from you as soon as possible to do a full account handover, and I'll need you to sign a document stating that you won't attempt to coerce any of our accounts over. Our legal counsel will be sending you that document within the next few hours, but if you do sign it, I would like to arrange the transfer of some smaller accounts to you. I think this can be a big win for you, Terence. What do you say?"

"I can't do anything Monday—I'm meeting with my new team and laying down the strategy, then I plan to hit the road the rest of the week meeting with my new clients. But I can come in tomorrow or Sunday if that works for you."

"Let me speak to Mike and check. He'll be taking over your accounts."

The phone went silent for a minute, and when Rudy returned, he confirmed that Mike could meet from noon to 4:00 p.m. Saturday to do the handover of all Terence's accounts and that Rudy would be present and have some smaller relationships to transfer."

"That works," said Terence. "See you tomorrow." Noon gave him enough time to be a baseball dad tomorrow morning and still get downtown for the handover meeting.

Terence spent the next few hours meeting with Lucy and Phillip and reassuring them that their roles were secure and that he was really looking forward to working with them both.

He left the office at 5 p.m. and took an Uber home. Julie had booked a celebratory meal out as a date night. He patted his stomach, thinking he would need to double down on the Peloton in the coming days and weeks.

Chapter 49

The Handover

Terence breezed into Creative PR's office a few minutes before noon on Saturday. Mike and Rudy were waiting for him in reception. Both were wearing jeans, crews and sneakers.

Mike had already moved into Terence's office. Terence's personal possessions were in two large boxes atop the conference room table.

They went through the account handovers in less than two hours. Mike had been promoted to Senior Account Manager the afternoon before after Terence's resignation. This was a massive opportunity for Mike.

As soon as he was up to speed on Starbucks, Publix, Universal and a bunch of other accounts, he retreated to his new office.

Rudy then closed the door and handed Terence a summary of much smaller accounts. These totalled more than $900,000 in annual billings.

"We're pivoting to purely Fortune 500 accounts, and these 12 accounts represent the smaller, regional clients from an acquisition last year."

"Strike Plan, right?" asked Terence.

"Correct," said Rudy. "I think these will be better placed with you. Unfortunately, I can't just give them to you."

"Okay, then, what do you want?" Terence asked.

"Two things. First, I need you to sign the non-solicitation agreement our legal counsel prepared."

"No problem," replied Terence. "I sent it to my attorney, Brittany, and she will communicate directly with you guys on that. Needs a few tweaks, but nothing earth shattering."

"Good," Rudy affirmed. "Now, on the client list, ideally we want to sell the book of business as a carve out. There will be no employees coming along with the clients, so you'll need to service them from within the JAT ranks."

"No problem. I would prefer to do that anyway. What do you have in mind, in terms of a deal?"

"Well, it's a $900,000 annual revenue stream, and we're running those accounts at a 25% margin, so it should generate the same cash flow for you. Around $225,000 per year. So, what do you say to $500,000?"

Having reviewed more than 20 deals in the past three months, Terence was becoming slick at mental math. "That's a 2.2X multiple," he quickly responded, almost to himself.

"I think that's too high, Rudy. However, I'll agree to $500,000 if I can make those payments over several years. Let me review the accounts and come back to you with an offer within the next few days. I want to discuss with my team over at JAT. I'm spending all day with them Monday and we will see if this is a fit for us."

"That works," Rudy said. "Can we say you'll let us know either way by the end-of-day Monday? We also need the exit agreement signed by then."

"Confirmed."

Terence left the office clutching the customer list and made a mental note to add this to his list of talking points during the strategy session tomorrow.

Chapter 50

Jacqueline and Jack's First Weekend Date

Saturday morning, Jack picked Jacqueline up in his BMW 840 M sport sedan and whisked her off into the countryside. The elegant hotel where they would stay was nestled in the Illinois countryside about a two-hour drive from Chicago.

She packed light. It was a spa resort, after all, but she included an elegant ensemble for the Saturday night dinner. They could only stay the one night, as Jacqueline was due back in her old business on Monday for the handover and strategic review with the team that Terence was leading.

During the scenic drive north up route 41, she gazed out at Lake Michigan in the distance and felt relieved that the deal had closed, although not on the original terms.

She had received over $350,000 by wire transfer on Friday, reflecting the reduced closing payment (under the annuity deal) and the first month's $35,000 annuity payment.

"What's on your mind?" asked Jack.

"Nothing much," she replied. "Just reflecting on the past few weeks and how relieved I am to have closed this deal."

Jack had been a stalwart in the previous few weeks, both on the original SBA deal and also the restructure.

"When is Terence expected to complete the refi?" he asked.

"He has 180 days to do it, under the revised agreement. However, we're at the mercy of the politicians who are still at stalemate over the shutdown."

"Let me ask you a question, then. Why not just keep up with the monthly payments?"

"I've thought about that myself. I'd ultimately receive much more money that way, pay a lot less tax, and since I'm connected to the business and have the covenants and liens in place, I do feel fully protected. And, I really like Terence. I'm looking forward to his strategic presentation.

"Anyway, he has the legal option to refinance the deal, so I think I'll let fate decide. If he wants to refinance, then I'm okay with that. But if for whatever reason I get an option to continue with the monthly payments, then I'll see how Terence and the business perform over the coming months."

Jacqueline and Jack thoroughly enjoyed the two-day break in the spa. It was the first time she had seen Jack not wearing clothes and the first time they made love to each other. Nothing beyond their current situation was discussed; however, Jacqueline could feel this would be a permanent new relationship for her.

Sunday evening, following an early dinner of prime rib, the loved-up pair drove back to the city. Jack ushered Jacqueline into the house and ended up staying the night before dropping her off back at her old business the following morning. They kissed gently before she got out of the car and promised to chat on the phone that evening. They did have a date planned mid-week at the opera, and both were really looking forward to it. Jack wasn't actually an opera buff. It was a passion Jacqueline had developed during her marriage to Bill. Jack was trying really hard to get into the same hobbies and passions as Jacqueline, and this really impressed her. He was big into fishing, but Jacqueline hated boats. She threw up three times on their one and only lake fishing trip. So, opera it was, together with gala dinners, the movies, baseball and Latin dance lessons.

Chapter 51

Terence Spends the Day with His New Team

Jacqueline actually felt awkward as she went into the conference room. Terence had abandoned the more corporate feel she had instilled, especially Monday through Thursday. Everyone was wearing crews, jeans and sneakers. A few even wore shorts.

Terence began the meeting by introducing himself again and then reviewed the current financials for the business. He also listed the top ten accounts and then announced his two-fold growth strategy.

First, he wanted to talk about strategy and structure.

Terence went to the whiteboard and drew five boxes. "This is the simple organizational chart I want for the business," he said.

"Every business is a three-legged stool." He cited the work done by Michael E. Gerber in his book, *The E Myth Revisited* as well as the EOS system designed by Gino Wickman.

"The first stool is sales and marketing. We need to generate leads then convert them into a customer. We make a promise to the customer to enroll them into our business. Next, we have an operations stool. Operations is all about fulfillment of the promise that's been made to the customer. Finally, there's a financial and administration stool. This is the 'glue' that holds the business together. It collects revenue, pays expenses, provides controls and watches the KPIs (key performance indicators) that we need to track the business weekly."

"Weekly?" asked Derek Smith, an account manager with five years tenure.

"That's right, Derek. Most small businesses (and we are still considered a small business) never track financial performance until, sometimes, it's too late. The typical business just hums along, and then approximately six months after the end of the financial year, the CPA sends in the accounts. If something's off, by then it can't be fixed. Those financial accounts are measuring past performance. There's no course correction possible, and that's why a lot of businesses fail.

"We are going to track all financial indicators, from revenue, margin, cash flow, accounts receivable through to sales and marketing metrics, including our marketing ROAS (return on advertising spend), our lead conversion ratios, the average cost to acquire a new customer (CPA) and something called lifetime customer value (LCV)."

Jeanelle, one of the sales people, was intrigued. "Terence, can you explain what these ratios mean and how we calculate them please?"

"Sure, Jeanelle. ROAS is a measure of our return on investment in advertising and marketing. If we spend $2,000 in marketing to acquire a new customer, that's our CPA, or cost per customer acquisition.

"If we then land a $10,000 contract to service that customer, that's called our AOV, or average order value. We spend $2,000 and generate $10,000. Are you tracking this?"

All the heads nodded.

"To calculate ROAS we simply divide our AOV by our CPA. In this example, $10,000 divided by $2,000 is a 5X ROAS. Got it?"

All the heads were still nodding.

"Finally, our LCV, or lifetime customer value, is the average spend of our clients. The $10,000 initial contract may lead to another $20,000 in additional revenue, on average, per client, so then our LCV would be $30,000. The initial $10,000 plus the $20,000."

The team was getting excited about all this. JAT had performed very well but without any of these metrics they would now be tracking.

"Some of these indicators are lagging. In fact revenue, profit, cash flow, accounts receivable, CPA, AOV, ROAS and LCV are all lagging indicators. These are important to track on a weekly basis, however we also need *leading* indicators." Terence paused to let the new term sink in.

Lucy, the financial controller chimed in. "What's a leading indicator?"

"Thanks for asking, Lucy. A leading indicator is something that will ultimately lead to one of the important lagging indicators I've just listed out. For example, to generate revenue, we need leads from our marketing. Therefore, the numbers of leads we're generating on a weekly basis, together with the conversion ratios are both leading indicators.

We're also going to be tracking our sales pipeline, and we'll be weighting that pipeline based on where the prospects are in the sales cycle, how hard we've vetted them and our confidence level on converting them to customers.

The energy in the room was building. Phillip was thinking about all this and realized he now worked for someone who was planning on growing this business to the moon. *Wish I had a piece of equity ownership*, he mused. The irony is that in the future, Phillip would get a small share of ownership, and it would be worth millions of dollars.

Terence went back to the whiteboard. "Sorry for the sidetrack," he said. "Let's get back to the organizational structure."

He drew on the board the three critical departments, then drew two additional boxes above these.

The Organizational Chart

```
        [ V ]

        [ I ]

[S&M]   [Ops]   [ S ]
```

DEALMAKER WEALTH

"I is the Integrator. That's the day-to-day General Manager of the business—the person driving the bus. The Integrator's job is to tie together the three critical functions.

"Finally, we have the V. This stands for Visionary. That's the person with the strategy and big ideas, who sets the culture and the beat of the business.

Terence filled in all the boxes with names.

The Organizational Chart

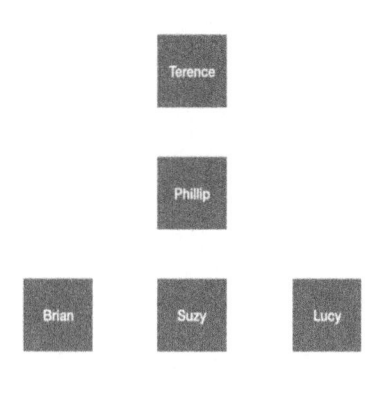

```
           Terence
              |
           Phillip
              |
    ----------+----------
    |         |         |
  Brian      Suzy      Lucy
```

DEALMAKER WEALTH

    Lucy was the current financial controller and would keep that role. She would be assisted by Jeremy, the fractional CFO and the rest of her team. This department included accounts receivable, accounts payable, payroll and HR.

    Suzy was the lead fulfillment person, taking care of all the marketing, advertising and PR work done for JAT's clients. She was the person everyone counted on, and Terence was very impressed with her. Clients loved her too. Terence had decided to promote her to Operations Director and she would lead all the fulfillment teams and customer service and also manage the internal IT function.

    Boris, the crusty, old IT manager glanced across at the much younger Suzy and smiled. He had a massive crush on her. Reporting to her would be fun, he thought.

    Finally, Terence promoted Brian to Director of Sales and Marketing. He was the top producing sales executive and also had crafted a lot of the marketing campaigns. As such, he was the natural choice. Brian would manage all the account managers, internal marketing executives, and the handful of outside agencies JAT used, including a media buyer.

    "Our growth is going to come from two sources," Terence continued. "We'll grow organically, as in more customers, and we'll also be acquiring more businesses. In fact, I plan for us to acquire a digital marketing firm in the next 12 months," Terence announced.

Terence then filled in the last two boxes. Phillip was the current GM, was solid and would stay in the role. "He's the one driving the bus, but I'm the visionary," Terence proclaimed. "I will be setting strategy, culture, the beat of the business, the big ideas and also closing more deals."

"So, that's our organizational structure. The leadership team can stay behind. The rest of you —back to work," he said with a smile. "Thank you for all you do for JAT, and I'm thrilled to be working with you."

The team filtered out of the board room in good spirits. The general feeling among them was that exciting times lay ahead.

Chapter 52

The One-Page Business Plan

After a short break, Terence convened with Phillip, Lucy, Brian and Suzy.

"Next," he told them, "I want us to create a one-page business plan. It will have our five-year financial goals and 12-month forecast, and it will define our target customers, market, core values and USP (unique selling proposition) in the market."

"Let's get started." First, he walked them through core values. "These are the values our business must have. It's how we feel about our business, and it's typically the case that these values are similar to the ones we have as leaders. This is important because we will hire and fire against these core values. People who don't exhibit most of these values can't stay within the business."

"We'll need three to five such core values," he said.

He then wrote down Amazon's core values on the whiteboard as an example.

Customer obsession
Passion for innovation
Commitment to operational excellence
Long-term thinking

This really got the juices flowing. The team started brainstorming, and Terence was writing so fast on the whiteboard his hand was burning.

After a healthy debate, the team settled on its own four core values:

Honesty and integrity
A passion for creativity
Relentless execution, or GSD (get shit done)
Creating long-lasting partnerships with customers

    The team agreed honesty and integrity were paramount and that as a creative design agency, creativity had to flow through everything they did. Terence was big on execution, and after a long debate and some fun, they all loved the GSD (get shit done) reference.

    Finally, Brian had suggested a big differentiation of JAT from other firms was its desire to be a partner to its clients—a partner in creativity, rather than just being a vendor.

    Terence underlined the four core values, then asked a very interesting question.

    "Do we all exhibit those core values?"

    The team looked at each other nervously. They went around the room and, yes, all five felt they exhibited those values.

    The next question was even more interesting.

    "Do any of you have people in your departments who do *not* exhibit these core values?"

    Suzy cited Jeff on her team, who was always late on deadlines. He didn't exhibit GSD.

    Lucy had issues with the accounts payable person, Toni, for the same reason. Some vendors complained they weren't paid on time and questioned Toni's integrity. She would reply to a vendor chasing payment with a "yes, we wired the payment earlier," but then it would not arrive.

    Finally, Brian had a salesperson, Simon, who was a 'hit man.' He was interested only in the initial sale. He wouldn't then build the relationship to solicit more business. He was a pure hunter, not a farmer, and sales people in creative services needed to be both.

    Terence made a note of the names and promised to chat one-to-one with the leaders later.

He then wrote the five-year plan out on the whiteboard:

Revenue $35 million
Profit $10 million
Margin 28%
Four acquisitions
125 employees
Offices in four major cities

Next, he laid out the plan for the current year:

Revenue $8 million
Profit $2 million
Margin 20%

Lucy chimed in. "Terence, that's more than double our current revenue run rate. How are we going to do that?"

"Well, first I'm acquiring a book of business from my previous employer, Creative. That deal will be locked up next week. Next, I have some solid relationships I'm going to transfer to Brian, and we'll implement Creative's LCV strategy. We can sell so much more to our existing clients. I'll walk you through it, Brian, in our next one-to-one meeting.

"Finally, I want to make one more acquisition this year. I'll be creating a shortlist that I'll run past you all in a future meeting. The top line revenue target will include all those initiatives."

The team wrapped up the marketing piece. The key USP was defined.

"Providing integrated marketing, advertising and PR services as a strategic partner, not a vendor."

It had been a very productive session. The leadership team now knew growth targets, USP, and core values, and Terence had architected a simple, yet effective management structure that was far better than the flat structure Jacqueline and Phillip had used prior to Terence acquiring the business.

The team was on cloud nine. They all bounded from the office and spent the next four weeks implementing the new changes. Revenue and profit continued to increase and JAT remained a fun, vibrant and fulfilling place to work.

Chapter 53

Federal Budget Signoff

The deadlock on the federal budget and resulting government shutdown entered its fourth week. The Speaker and President had met six times in the West Wing with neither side backing down. The media was all over the pair and tensions remained high. The country (and more importantly the voters) were sick of the debacle. It was time to make a deal.

The President was sitting in the Oval office reading the latest security briefing on Taiwan when his secretary, Mrs Lewis buzzed his intercom to say his Assistant Chief of Staff, Josh Parker, wanted to see him. His boss, Larry, was on the Hill still trying to negotiate a breakthrough in the budget negotiations.

Josh rushed in with a plan.

"Good afternoon, Mr President."

"What's up Josh?"

"I just heard the Speaker of the House and his team are locked in discussions up on the Hill. I recommend we march up there, you and me, and insist on a meeting.

"Are you crazy?" replied the President.

"Not really, Sir. The public is mortified with what's happened. I think it would be a great PR exercise for you to actually go to the Speaker's office, demand a meeting and break this deadlock. Asp (i.e., the nickname of Martin Aspir, the White House Press Secretary) will leak it that we're going up there, and we'll get fantastic coverage."

"Josh, I'm more concerned about reopening the Federal Government than I am about PR and scoring some cheap points with the press. Asp has plenty to be working on with the upcoming G-8 summit."

"I know, Sir, so am I, but I think this will force the Speaker's hand. I really do believe this will work, just trust me, Sir. I spoke to Larry and Asp, and they're both onboard. Even the Veep signed off."

The President, concerned that Josh had canvassed everybody else before confronting him (but he knew why), closed his eyes and rubbed his fingers vigorously through his thick, gray hair.

"Okay, Josh, let's do it. I have a briefing on Taiwan in a few hours. Tell the Secret Service to get the car ready. We leave in five minutes."

The President and Josh got into the Presidential Limousine, and the car, surrounded by Secret Service agents in SUVs, inched the distance between the White House and Capitol Hill. About half way, traffic was at a gridlock.

"Sir, let's walk the last half mile. There are cameras everywhere. Asp has the press all fired up. It's going to be amazing."

"Okay, 'In for a penny, in for a pound.' Let's do it."

"Excuse me, Sir?"

"Sorry, it's an old English saying. Roughly translates, 'It's game time, let's go.'"

The Secret Service exited the SUVs like ants and quickly surrounded the president.

As they all walked the half mile to the Capitol Building, camera crews were swarming. CNN, ESPN, even MSNBC were broadcasting live. It was everywhere on national television.

At that very moment, an aide barged into the Speaker's office and told him what was happening. The Speaker of the House grabbed the remote control and instantly CNN streamed on the 42-inch LCD television.

The President was walking to him. This was a stunt, it had to be.

"Let's quickly wrap up this meeting," the senior Representative from California, Doug Leeson, suggested. "Our President is coming, and we won't make him wait."

The Speaker suddenly felt under a mountain of pressure. The President had made a stunning move. The entire country was watching. Now he had to close a deal, and he needed to know what that would look like in the next ten minutes.

The assembled cast of the Speaker, five congressmen and their aids quickly agreed to split the difference. A $50,000,000 cut. The President could take it from anywhere, but there had to be a cut.

At that moment, there was a loud bang on the door. Doug Leeson opened it to see his nemesis, Josh Parker, White House Deputy Chief of Staff, glaring at him.

"The President is here to see the Speaker," Josh proudly announced.

"We know," said Doug. "It's all over CNN. Just give us a few minutes."

Josh and the President sat down, and the President looked at his watch. It had been years since he'd had to wait for anyone. He was the President, after all.

Suddenly, the Speaker came out, greeted the President warmly and ushered him and Josh into his office.

"Just me and you, Mr. Speaker," boomed the President.

Everyone else left, and the President laid down his terms.

"Mr. Speaker, we had a budget agreed, and I'm not cutting $100,000,000 from it. I'll leave the Government shut down indefinitely, if I have to.

"Let's meet in the middle, Sir. $50,000,000, and we can sign the budget today and reopen the Federal Government."

"No. I'm not cutting anything," the President said with finality.

After a pause, his left eyebrow raised slightly. "There is, however, a $50,000,000 program on welfare incentives that's going to take at least six months to roll out. We can move it into next year, and that will save $50,000,000."

"Deal!" said the Speaker. The two men shook hands, and the President left. The next few hours would be a frenzy of editing documents, but the deal was signed later that evening. The following morning, all furloughed Government employees went back to work.

Chapter 54

The SBA Reopens

It was 10 a.m. inside the SBA. In the past four weeks during the shutdown, more than six thousand new SBA loans had been submitted, and the current processing time was an estimated nine-weeks on a new loan.

Felix Walker, a senior loan officer, was scanning the list of pending applications that would, prior to the shutdown, have closed in a week or less.

"Terence Turner to acquire JAT PR LLC."

He smiled. The shutdown had been a total, PR nightmare for Congress. The President's approval ratings had shot up overnight following his walk on Capitol Hill to confront the Speaker and his henchmen.

Let's quickly resurrect this deal.

He opened the file, then placed a call to his contact at Live Stem. Each SBA deal gets assigned a closer in the final stages to get the deal across the line. It's primarily an admin function but still critical to pull everything together between the buyer, seller, sponsor bank and the SBA itself.

Within a few minutes, Marlyn Day (the closer) was on the phone.

"Where are we on JAT," he asked. He quoted the SBA PLP loan number.

"We're still waiting on some ancillary documents," she said. I should have them within the next few days. I'll call the buyer and see if the deal is still active."

Terence was walking back from a new (and major) client presentation with Phillip when his iPhone buzzed violently in his pocket.

He noticed it was "caller withheld."

He let the phone continue to buzz. He was half day dreaming.

With the annuity acquisition of Creative PR's unwanted smaller client list and some big wins, revenue was up more than 30% in the first month, year-on-year.

Terence thought back to the day Nike replaced him as Senior Account Manager in favor of his subordinate, Mike. If that hadn't happened, he wouldn't be in this fantastic new position.

Terrence suddenly realized the phone was still pulsing in his pocket. He answered it.

"Hello, this is Felix Walker, from the SBA. Is this Terence Turner?"

"Yes, it is. How may I help you?"

"As I'm sure you're aware, the shutdown put us all in a holding pattern. However, as you also know, your loan was approved, and we're now ready to move to a close within the next seven days. I assume you're still looking to acquire JAT PR LLC? Where are you with the deal?"

"Thanks for calling me. But I actually acquired the business creatively, on an annuity deal, not long after the shutdown started."

"An annuity deal?" replied Felix. "What's that?"

"Sort of like a lease purchase. I'm paying for the business monthly with a promise to refinance with the SBA once you guys are back up and running."

"Well, we most definitely are. There's a major backlog, as you can imagine, but I scanned my list of open deals and decided to jump on yours first, as it's a good deal for us."

"Great, what are the next steps?"

"Can you send me the stock purchase agreement you signed? I'll review that then reposition the loan as a refinancing (of the seller financing promissory note) versus an outright acquisition. It won't be a problem. Do you still have the equity required?"

"Yes, it's in escrow, My investors have been very understanding. I'm going to give them both an extra point of equity each for hanging on and tying up their capital in escrow for the past month."

"That's fine."

Terence smiled. The refinancing would save him $9,000 per month and change. The SBA loan would amortize over the same 10-year term, but since the SBA valuation was lower, it would save him some serious monthly cash. *Money in my own pocket*, he thought to himself. Now he was really smiling.

He ended the call and quickly placed a call to Brittany, instructing her to re-engage with Live Stem and the SBA and trigger the refi. Since Jacqueline had already received the $350,000 closing payment and two months of the annuity, the resulting SBA refinancing would be lower than originally underwritten, so it would be an automatic reapproval following Terence's submission of management accounts for the past two months, in which he had grown the business by more than 30%. Current monthly cash flow was up to $112,000 and change. The refi would save Terence $9,180 per month and would give him a net free cash flow of almost $90,000 per month. Not bad. His share of that was around $80,000 and that was nearly six times what he was earning in his corporate role.

Why didn't I do this years ago? He mused.

Cash Flow Comparison

	Annuity	SBA	Difference
Valuation	4,160,000	2,800,000	1,360,000
Deal Debt	3,740,667	2,100,667	1,640,000
Monthly Debt Service	34,667	25,487	9,180
Current Cash Flow (month)	112,740	112,740	N/A
DSCR, X	3.25	4.42	
Free Cash Flow	78,073	87,253	9,180

DEALMAKER WEALTH

At the management meeting the next morning, Terence pulled Jacqueline aside and told her the refi would be happening imminently, like within a week.

"That's a shame, Terence," she grinned. "I do like the monthly cash flow but totally understand the refi will save you close to $10,000. I'm happy to stay in the annuity but respect your decision."

"Yes, I want to do it, and I can use the balance of my $5,000,000 SBA cap to close some more deals. As you still own 10% of the business, it's all upside for you."

"I get it. I'll let Herb know it's imminent."

The SBA loan refinancing went through a few days later. The annuity debt was removed from the balance sheet of the business and the lien Jacqueline had over the business was replaced by the UCC filing imposed by Live Stem Bank. Terence decided to invest the $9,000 per month additional cash flow on a new account manager and a new company car, a gleaming blue Audi RS Q8. He was bored with the Tesla X so would trade that in to get himself out of the personal note.

Chapter 55

The Next Acquisition

Over the next 12 months, Terence wanted to close three more deals. After the quick tuck-in of the smaller accounts of Creative PR, the recasted financials were as follows . . .

TTM Recasted Financials

Recasted Financials, $	TTM
Revenue	4,883,774
COGS	-405,353
Gross Profit	4,478,421
GM, %	91.7%
Overheads	-3,171,877
EBITDA	1,306,544
Margin, %	26.8%

DEALMAKER WEALTH

Terence decided to recruit a dealmaker to do a lot of the heavy lifting for him in terms of deal flow and management.

With two tombstones in the bag from Dealmaker Wealth Society, he was hungry for more. Phillip was doing a great job running the day-to-day, and apart from winning some big, new key accounts, Terence had a lot of time to devote to raising additional capital and closing more deals. He had over $3,000,000 left in

SBA financing available to him, and when he sent the latest financials to Lisa at Live Stem, she reiterated the bank's desire to support Terence on additional acquisitions.

He asked Carl the question on a Friday group Q&A call.

"Where can I find a dealmaker to help me?"

"Simple," said Carl. "You can recruit someone full-time using LinkedIn, or, if you have the budget, use a recruiter (Carl surprisingly never did this) or use Upwork. Carl was a massive fan of Upwork and had recruited lots of people through that platform over the years.

Terence also knew he didn't need anyone full time, so having a part-time 1099 contractor sounded like a good idea.

Terence created a post and listed it both on LinkedIN and Upwork.

Creative dealmaker wanted

JAT PR LLC, a growing and profitable Chicago-based PR firm, is seeking a part-time dealmaker to assist in the origination, vetting and closing of small to medium PR firms. Please respond with your resume, two references, salary requirements and availability.

Regards,

Terence Turner

CEO. JAT PR LLC

Within a week, Terence had received over 50 applications, and, following a shortlist of six, he hired Daniel Suttar, a recently graduated MBA from Baylor University Business School in Waco, Texas. Daniel was already doing some consulting for an SAAS business he interned with during his MBA and had 25 hours per week available.

Terence really liked Daniel. He was working on deals for the SAAS company and also had an expertise in equity investor pitch decks. As a bonus, he boasted a nice rolodex of equity investors he was building up in the SAAS firm and offered to leverage that for JAT.

Terence hired him on a $5,000 per month retainer with a $25,000 bonus for every deal closed and 5% of any capital he could bring into the business in the form of equity.

Daniel would work remotely but come to Chicago three days a month to get rub time with the team.

Daniel initially worked on a target list, comprising a new round of broker outreach, some LinkedIN direct approaches and a deeper dive into the deal intermediary network in and around Illinois, Indiana, Ohio, Michigan and Wisconsin. As a result, he sourced 25 deals. After preliminary vetting, the list was down to the final eight.

New Acquisitions Shortlist

Deal	Revenue	EBITDA	Margin	Ask	Multiple	Location	Source	Founded
Human Media	6,736,281	754,463	11.2%	2,565,176	3.4	Chicago, IL	Broker	2001
Luxe Creative	4,837,261	759,450	15.7%	4,101,030	5.4	Gary, IN	Broker	2015
Light Surge	7,384,939	1,661,611	22.5%	10,301,990	6.2	Detroit, MI	Broker	1998
Strike Pin	2,837,462	658,291	23.2%	3,488,943	5.3	Cleveland, OH	LinkedIN	2019
Medical PR & Advertising	11,928,372	3,721,652	31.2%	14,142,278	3.8	Dayton, OH	LinkedIN	1995
Showman Media	10,992,883	1,033,331	9.4%	9,713,311	9.4	Chicago, IL	Network	2007
Stellar Creative	3,827,485	176,064	4.6%	1,267,663	7.2	Madison, WI	Network	2002
Plug Works	5,637,281	490,443	8.7%	3,236,927	6.6	Atlanta, GA	Network	2010

DEALMAKER WEALTH

All were solid businesses, for one reason or another. Terence decided to strike out Showman Media and Stellar Creative on the grounds that he didn't want to acquire anything above a 7X multiple. He also eliminated Plug Works due to the low 8.7% margin. Out of the ones left, he wanted to spend his $3,000,000 SBA budget, so that would give him a $3,600,000 budget for the next deal, combining the 80% SBA financing plus the 10% seller note and cash equity.

Lisa had mentioned to Terence that he could do bolt-on acquisitions for only a 5% equity downpayment, with the SBA willing to go up to 90% loan-to-value. However, if the seller would carry a 15% seller note, that would be even better.

Terence worked on a strategy:

5% equity (using the solid cash flow the business was currently generating; he wouldn't need an equity investor just yet)
80% SBA financing (to take Terence to his $5,000,000 cap)
15% seller note

On that basis, he decided to make Luxe Creative his number one pick. At a $4,100,000 ask, Terence believed he could get it for max $3,600,000 using the tried and tested two-offer structure.

He called the broker (this was a broker deal) and asked to schedule an on-site meeting in Indiana.

The broker's name was Leanne Deakins—someone he liked and had collaborated with on a deal last year before buying JAT.

"Hey, Leanne, it's Terence. When can I come to see Luxe? I've had a few calls with Ryan (the owner), but I want to inspect the business personally."

"Sure. The business is still available for sale. The deal just came out of LOI, as the buyer couldn't raise the financing. Match the terms and you can have it."

"What are the terms?"

"Well, the buyer was doing an SBA 7a loan at $3,700,000 but couldn't get the $370,000 of equity."

"That's too rich for me. I'm probably at $3,500,000 but can put 85% of the money down at closing. Will that work?"

"I think that's in the ballpark. Do you have proof of funds?"

"Yes, I have $3,000,000 available from my SBA cap and can connect you to Lisa at Live Stem—she'll vouch for that. I used Live Stem to finance the acquisition of JAT."

"I thought you did an annuity deal? I heard it was some creative magic you worked up when your SBA loan stalled in the shutdown?"

"Yes, we did go for that, but I refinanced the deal using the SBA when it came back online. Would Ryan consider an annuity deal? I could certainly do $3,700,000, probably north of $4,000,000 over 10 years?"

"No, he's not interested in that. He's only 36, as you know, and he's bored of creative services. He wants the cash at closing to go buy something in the IT sector, something in AI, and those multiples are high right now, so he needs a lot of equity."

"Okay, let's have the meeting and see if we can do the deal."

Leanne called back within the hour, suggesting an on-site meeting the day after tomorrow. She would also be in attendance, and since Daniel was in Chicago, he would make the trip as well to even up the numbers.

Terence called Daniel into his office and asked to see the bolt-on analysis for Luxe. Luxe was the perfect bolt-on for JAT, as it was a pure advertising agency that did no marketing or PR work. It offered a perfect cross-selling opportunity for JAT to promote its own marketing and PR services into Luxe's advertising accounts.

Luxe also gave Terence a foothold in Indiana. Gary, Indiana was becoming a booming hub for both the medical and consumer ecommerce industries, and those were sectors JAT was strong in, especially in PR, so there was a lot of potential upside.

Terence would not need all of the admin personnel in the business, as he could manage a lot of it from JAT in Chicago, which meant there would be a lot of cost synergies. Terence didn't like to fire people. However, he knew Ryan's wife, sister-in-law and best friend currently occupied those positions, and all wanted to leave to join Ryan in the new AI venture. Collectively, that would save him $150,000 per year in salary, and there would be another $250,000 in other cost synergies he could conservatively save across both businesses.

Daniel presented the analysis:

JAT & Luxe Combined

$	JAT	Luxe	Cross Selling	Cost Synergies	Combined
Revenue	4,883,774	4,837,261	1,000,000	0	10,721,035
COGS	-405,353	-865,870	-83,000	25,000	-1,329,223
Gross Profit	4,478,421	3,971,391	917,000	25,000	9,391,812
GM, %	91.7%	82.1%	91.7%	N/A	87.6%
Overheads	-3,171,877	-3,211,941	-649,472	400,000	-6,633,291
EBITDA	1,306,544	759,450	267,528	425,000	2,758,522
Margin, %	26.8%	15.7%	26.8%	N/A	25.7%

DEALMAKER WEALTH

Terence had attended the advanced track Protégé training on bolt-on acquisitions and shared the recording with Daniel. The latter had downloaded Carl's synergy model and populated it for combining JAT and Luxe.

The results were amazing. The combination of businesses could generate at least $1,000,000 in new business by offering JAT's PR and marketing services across the Luxe customer base. Together with $25,000 savings in cost of goods sold (COGS) and $400,000 in overheads, this would create a combined entity with almost $11,000,000 in revenues and $2,800,000 in EBITDA.

Terence emailed the sheet to Lisa at Live Stem, and she replied within five minutes

"Fantastic. Let's do it."

Terence and Daniel went to see Luxe, and all four went out to dinner following a great session in the business. Terence determined this was a much better business than the numbers were telling him. He could fix the margins overnight; however, he decided not to share that with Ryan and Leanne and didn't want to update the bolt-on analysis model. The numbers in there were already fantastic, as Lisa at Live Stem had acknowledged.

Ryan and Terence shook hands on a $3,500,000 purchase price. With $3,000,000 at closing and a $500,000 seller note, Terence was within the SBA cap on his remaining financing. To sweeten the deal, Terence offered free creative services for the next three years on Ryan's next venture, to a total of $100,000. This would be kept out of the main deal legals and would be done via a side agreement the SBA didn't need to see.

The deal would be:

Equity = $175,000
SBA = $2,825,000
Seller note = $500,000

    Terence confirmed he would get the term sheet from Live Stem within 48 hours, and since the capital had been pre-allocated, they could close within 30 days, subject to due diligence and the legals.
    This deal had turned out even better than Terrence had hoped.

Chapter 56

Closing Luxe

What amazed Terence was how much he had learned in the past year. Carl had always said, "You're only one deal away, and that very first deal—the emotion, psychology, process and deal management—will radically accelerate your experience in the world of dealmaking."

He was right.

Luxe closed without many issues at all. However it took 45 days from signing the LOI. Ryan's attorney was extremely rigid, and his CPA, Bob Franks, completely useless. He knew he was going to lose the account, as Jeremy would take over the CPA and fractional CFO duties across both businesses, so Bob dug his heels in and made the financial due diligence and requests from the bank a nightmare.

Ryan was on vacation in the Cayman Islands when it came time to close, so the process was handled by DocuSign. Terence signed the documents in Ryan's office at Luxe. He wanted to meet the rest of the team immediately and handle the integration. Both Lucy and Phillip had made the trip. Phillip would oversee the day-to-day operations from Chicago, but with all admin, IT and financial functions transferring to HQ in Chicago, the Gary office would merely serve as a sales hub and fulfillment center for the Indiana clients. This would add another $150,000 of cost synergies over and above what was modeled initially, and including the continued organic growth of JAT—thanks to some amazing referrals from Jacqueline and even Jack (he plugged JAT into his own family business to run all the marketing)—the combined entity hit $3,000,000 of EBITDA on a TTM (trailing, 12-month basis).

Jeremy and Terence were spitballing valuations on the drive back to Chicago, and Jeremy was convinced the business would command an 8X multiple, considering its size, sophistication, profit margins, customer diversity and new recurring revenue streams. Terence had implemented an impressive growth rate.

At an 8X multiple, this would give an enterprise value (EV) of $24,000,000, and there was roughly $5,000,000 of net debt on the balance sheet, including the total SBA financing. This provided a stock value (debt free, cash free) of $19,000,000.

"So, Jeremy, I'm tapped out now at the SBA. Lisa has offered non-SBA financing for the next few deals but only an additional $5,000,000. I want to do bigger deals, so I'm going to find a debt partner who can write the bigger checks. I want to raise around $3,000,000 of equity as well."

"Where are you going to get the equity from?" asked Jeremy. "Crowdfund?"

"Not sure yet. I'll ask Carl on the next Protégé Q&A call."

Chapter 57

Terence Needs More Capital

The next deal on Terence's hit list was Medical PR & Advertising, in Ohio. Terence loved this deal for three reasons:

1) It was generating almost $4,000,000 in EBITDA.
2) It specialized in the medical sector. This was the fastest growing market for creative services, and Terence desperately needed more account managers and creative fulfillment personnel to support his own flourishing medical accounts.
3) The deal was in a new state, Ohio. JAT was crushing it in Chicago, and Luxe was continuing to scale in Indiana, as the cross-selling of services into the Luxe accounts was going really well.

    The asking price for Medical PR & Advertising was $14,000,000 and change. Carl had provided the names of some big-ticket debt financing companies, and he could raise up to $15,000,000 in debt. This would pay off the existing SBA financing (since two banks couldn't have liens on the business without complications) and provide just over $10,000,000 in additional debt for deals.

    The problem, however, was that he would need 20% in equity, so $3,000,000.

    The combined businesses had just over $900,000 in cash in the business, and Terence didn't want to dip into that. He could use the $3,000,000 in equity plus the debt to buy Medical, pay back the SBA and still have all the working capital he needed to continue to grow.

He was concerned about dilution and needed some advice. Luckily, Terence had graduated from Protégé and recently joined the Upper Echelon Mastermind. The next event was at a lavish mansion in Orlando in two weeks. Terence looked at the speaker list and agenda and saw a session on equity raising. *Perfect timing*, he thought.

He spent the next few days vetting the Medical PR deal. Jeremy, Lucy and Daniel had scoured the numbers and were confident in the validity of the financials. The issue, however, was that the founder and CEO, Nick Alison, wasn't really a distressed seller. He was a serial entrepreneur, was making $4,000,000 per year and wouldn't budge on the $14,000,000 ask.

Time to get creative again, thought Terence. However, in one of their first meetings, Terence had explained the annuity deal structure to Nick when explaining how he originally acquired JAT.

"Just don't try that shit with me," Nick had warned.

Terence decided to use another tool from the endless bank of Protégé resources, the offer sequencing stack. This was a psychological tactic that Carl used in which the buyer would prepare a sequence of five or six offers in advance before ever making the very first actual offer on the deal. This was designed to keep the buyer multiple steps ahead of the seller (and the broker, as this was a broker deal) and stay in control of the negotiations. Carl always said to send in offers on a Friday or a Monday. Friday, because it left the seller stewing on the offer over the weekend, or Monday, because it was typically the worst day in the week for a distressed business owner. Since Nick wasn't a distressed seller and actually loved his business, Terence would send in the offers on Fridays. Every Friday until one got accepted.

Terence applied the coaching to the Medical PR deal and had Daniel populate the chart downloaded from the Protégé resources section.

Terence knew he could probably pay up to $12,000,000 at close, combining $10,000,000 of new debt and $3,000,000 of equity (allowing for $1,000,000 in closing costs and additional expenses), and top up working capital and some additional headroom across the group. Ideally, he wanted $10,000,000 at close so he could close another deal as well from the same financing pot.

Terence and Daniel went through the stack.

Offer Sequencing Stack

Medical PR	Closing	Seller Note	Earn Out	Retained Equity	Total
Offer 1	9,000,000	3,000,000	0	0	12,000,000
Offer 2	9,000,000	3,000,000	0	0	12,000,000
Offer 3	10,000,000	3,000,000	0	0	13,000,000
Offer 4	10,000,000	4,000,000	0	0	14,000,000
Offer 5	10,000,000	4,000,000	1,000,000	0	15,000,000
Offer 6	10,000,000	4,000,000	1,000,000	1,000,000	16,000,000

DEALMAKER WEALTH

Terence directed Daniel to create all six offer letters. He waited until 4:45 p.m. Central time on Friday, then duly dispatched the first offer by emailing the offer letter directly to Nick, the seller, as there was no broker involved. Terence had collaborated with both Nick's CFO and external CPA in gathering the numbers but didn't feel it appropriate to copy either of them in on the offer.

To: Nick Alison
From: Terence Turner
Subject Line: Offer for the purchase of Medical PR & Advertising, Inc.

Dear Nick

As discussed, I attach an offer letter for the above.

I look forward to hearing back in due course.

Sincerely,
Terence Turner

The attached letter read as follows:

Nick Alison
Medical PR & Advertising, Inc.
77 Main Street
Dayton, OH 45428

Dear Nick,

Further to our conversations and your kind provision of financial information, I have the pleasure of enclosing an offer to acquire 100% of Medical PR & Advertising, Inc.

Closing payment = $9,000,000
Seller note = $3,000,000 paid over 36-months from closing
Total offer = $12,000,000

Closing is anticipated to take between 12 and 16 weeks depending on the bank's due diligence process, legal process and internal credit review process.

This is a fully-funded offer. Proof of funds will be provided with a subsequent LOI.

This offer is valid for 72 hours.

Upon your acceptance of this offer, we would move to a full LOI within 48 hours to incorporate working capital requirements and any retained involvement from your side.

Sincerely,
Terence Turner

  By 5:30 p.m., Nick had responded acknowledging that he had received the offer.
  At 9 p.m., Nick texted in an aggressive tone saying the offer wasn't acceptable and expressing his doubt that Terence was actually serious about making a deal.
  Terence was dying to respond but remembered Carl's advice. Let the offer stew. By Sunday night, the offer will look much more appealing.
  Carl was right. Sunday at 6:30 p.m. Nick texted to say he had reflected on the offer and that although it wasn't enough to get the deal done, he was willing to negotiate and would submit a counteroffer the next morning once he had spoken to his CPA.
  Monday morning around 11:30 a.m. Terence was in the midst of reviewing the new business pipeline with Phillip, his GM, and his head of sales, when his laptop, Apple Watch and iPhone all pinged with an incoming email at

the same time. Terence wrapped up the meeting quickly and ushered his two trusty lieutenants out of his office. He opened the email.

To: Terence Turner
From: Nick Alison
Subject Line: Counteroffer for the purchase of Medical PR & Advertising, Inc.

Dear Terence:

Following up on my text message last night, below is my counteroffer for you to acquire my business.

Closing payment $11,000,000
Seller note $2,500,000 payable within 24-months
Total consideration $13,500,000

I will leave $2,000,000 of working capital in the business at closing, and I will repay the $300,000 of non-current liabilities immediately prior to closing.

Sincerely,
Nick Alison

 Terence reflected on the counter offer. At least it was lower than the $14,000,000 asking price indicated by Nick in their first meeting, and the good news was that Nick was prepared to accept $2,500,000 in seller financing. No mention of interest, although the term was only two years.
 This was a solid counter. Terence was ready to submit offer two, but as per Carl's instructions he waited the full week.
 Later on Monday, he texted Nick to say he had received the counter and needed to talk to his investor partners and bank financiers to see if there was scope to improve his initial offer. He would get back to Nick by the end of the week. Friday Terence would be at the Upper Echelon Mastermind in Orlando, and he was due to fly down there Thursday afternoon. The attendees and speakers would arrive early in the evening.
 Terence called Jeremy to check in on a likely valuation for the equity raise. He was going to use the Mastermind this weekend to devise his capital raising strategy, as Carl was leading a half-day session on the very topic.

"You'll need to model up the deal, Terence. Daniel can do it based on the model he used for Luxe. Just take the combined revenues of the businesses and model out the deal synergies as before."

Terence called Daniel (who was back in Texas) and directed him to build the model by close of business tomorrow. They brainstormed on cross-selling opportunities and cost synergies, and Daniel promised to have the model finished by the end of tomorrow.

Terence left the office early and drove his new Audi RS Q8 home. He and Julie had a parent-teacher conference that evening, and it was also movie night, so he tried to put business out of his mind and spend a relaxing evening with the family. They watched the new *Top Gun Maverick* movie, which was great, except that Terence became mildly irritated with Julie constantly gushing over Tom Cruise, especially during the beach scene when he was running around semi-naked throwing a football.

Chapter 58

The Medical Deal Model

The next day Daniel emailed Terence the model by 1 p.m. Terence was devouring a Subway chicken wrap in his office at the time and reviewing the monthly financials. As before, his watch, phone and computer all pinged at the same time to acknowledge the email.

He pulled up the model and was blown away by the numbers:

Combined With Medical PR

$	Current Group	Medical	Cross Selling	Cost Synergies	Combined
Revenue	12,372,664	11,928,372	2,000,000	0	26,301,036
COGS	-1,937,282	-2,135,179	-166,000	75,000	-4,163,461
Gross Profit	11,345,733	9,793,193	1,834,000	75,000	23,047,926
GM, %	91.7%	82.1%	91.7%	N/A	87.6%
Overheads	-7,708,493	-6,071,541	-1,246,052	750,000	-14,276,087
EBITDA	3,637,240	3,721,652	587,948	825,000	8,771,840
Margin, %	29.4%	31.2%	29.4%	N/A	33.4%

DEALMAKER WEALTH

The combination of the existing group with Medical PR would be a business with more than $26,000,000 in revenues and almost $9,000,000 in EBITDA. Terence was dizzy. At that level of profit, he would easily command an 8X multiple of profit in a valuation, so he would be somewhere north of $60,000,000. He only needed $3,000,000 in equity to close the deal, so his dilution would be somewhere in the 5% to 10% range. *That's amazing*, he thought.

He suddenly felt anxious. He'd never pitched to an equity investor before and knew it was going to be much harder than pitching to the bank. Luckily, he had the weekend with Carl on equity capital raising and vowed to not leave the Mastermind until he had a fully baked plan to make this work.

Chapter 59

The Upper Echelon Mansion

Terence flew first class on United from O'Hare direct to Orlando. He sat in seat 2A and drank Old Fashions on the flight down as he watched the final season of Ted Lasso from the inflight entertainment.

He was really excited about the weekend. Carl, his business partners and coaches would all be at the Mastermind, and there would be fewer than 30 attendees, so he knew he could get some quality one-on-one time with Carl to pick his brain on the capital raising.

He landed in Orlando, picked up his bag from the baggage claim and hailed an Uber to take him to the mansion, 30 minutes south at Davenport.

When he walked in, he was blown away by the size of the house. It was by far the biggest house he had ever seen, let alone entered. It had an indoor bowling alley, basketball court and the most amazing pool you could imagine. It even had a lazy river.

A DJ was outside spinning the decks at the welcome mixer, and Terence could smell the spine tingling aromas of the BBQ being prepared. Beers, wine and cocktails were flowing.

Not unexpected, many of the guests were swarming around Carl. As he excused himself to grab another beer, Terence went to introduce himself. "Hey, Carl, it's Terence Turner. Thanks again for your ninja move on the JAT deal. I've made two more acquisitions and am in negotiations for the third, which will take my EBITDA close to $9,000,000."

"Wow," said Carl. "Not bad for a year's work. How are you funding the latest acquisition? I heard you triggered the refi, so you must be close to the SBA cap by now?"

"Yes, I'm working with Centrix Capital for the debt. This will also allow me to discharge the SBA financing, but I'm going to need $3,000,000 of equity as part of the funding mix, and I have no idea how to do that."

"Well," said Carl. "Your timing is impeccable. I'm running a breakout session tomorrow on that very topic, so make sure you attend that. Also, let's connect tomorrow evening, and I can show you how to apply it to your business and next deal."

Carl was pulled away by his assistant, and Terence spent the rest of the evening drinking, eating and networking with Carl's top 1% of dealmakers, of which he was now an exclusive member.

The following morning, all the attendees ate breakfast, freshened up their coffee and gathered in the main room for Carl's equity masterclass.

Chapter 60

Carl's Equity-Raising Masterclass

Carl started the masterclass by making a profound statement.

"Equity investors really only care about five things, and five things only. They are …

The story or big idea
The strategy or plan
The team
The exit
The risk-adjusted return on investment."

He then explained each in turn.

<u>The story or big idea</u>

"Investors are pitched deals every day. It's important for your deal to pop. To stand out. Investors don't like 'me-too' investments. Your story, your idea, your deal needs to be different. Differentiated. Your deal needs to have a solid USP, or unique selling proposition."

Terence noodled on this. There was nothing unique about PR itself. However, surely he was doing things in his project that made it unique. Terence thought back to the "three uniques" he walked his team through in the initial post-closing planning session for JAT. *Perhaps I can apply the "three uniques" to my roll-up project?* he thought. This led him to three unique differentiators of this new project:

1) He was integrating PR, advertising, design and marketing services for mid-market businesses with a specific focus on the medical sector. That was unique. The next phase would be to introduce a non-creative service that would have massive cross-selling capability, for example IT services, all under the umbrella of integrated and unified professional services for the mid market.
2) He was now geographically expanding into Michigan, Indiana and Ohio yet leveraging the mothership (JAT HQ in Chicago) for both back-office support and also design and creative fulfillment, most of which was done back at HQ. The satellite offices (from the acquisitions made) could thus serve primarily as sales offices, an arrangement which would result in lower overhead costs, higher margins and efficiency.
3) Nobody had done this before. All the consolidation and aggregation of creative businesses was being done at the $100 million and above level. There were lots of trade buyers and large private equity funds buying up the larger businesses. His plan was to create a business worth $100 million then flip it to one of the bigger fish.

The strategy or plan

Carl continued. "Once the big idea is formed and differentiated, then the investor is now concerned how this will work. What needs to be true for this to happen? If it's a roll-up, how many deals need to be closed? To drive shareholder value, can you measure and execute on the cross-selling? Generate significant cost synergies?" Carl also talked about "superpowers": "In every business I've acquired, even every business I've vetted over my 30 years as a dealmaker, each one of those businesses did ONE thing very well. They may do 29 other things badly, but there's always ONE thing that is a superpower. Now, when you buy multiple businesses, the key is to leverage all the individual superpowers across all the businesses in the roll-up." He used the example of TikTok marketing. He had recently acquired a business into his ecommerce rollup for women, and it had cracked the code on TikTok marketing for lead generation. None of his other businesses could do that, so he was able to cross-skill every other business in the roll-up to generate leads on TikTok.

He also discussed organic growth: generating more leads and conversions, then repeat customers. "Investors want scale," Carl pointed out, "so what resources—human, system and financial—would be required to make the growth happen?

Terence was furiously writing notes. He had been quickly growing the businesses he was acquiring. Cross-selling, cost synergies and—although he hadn't used the term—"superpower" . . . he was actually doing all of those. The Luxe acquisition had the best lead generation funnel using Google Adwords he had ever seen, and when he deployed the same funnel into JAT, his cost per customer acquisition (CPA) dropped 28%, so it was now less expensive for him to acquire a customer. That's why his margins were increasing.

His strategy was clearly working. This would look good to investors.

The team

"Even with a solid, differentiated big idea and a winning strategy to make money, your team will be critical for the execution of the strategy." This is where Terence believed he was particularly strong. He was from the industry, was a natural born, big-ticket sales person, a great leader, was building and mentoring a great team of lieutenants, and was retaining the previous owners (Jacqueline, Ryan and hopefully Nick) to create a slick advisory board to brainstorm with on big ideas and big strategic moves. Ryan (former owner of Luxe) was providing killer value in the ongoing Medical PR deal. Terence was proud of his team. They were all A players, and although a few people had left, the vast majority of his employees were all the right people in the right seats.

The exit

"The only way an investor will get their money back (plus a premium)," Carl said, "is when you sell, or you can recapitalize the business to return that capital back. This could be another investor or your ability to raise increased levels of debt.

"The most common form of exit for business owners and investors is to sell the business, and trade buyers typically can pay the highest amounts for businesses due to their ability to generate financial synergies in the deal. Large private equity funds are also solid buyers for larger businesses, and really sexy businesses with high growth and massive future potential could exit via an initial public offering (IPO) by listing the business on a public stock exchange, like the Nasdaq.

"So, an investor will want to clearly understand the exit options. Who will buy the business, why and when?"

Terence had nailed this. He knew as soon as he got the business to $100 million in revenue, it would be a feeding frenzy. He didn't feel his roll-up would qualify for an IPO (but you never know), but he knew large private equity and some of the major PR brands were constantly acquiring businesses north of $100 million.

The risk-adjusted, return on investment (ROI)

"Investors are different from banks," Carl proclaimed. "Banks are only concerned with you returning their capital over time, with interest. You need to have cash flow for debt service and often security to collateralize the investment. Therefore, it's much lower risk. However, investors are taking bigger risks. They're putting capital into your deal: unsecured and in the hope that equity increases in value. Most investors will not consider an investment unless the story, strategy and team can likely generate at least a 3X return over a period less than 10 years. Probably closer to 5X. The riskier the investment, the bigger the return the investor will seek.

"For example, let's say you need to raise $1,000,000 in equity. If your plan doesn't forecast to return 3X to 5X in around five years, then the investor will not pursue this opportunity.

"There are two measures of return," Carl said, and he started doodling on the whiteboard.

"The first is cash-on-cash (CoC) return on investment, or ROI. If the $1,000,000 goes in for, say, 25% of the business, and you then sell the business for $20,000,000 in four years, then 25% of that is $5,000,000, a 5X ROI during the period.

"The second measure is the internal rate of return, or IRR. This calculates the compounding growth of that investment over the period." Carl scribbled the formula on the whiteboard.

$IRR = (CoC)$ ^ $(1/N)$, where N is the number of years the equity is deployed.

"In our example, this would be

$IRR = (5)$ ^ $(¼) -1 = 0.495$ or 49.5%

"Anything above 20% is good, and anything above 30% is excellent.

"This means the investor is growing his or her equity at a compounded rate of 49.5% per year. In this example, this would be an excellent investment, provided the strategy, plan and team to create the exit looks sensible and highly achievable."

Terence's head was spinning. He had already nailed one through four on the list. What he really needed help with was number five: how to calculate the true value of his business once he had acquired Medical PR and then how to negotiate an equity investor buy-in to give him the capital he needed to leverage the amount of debt he would require to close the deal.

Carl spoke for a few more hours using case studies and examples, and a couple of the Mastermind attendees showcased their roll-up projects, which Carl vetted and gave solid advice on. Mark Holt was building a construction company roll-up in Georgia (Carl was actually a partner in this) and Erin Grimes was building a marketing services roll-up in the Pacific NorthWest. This second one had synergies with his own roll-up, thought Terence. He definitely needed to chat with Erin over lunch or drinks out by the pool at the end of the day.

Chapter 61

Deal Synergies

The rest of the day was filled with different presentations on topics covering mindset, health, deal origination, ESOPs (employee stock ownership plans), advanced seller role-play discussions and a really cool session called "Stand up and Connect," where each attendee listed their one superpower and one area in which they needed help. It was a true Mastermind. People would help each other in areas where they were strong and get help back from others to plug gaps in their experiences and skills.

Terence's superpower was high-ticket selling (several members wanted his help on that), and his proclaimed weakness was determining the right levels of equity to offer investors. Carl winked at him and mouthed, "Come see me before dinner—I've got you."

Carl grabbed a couple of ice cold beers. His favorite, Birra Moretti. Italian. Founded by Luigi Moretti in 1859, it was acquired by Heineken BV in 1996. Roll-ups were rife in the alcohol industry, a fact Carl had mentioned in his masterclass earlier.

Carl and Terence found a secluded table out beyond the pool and started sipping the beers. Terence opened his laptop and showed Carl the consolidated model.

Combined With Medical PR

$	Current Group	Medical	Cross Selling	Cost Synergies	Combined
Revenue	12,372,664	11,928,372	2,000,000	0	26,301,036
COGS	-1,937,282	-2,135,179	-166,000	75,000	-4,163,461
Gross Profit	11,345,733	9,793,193	1,834,000	75,000	23,047,926
GM, %	91.7%	82.1%	91.7%	N/A	87.6%
Overheads	-7,708,493	-6,071,541	-1,246,052	750,000	-14,276,087
EBITDA	3,637,240	3,721,652	587,948	825,000	8,771,840
Margin, %	29.4%	31.2%	29.4%	N/A	33.4%

DEALMAKER WEALTH

"So," Terence observed, "when I close this deal and push through all the synergies, the business will generate almost $8,800,000 in EBITDA. What type of multiple can I expect at that level? I can then calculate the valuation and negotiate an equity split."

"Well, it doesn't really work like that. Because the equity investment is going to help you generate those levels of profitability, you need to factor that into the math.

"Right now, you're delivering $3,700,000 of EBITDA. You're easily worth a 7X multiple.

"Your enterprise value is about $26,000,000, and you have $5,000,000 or so of debt, so your stock value is $21,000,000. We'll work it out exactly in a minute, but for now, bear with me.

"At $8,800,000 of EBITDA, you'll be in the 10X multiple range. So, $88 million in enterprise value, and your total debt load will be, say, $15 million. That stock value will be $73 million.

"Now, your new equity investor won't subscribe to a $73-million valuation because his or her equity capital is critical for you to hit that mark. In the same vein, you can't sell your equity at a $21,000,000 valuation because that's not fair to you. You and the team need to execute to turn that equity into a much bigger valuation, so, typically, you'll negotiate somewhere in the middle. In my experience, and if I was investing in this deal, at this stage I would be about one-third the way between $21 million and $88 million. Say, $43 million. That would be the pre-money (or pre equity) valuation. If you need $3,000,000, then the post-money valuation would be $46 million.

"You'd be selling 3/46 of your stock, which is around 6.5% unless this fine Italian beer hasn't clouded my mental math skills." Carl was giggling now.

"What's the difference between pre-money and post-money?" asked Terence.

"Simple," replied Carl. "When you raise equity, if it's to cash out another shareholder, then the deal would be done on a pre-money basis, so $43 million—because the equity cash isn't being used to grow the business. That would be a higher dilution of 7%, or 3 divided by 43.

"In your case, the equity is to buy another business, so we use the post-money valuation of $46 million. The $3 million equity cash is added to the $43 million of negotiated, current value. Right?"

"I got it," said Terence. "So, I can model this up and create a pitch deck from what I've learned this morning. I can answer the five investor questions."

"Great," said Carl. "You also need to look at any other acquisitions you want to make in the next five years and forecast the organic growth of the entire group post-acquiring Medical PR. From what you were saying in the session Q&A, the exit level is at $100 million of value, and if you use the 10X multiple, that's only $10 million of EBITDA for two consecutive years. You're almost there with this deal, so I expect you can probably flip this within three years max."

A long line was forming to chat with Carl, and Terence excused himself. The cookout was in two hours. He sent a group text to Jeremy and Daniel asking for a quick Zoom so he could share his notes on the day and tell them about his meeting with Carl. He also wanted a deck and model completed before the end of the weekend so he could run it past Carl before everyone scattered from the Mastermind.

The guys weren't thrilled being summoned to the Zoom meeting over the weekend but agreed to divide and conquer over the next 36 hours. Jeremy would build the forecast model for three years, and Daniel would create the draft of the pitch deck.

They agreed to have another Zoom meeting again in 24 hours, at the end of the second day of the Mastermind.

Just before the call ended, Terence said he needed to say something important.

Both Jeremy and Daniel stared intently into their computers.

"Guys, something really hit home with me today, and it's the power of the team. In understanding how to raise equity capital, it's critical my team is aligned and incentivized to be on this journey with me. To that point, I'm going to free up a total of 15% of the equity in this group to the key leaders in the team.

"Philip will get 4% as GM. Jeremy, Daniel and Lucy will each get 2% (so, 6% total) for the amazing work and dedication you're showing, and I'll allocate the remaining 5% to the rest of the employees, based on tenure, role and importance. There was a session on ESOPs (employee stock ownership plans) earlier today and I want to do that for all you guys. I can't give you real equity, unfortunately, as it would cause a tax charge for you, but at least you'll get to share in the exit of this roll-up, hopefully within three years."

The guys lit up on the screen.

Jeremy and Daniel both did the mental math. A $100 million exit in three years: 2% of that would be $2,000,000.

Life-changing money for both of them, especially for Daniel, as he was still in his twenties.

Both vowed to have their work done within 24-hours. Daniel had no plans for the weekend, so this was easy for him. For Jeremy, he would have to cancel a tennis game and some family plans tomorrow, but the $2,000,000 bounty would certainly make it easier for his wife to accept. Tomorrow was his wife's sister's birthday party. He didn't want to go anyway.

Chapter 62

The Pitch Deck and Forecast Model

Following a very enjoyable evening of eating, drinking and networking, Terence went to sleep around midnight but woke up around 7 a.m. to do some group Wim Hoff breathing exercises with the in-house health and wellness coach for Upper Echelon, Justin Morris.

Feeling refreshed, he showered, ate breakfast and settled into day two of the Mastermind. There was a guest speaker from EOS, Shannon Potts, an equity capital raiser, Devon Jones, who ran Dark Moon Capital, and several other masterclass presentations by Carl and his team.

Over lunch, Terence ate the delicious, catered-in Chipotle with Devon, and he pitched her his deal. Devon confirmed what Carl had told Terence the night before. Investors will want to get a valuation closer to the current mark versus the enhanced valuation after using the equity.

At that moment, Carl breezed past, and Devon stopped him.

"Carl, have you looked at Terence's deal?"

"Yes, ma'am," replied Carl. He was trying to be an American now that he had his visa. He was originally from the UK.

Devon hated being called "ma'am," but she let it go.

"Great. Terence is expecting his pitch deck and forecast model later this afternoon. Can the three of us meet before dinner and go through them? I'd like to pitch this to my equity investor network."

"Absolutely," replied Carl.

Carl had promised one of the attendees, Christian Bloomingdale, a game of indoor basketball, so he was running around sweating when the pitch deck and model arrived on Terence's laptop. Terence informed Devon, who located Carl, who, in turn, went for a quick shower and change before meeting her and Terence outside. Devon had arranged a table for them in one of the lounging areas, on which three ice-cold Birra Morettis awaited them. Devon made a spur-of-the-moment decision to switch to a margarita. Carl, however, thirsty from the exercise, claimed her bottle and having skulled his own in two gulps, slowly began sipping on the second bottle.

Terence spun his laptop around and walked Carl and Devon through the numbers.

Forecast Model

$	2024 Stand Alone	2024 Synergies	2025	2026
Revenue	24,301,036	26,301,036	30,246,191	34,783,120
Y-Y Growth, %	N/A	N/A	15.0%	15.0%
COGS	-4,072,461	-4,163,461	-3,327,081	-3,478,312
Gross Profit	21,138,926	23,047,926	26,919,110	31,304,808
GM, %	87.0%	87.6%	89.0%	90.0%
Overheads	-13,780,034	-14,276,087	-16,332,943	-18,782,885
EBITDA	7,358,892	8,771,840	10,586,167	12,521,923
Margin, %	30.3%	33.4%	35.0%	36.0%
Acquisitions	4	4	5	5

DEALMAKER WEALTH

"Here are the stand alone numbers when I just add Medical PR to the existing group, then here are the full-year 2024 numbers once I've integrated the business, done the cross-selling and generated the planned deal synergies on overheads and cost of sales."

Devon wanted to see that analysis, so Terence pulled up the earlier model.

Combined With Medical PR

$	Current Group	Medical	Cross Selling	Cost Synergies	Combined
Revenue	12,372,664	11,928,372	2,000,000	0	26,301,036
COGS	-1,937,282	-2,135,179	-166,000	75,000	-4,163,461
Gross Profit	11,345,733	9,793,193	1,834,000	75,000	23,047,926
GM, %	91.7%	82.1%	91.7%	N/A	87.6%
Overheads	-7,708,493	-6,071,541	-1,246,052	750,000	-14,276,087
EBITDA	3,637,240	3,721,652	587,948	825,000	8,771,840
Margin, %	29.4%	31.2%	29.4%	N/A	33.4%

DEALMAKER WEALTH

"Walk me through your cross-selling and synergy plan," asked Devon.

Terence spent the next ten minutes taking Devon through the income statements of both businesses and the customer lists, walking her through the way he could use the Medical PR customer base as a platform to sell in his advertising, design and marketing services. Medical PR didn't do any of that, and he had built an integrated creative service model for other medical clients in Chicago and Indiana that he could reference.

Then, Terence walked through the next two years. "After Medical PR, I'm going to make one more acquisition. That will make five in total, and that will allow me to maintain a 15% minimum annual growth rate for revenues. With that scale I can increase my gross margin and lower overhead as a percentage of revenues. We're conservatively looking at $34.8 million of revenue by the end of 2025 with 36% margins, so $12.5 million in EBITDA."

Carl interjected. "Those margins will put you at best-in-class, and, as such, you should command a multiple in the higher end of the range."

Carl logged into his Deal Data database on his phone. He looked at the NAICS codes for creative professional services, and with that level of profitability he saw a range of multiples between 4.7 and 11.4 of EBITDA.

"I think 9X is absolutely achievable as an exit, maybe even 10X if interest rates continue to fall and the cost of capital becomes cheaper."

Terence then pulled up another model Jeremy had built populating the numbers. He changed the exit multiple to 9X.

Forecast Model

$	2024	2025	2026
Revenue	26,301,036	30,246,191	34,783,120
Overheads	-14,276,087	-16,332,943	-18,782,885
EBITDA	8,771,840	10,586,167	12,521,923
Margin, %	33.4%	35.0%	36.0%
3-Year Average			10,626,643
Multiple			9.0
EV			95,639,790
Debt load			-15,000,000
Equity Value			80,639,790

DEALMAKER WEALTH SOCIETY

Taking a three-year average of EBITDA, applying the 9X multiple on that average and deducting the forecasted net debt load at that time, the valuation was north of $80 million.

"Not bad," said Carl.

Devon agreed. "I'd like to pitch this to my investor community as soon as I get back to Nashville next week," she said. "We'll need the signed LOI for the Medical PR deal."

"I should have that locked up within a week," replied Terence.

Devon, Carl and Terence then went through the pitch deck and made some minor changes.

The rest of the evening Terence ate, drank, networked—even danced and hung out in the hot tub for a while. This was an amazing event.

He had learned a ton.

He'd spent some quality time with Carl, the speakers and the attendees. And he'd formulated his pitch deck and forecast model and developed a channel into hundreds of equity investors.

This was proving to be the most amazing weekend of his life.

Terence was lying on the bed in his room when his phone buzzed. It was Julie. They hadn't spoken since the mid-morning break when she was at the baseball field with their son.

"Hi, honey, how are you?" How was your night?"

"Amazing. Lots of fun but more importantly, I have all my shit together to be pitching investors next week so I can close the Medical PR deal and take the business to exit within two years at a $80 million exit, net of debt."

"Oh my God, really? And how much of that will we get?"

"Probably about 60%, so $48 million, give or take."

"Does that mean we can retire?" Julie said in a hopeful voice.

"Yes, we can. But this is so much fun, I'm not sure I'll want to. Let's see in a few years, but I love this stuff, and being around some amazing other dealmakers this weekend wants me to stay in this club for a long time."

They said goodnight. Tomorrow was the final day, and the event finished at 3 p.m. Terence was flying back to Chicago at 6 p.m. and would spend next week focusing on getting Medical PR under LOI and pitching investors for the $3,000,000 equity he would need alongside the bank debt he already had a term sheet for.

Chapter 63

Medical PR Goes Under LOI

Since Terence was due to pitch equity investors by the end of the week, he went back to Nick early Monday morning with his second offer from the offer sequencing stack.

By the end of Monday, Nick had countered again:

To: Terence Turner
From: Nick Alison
Subject Line: Counter offer for the purchase of Medical PR & Advertising, Inc.

Dear Terence:

Thank you for your counter offer. Upon reflection, I will agree to the following terms. This is my best and final offer, and I would like to have an LOI signed within 24-hours.

Closing payment $10,000,000
Seller note $3,000,000 payable within 36-months
Earn out $1,000,000 based on minimum 90% retention of clients within a 12-month period
Total consideration $14,000,000

I will leave $2,000,000 of working capital in the business at closing, and I will repay the $300,000 of non-current liabilities immediately prior to closing.

Sincerely,
Nick Alison

    Terence liked this counter offer to his counter. He had never seen the words "best and final" before. *I guess that's the same as "take it or leave it."*
    He went back to his offer sequence. Nick had landed somewhere between offers 3 and 5 on the sequence.
    The key to this deal was that Terence needed only $10 million as the closing payment. He had a term sheet for $15 million from the bank, and he would repay the $5 million of SBA.
    Therefore he needed only about $2 million of equity to give him $1,500,000 or so of working capital left after closing costs, etc.
    Terence waited a few hours then called Nick to accept the offer. He had Jeremy draft and submit an LOI, and after a few tweaks this was signed the following day, just before his first investor pitch.

Terence had lots of ammunition now.

A refined pitch deck.
A term sheet for $15 million of debt.
A forecast model.
An LOI to buy Medical PR.

    He was on a roll. All he needed was $2 million of equity, and he would offer a sweet deal to get it. It was the only thing standing in his way of an $80 million exit in two years.

Chapter 64

Terence Pitches to Equity Investors

Over the course of the next three days, Terence and Devon pitched to eight equity investors. Some were private equity firms, some were family offices and one was an ultra-high-net-worth individual who wanted to not only invest the $2 million but also be Chairman and lead the exit in two years' time.

This was very appealing to Terence. Not only did the private equity guys want control of his business for less than a 10% equity stake, they didn't appear to really understand the market or have any real strategic value-add to the business.

The ultra-high-net-worth investor was Bryan Scott. Worth about $100 million, he had made his money when he sold his large Madison Avenue advertising agency to private equity a few years back. He knew the market, and he knew how to get a nine-figure exit.

The issue, however, was the terms he wanted.

Bryan had no interest in the $46 million valuation that Terence and Carl had spit-balled at the Mastermind last weekend.

He was only interested in the current valuation of JAT, although he agreed to take the current trailing 12-months numbers rather than an average.

EBITDA was $3,637,240
Multiple agreed was 7X
EV was $25,460,680
Less SBA debt load of $4,500,000 at the current time
Equity Valuation of $20,960,680

Bryan also agreed to the post-money valuation by adding the $2 million cash, so ordinarily, the equity purchased would have been

$2 million / $22.96 million = 8.7%

However, Bryan wanted double that equity to act as Chairman of the Board and drive the exit in two years.

So, the $2 million would cost Terence 17.4% of the equity. He and Jacqueline would dilute, and the 15% he had allocated to the team via options would get set at the time of this equity investment.

Jeremy had pulled together a cap table for him, for both before and after this deal.

Cap Table

Shareholder	Before	After
Terence Turner	90.0%	60.8%
Jacqueline Turley	10.0%	6.8%
Bryan Scott	0.0%	17.4%
Team	0.0%	15.0%
Total	100.0%	100.0%

DEALMAKER WEALTH

Terence couldn't get his mind around this. 17.4% of the business would represent around $14 million in exit proceeds for Bryan at an $80 million exit. That would be a 7X return over three years. *That's crazy*, he thought.

But he needed the capital, and he liked Bryan. He had himself previously done what Terence needed to do: Scale up and exit to private equity. Having pitched to a bunch of them that week, Terence decided he was in the lion's den and would welcome both the mentorship and protection Bryan could offer.

Bryan sent his term sheet for the investment, along with a draft operating agreement.

$2,000,000 of ordinary shares
17.4% equity
Chairman of the Board
$150,000 annual salary

Terence would maintain control of the business; however, Bryan was recommending a new five-person board comprising himself, Terence, Jacqueline, Jeremy and an independent director Bryan would choose. *Probably his attorney, Kyle Parsons*, Terence thought.

Terence called Bryan confirming receipt of the offer and promised to have an answer back within 24 hours.

He needed advice from Carl. Devon had told him to go for it, but this was one of Devon's connections.

The beauty of the Upper Echelon Mastermind is direct access to Carl. Terence had his cell phone number, so he texted him.

Carl was on a Virgin Atlantic flight from Manchester, UK back to Orlando, Florida. He had onboard Wi-Fi so could communicate but couldn't chat.

Terence sent him the offer documents, which Carl received via email on his phone. He promised to review them and have a call with Terence early tomorrow.

About an hour later, Carl texted Terence back.

"Go for it. Will explain tomorrow."

The following morning, Carl was on his morning walk to Starbucks. A four-mile round trip. It was his thinking time. He strategized his day on the walk there, had his caramel macchiato, then walked back and usually took calls on that 40-minute walk back.

It was 6:45 a.m., and Terence had just gotten off his Peloton. He was toweling the sweat off his face when Carl called.

"Morning, mate," Carl said in his broad, Northern UK accent. "I would do this deal."

"First, you get your equity, and you get to close on Medical PR. Then, you're on your way to a $80 million, maybe even a nine-figure exit.

"Two, this guy can help you, not only with the exit (since he's done it before), but this guy is from the industry. You two may decide to keep rolling and build something even bigger.

"Three, I bet he has tons of connections in the industry both for additional acquisitions or high-ticket sales relationships.

"Four. You keep control—unlike the terms Devon told me were on offer from private equity.

"Five. Who do you want on your board? A kid from Harvard Business School who works for the private equity partners or a seasoned, wiley entrepreneur and executive who can add a ton of value to your business and even be another solid mentor for you?"

Terence smiled. Carl was always right.

"Okay, coach," he replied. "I'm going to do it. Thank you for your advice and counsel."

"Oh, and I almost forgot," Terence added. "Carl, I want to give you 1% of the equity in the group for all your help, advice and counsel."

"No need," replied Carl. "I don't want it. I don't do this for money. I do it to change lives, and your life, my friend, is definitely changing for the better. But I'll tell you what: Close on the deal, then, if you want, send me some nice wine. But I don't need any equity."

"Deal," replied Terence. He remembered Carl being a big fan of Caymus, Barolo and that delicious white Burgundy called Montrachet. He would send him a bottle of each.

Chapter 65

Double Closing

The next six weeks were a whirlwind of activity. Although the existing group of businesses continued to expand at a pace, Terence needed to do three things, none of which involved the day-to-day running of the business.

He needed to:

Close the $2,000,000 equity investment with Bryan
Close on the $15,000,000 debt funding package from Matrix Financial Partners
Close the Medical PR acquisition

He first signed the term sheet Bryan had sent him. Nick had been chasing that alongside the $15,000,000 term sheet from Matrix.

Jeremy and Brittany had started the due diligence on the Medical PR deal, and Bryan was going pretty heavy on the due diligence both for Medical and also the existing portfolio of businesses. He had hired Deloitte to scour the numbers, and it was almost a full time job for Jeremy to quarterback all this deal activity. However, aided superbly by Phillip, Daniel, Lucy and a new financial analyst Terence had hired named Samantha Reeves, the team powered through.

JAT had recently leased a larger office three floors above the old suite. It was 50% bigger, and it now had a war room where all the deal documents were worked on. Brittany, Terence's attorney, had worked in the room that day for three hours. By 5 p.m., Terence was exhausted. Lunch had been over four hours ago. He ate a ham sandwich in three bites while standing over Daniel's shoulder as he ran through financial due diligence protocols on Medical PR.

The team would stay a few more hours, but it was time for Terence to drive home to go watch baseball. His beloved Cubs were playing tonight, and he planned on switching off, having a few beers and enjoying some time with his family. Carl was also in town. He had spoken that afternoon at his alma mater, the University of Chicago Booth School of Business, and Terence had invited him to the baseball game.

Terence drove home in his Audi RS Q8, cleaned up, then drove Julie and the kids to Wrigley Field to the stadium. As a ballpark, it had the notoriety of being the world's largest open bar. Favored by the white-collar workers of Chicago who liked to party, it was a stark contrast to the neighboring White Sox stadium, which was frequented more by Chicago's blue-collar workers.

The Cubs were playing the Atlanta Braves. Carl had become a Braves fan, visiting games with his business partner, Mark Holt. Terence had met Mark at the Upper Echelon Mastermind several weekends ago. Mark was also in town with Carl; they were scouting construction deals to buy.

Both teams were in great form. Each had lost only one of their last six games, so this would be an excellent matchup.

At the bottom of the ninth, the score was 8-5 to the Cubs. The Braves were in to bat. Epic game of cat and mouse. All the bases were loaded. The Braves needed four runs to win, and Ronald Acuna, Jr. stepped up to the plate. A home run would win the game.

He missed the first two pitches, but then on the third pitch he swung the bat, and all you could hear was that incredible, resounding whack as wood hit leather and the ball shot to the moon. Home run.

Fewer than 5,000 of the 40,000-strong crowd were Braves fans, so you could hear more groans than cheers. Carl and Mark jumped around like crazy cats. Carl was even wearing his Acuna replica jersey.

They ambled out of the stadium. Terence took his family home, while Carl and Mark had their driver take them back to the hotel.

The next four weeks continued at a pace. All the due diligence and legals were completed. However, Nick's attorney on the sell side of the Medical PR deal was an absolute nightmare. Nonetheless, Brittany, known for her cool head and commercial savvy, managed to get the legals locked. Everything was set for a Friday double closing.

The equity investment would be ratified in the morning, and then those funds, together with the $15,000,000 debt financing package, would be used to pay back the SBA loans and close on Medical PR.

By 4 p.m. that Friday afternoon, everything was completed. This had been a huge series of experiences for Terence. He now had a business at almost $8 million of EBITDA, and he owned 60.8% of it. He now owned four businesses, had a new chairman and board and a big opportunity ahead of him to scale up for two years and then retire with at least $40 million pre-taxes. The business had also been rebranded as the JAT Integrated Media Group.

Let's do this, he thought. *Piece of cake.*

Chapter 66

Two Years Later

Ross Thompson and his leadership team of PR Empire Inc. sat in their monthly board meeting. The business was performing admirably. The Austin-based PR firm was a roll-up. It was the creative and scientific combination of thirteen brands that were all centered around the same customer avatar: the small- and medium-sized business who needed PR, advertising, traditional and digital marketing services. It was a one-stop shop for clients with $10 million revenue and above across multiple industries: financial services, technology, ecommerce, healthcare and some brick-and-mortar leisure and retail. It was a very similar business to the JAT group

Sarah Lewis, the CFO reported on the latest numbers.

Trailing 12-month revenue was $163,500,000 and EBITDA was $32,300,000. The business would easily command a 12X multiple in an exit, so the business was easily worth $350 million.

Beyond that, the business had just secured a $125-million line of credit from Knights Capital to make additional acquisitions. Ross and the team had made smaller acquisitions to date but now wanted to spend the money on only two more deals to get the business to at least $200 million in revenue and $50 million in EBITDA with synergies and cross selling. Then, he would take the business through an IPO and probably command a 20X multiple as a public company.

Ross did the mental math. 20 X $50 million was a billion dollar valuation. He sat there for a few minutes with the goofiest of grins.

Sarah was a mathematical genius. She brain-calculated the amount of EBITDA the business would need to acquire ($17,700,000), and with a net $125,000,000 of capital to deploy (after working capital requirements and closing costs), they would need to be buying at around a 7X multiple. She walked over to the whiteboard and wrote it down.

"Easy," said Ross. "We can put some of the deals into seller financing like we did with Toto PR and Flaming Creative Media. Also, we'll generate additional EBITDA through cross-selling and deal synergies."

Jess Thompson and Chris March walked through the integration plan following tweaks they had made from the last few acquisitions. Both had hired understudies for the operations and marketing teams, respectively, so they could tag team on integrating new acquisitions and setting strategy before handing it over to their understudies to execute the plan. Jess and Chris were masters of strategy, and developing the KPIs to the businesses could be tracked in real time. This was a major reason why PR Empire was crushing it in the market and was the target of some major players for an acquisition.

However, Ross was highly ambitious and wanted to create that $1 billion business (by market capitalization). He and Sarah had a plan to list the business on the NASDAQ soon by IPO. The $50,000,000 of EBITDA was at least double what the NASDAQ would perceive as a credible business, and there was an investment bank and market maker (with a share subscription facility) standing by. Ross had signed that contract on stage at an event last year.

Ross asked Sarah to put the target list on the giant screen. Sarah was fumbling with the Apple play settings to connect her MacBook and dropped a few F-bombs, as technology wasn't her forte. Chris was the jack-of-all-trades (and, ironically, master of them all), and he got the presentation on the big screen in under ten seconds.

The list was impressive.

None of these businesses had been approached yet. Through a detailed process of pulling data from Hoovers, Pitch Book and several other online databases Empire subscribed to, it had an accurate picture of who was out there and the high level numbers.

"What do we think, guys?" Ross asked the team.

Next followed a solid debate lasting an hour about the strengths and weaknesses of each of the target businesses. One had been in a sexual harassment lawsuit, so Ross quickly called his attorney, David Gifford, for his input. "Strike it off the list, Ross. It's not worth the brain damage of figuring out the legal liability."

Ross went round the table for a show of hands. Two businesses really stood out.

Foxtree Creative Services LLC.
Dallas TX
Revenue = $26,000,000
EBITDA = $4,600,000
Margin = 17.7%

JAT Integrated Media Group LLC.
Chicago IL
Revenue = $34,783,120
EBITDA = $12,521,923
Margin = 36.0%

Both were solid businesses.

Foxtree was more of a tactical acquisition. Empire could consolidate its position in the Texas market. Foxtree had been chipping away at Empire's customer base, and it was starting to annoy him. This was a no-brainer deal and should happen first.

The big future deal would be JAT.

Ross was shocked at the performance of JAT. He recalled being sent the deal from a CPA less than three years ago, and the revenue then was a fraction of what it was today. Both revenue and EBITDA seemed to be around 10X what it had been back then. *It's obviously been going through a roll-up*, he thought.

"That's some crazy growth," said Chris.

"They've made some bolt-on acquisitions," explained Sarah. "I found them on Pitch Book. The owner is named Terence Turner. He bought the business and has acquired four other businesses since. The guy is clearly a dealmaker. He may be a tough negotiator."

"Sure," said Ross, "but he'll have a number, and if we can get creative, I think that's the deal we target after Foxtree. But let's feel him out. He may want the $1 billion moonshot like us, but let's see where his head is at.

"I know Brian Cowans, the owner of Foxtree. We sat next to each other at Creative Con last year. I wasn't aware his business was that big, but he's miserable and tired. I know he'll sell on sensible terms. That's an easy deal for us. I'll just call him and feel him out.

"But I don't know Terence. We need to find a mutual contact, or send him a direct approach letter."

Chris fired up LinkedIn and found Terence was two links away from him. Sarah had three mutual connections with him, including the CPA who had sent them the Creative PR deal a few years ago. She clicked on his profile.

Jeremy Brown, CPA.
CFO, JAT Integrated Media Group LLC
Former Managing Partner, Jeremy Brown & Associates.

That's interesting. He sold his CPA firm, she thought. Maybe he had gone full-time into JAT considering all those acquisitions and explosive growth.
She sent Jeremy a quick in-mail while it was on her mind.

Jeremy,

Hope all is well.

You pitched the JAT PR deal to us a while back. We passed at the time because it was too small; however, we have been tracking its growth, and it looks a great fit for us now.

I believe you exited your practice and went full time there as the CFO.

Can you chat with Terence and see if he's interested in selling at this point?

Feel free to give me a call. 737-999-1234.

Best regards,

Sarah

The team wrapped up the rest of the afternoon agenda then went out for happy-hour cocktails. Ross was four margaritas in before they decided to order food.
He was thinking a lot about JAT. Terence could be an ally: He knew how to do roll-ups. JAT would be a great new piece to the puzzle.
The Mexican food and wine kept coming and coming. All the team was well oiled. About 9 p.m., Sarah received a text from Jeremy. He was responding to the LinkedIn message.

Hi Sarah,

Jeremy Brown here. Got your message. Are you free to chat tomorrow morning?

Regards,

JB

Sarah replied:

Sure, 9 a.m.?

Jeremy agreed

Confirmed, chat then. Call my cell. JB

Chapter 67

The First Seller Call for JAT

Sarah Lewis was a CPA with 20 years of experience. She had worked in practice and in private equity and now served as the CFO of Empire. She was a single mom of twin girls, and after dropping them off at school, ordered her daily ritual of a venti oat milk latte and drove the five minutes to Starbucks. She sat patiently in the drive-through line; it was 8:15 a.m., after all. Coffee finally in hand, she zoomed the ten-minute drive to the office in Bee Cave, about 40 minutes northwest of downtown Austin, and ventured into the Empire offices.

Walking into her office, she plugged in her laptop and went through her power list items for the day. Top of the list was to engage with Jeremy Brown and try to get Terence Turner to the table. Ross had already texted her three times this morning confirming his strong desire to acquire JAT.

As soon as it hit 9 a.m., Sarah found Jeremy's last text message and, using her iPhone, clicked the call button. After four rings, Jeremy picked up.

"Hey, this is Jeremy."

"Good morning. It's Sarah, calling you as we agreed last night."

"Yes, Sarah. What can I do for you?"

"As you know, I'm the group CFO of Empire. We're building a roll-up of creative professional services businesses, currently only in Texas. As a board, we want to expand, and Chicago and the Midwest is top of our list.

"Ross, my CEO, was pitched JAT about three years ago, but at that time it was too small. However, we've seen your numbers online in our deal database, and, clearly, you've been on your own buy-and-build strategy. I'm not sure of your exact numbers, but would Terence be interested in selling anytime soon?"

Perfect timing, thought Jeremy. Only last week, the board of JAT had determined now was the right time to sell and he had been instructed to hire a boutique investment banking firm to handle the sale. He was currently interviewing a bunch of them from across the country.

Jeremy decided to play it cool.

"Well, you never know. I can ask him. How much capital do you have lined up?"

"We have a $125,000,000 line of credit to do multiple acquisitions, and if there is interest in selling, I can provide that as proof of funds. Clearly, we can't spend all that on JAT, though."

Jeremy laughed. "Well, that would be nice. Let me chat internally and get back to you."

He actually didn't need to chat internally. He would just add Empire to the buyer's list.

The following morning he called Sarah back and confirmed that, yes, the business was going to be put up for sale, and the board had indeed instructed him to hire an investment bank to handle the sale.

"Really?" said Sarah. "Why not just let us take a quick look at it. We could potentially make you an offer while you are interviewing banks, and if it's in the ballpark, you can save yourself the time and cost of sell-side broker fees."

Jeremy knew the benefits of having multiple suitors and how that could bid the price up. However, all the banks he had spoken to so far wanted $50,000 per month as a retainer and a 10% success fee. So that would be around $9 million in fees just to represent them. Between himself, Terence and Bryan the Chairman, they had a ton of dealmaking experience.

"Let me chat to my CEO and Chairman," Jeremy replied. "I'll get back to you shortly."

Terence was in the office reviewing the current sales forecast and reviewing the integration progress of his latest acquisition, a small digital marketing agency business in Chicago that specialized in Facebook marketing. This had been a weak link for JAT, and he outsourced all that work to Stern Media Inc. down the street. When he was drinking Guinness with Russell Stern, the owner, six weeks ago, Russell had mentioned he was going to sell, so Terence acquired it. 50% cash at close and a two-year seller note. He used some of the cash in JAT for the closing payment. He didn't need additional equity or debt financing.

Jeremy popped into the office. "Got a minute, boss?"

"Yes, what's up?"

"I just spoke to Sarah Lewis. She's the CFO of Empire, out of Austin. They want to buy us. Have nine figures in capital to deploy."

"Ah, yes, I know them. Their CEO Ross Thompson is a legend. Really great guy. Likes a drink. I chatted with him briefly a few years ago at an event. They're doing what we are in Texas—only larger, I think."

"Sarah's asking if we can get them financials so they can give us a ballpark offer. If that's significant, then we may not need to hire an investment bank to run the process for us. Could save us $9 million."

"Let's call Bryan. He's fishing, I believe, but he texted me an hour ago, let's see if he'll take our call."

Terence called Bryan and put the phone on speaker, turning up the volume so Jeremy could hear.

Bryan picked up immediately. "Hi, Terence, what's up?"

"Hi Bryan, how's the fishing?"

"Good. What do you need?"

"Well, JB is with me, and you're on speakerphone. He was approached by the Empire guys over in Austin. They want to potentially acquire us. We're still interviewing investment banks, but are you happy for us to give them a shot to see how serious they are?"

"Yes, no harm in that. Let's get them under NDA, then we can share details with them. Clearly, we don't have a CIM prepared yet, so have Jeremy prepare a management presentation and start a data room. I will also put some calls in to my friends in private equity and get a few other bites. I was thinking just this morning, *why hire an investment bank and pay all those fees when we can do this ourselves and save ourselves millions of dollars in fees?*

"So, absolutely. Let's do it."

Chapter 68

The Proposal

Jack's birthday present to Jacqueline was a five-day cruise around the Northern Caribbean, sailing from Miami.

They boarded the flight from Chicago O'Hare and flew directly to Miami. After the obligatory overnight hotel stay (so that pesky airline delays wouldn't cause a missed departure) the two love birds walked onto the ship, purchased the Royal Caribbean drinks packages and found the lunch restaurant. Check-in to the rooms wasn't for a few more hours.

Since Jack had booked a loft suite, they would eat most of their meals in the secluded Coastal Kitchen. It was waiter service, not like the crazy Windjammer Cafe that tended to be carnage.

"Where do you want to go for dinner, my dear? Jacqueline asked Jack.

"I've booked us into the grill. Private booth. I hear the filet mignon is outstanding," he replied.

"You're so sweet. I would love that."

They wrapped up lunch, checked into the suite and unpacked.

The ship was amazing and huge. Serenade of the Seas. It had this wonderful bar that actually moved up and down every thirty minutes, so you could enter the bar on one level and get out on another. The Rising Tide. Hopefully Jack's life was going to rise on this cruise.

The two of them sipped cocktails and, at precisely 7:50 p.m., walked the short distance to the grill.

As soon as they sat down, Jack became nervous and edgy, seemingly messaging the waiter in code. He also went into hiding for a few minutes (with the waiter) then came back looking very sheepish.

"What's the matter, Jack?" she asked inquisitively.

"Nothing, my dear," he replied.

The waiter handed out menus and took drinks orders, then returned with water and bread and took the food order.

"Two caesar salads and chateaubriand for two, medium rare," Jack rattled off like an army general giving out battle orders.

The next ten minutes were awkward. Jack kept looking around and Jacqueline was starting to get irritated. *He's never been like this*, she thought. They'd been out for dinner many times, and she couldn't remember him ever acting so strange.

Then, it happened.

A violinist approached the table and started playing a beautiful piece. Edward Elgar's classic Salut d'Amour. Love Letter.

She knew the piece instantly. At that very moment, Jack lifted up the placemat, and there was a letter addressed to Jacqueline. She smiled awkwardly and ripped it open.

It contained a plain card with just four words on it.

"Please Close Your Eyes."

Puzzled, she closed her eyes, with absolutely no idea what was happening.

Thirty seconds and a few giggles later, Jack asked her to open them. When she did, Jack was no longer sitting in front of her.

Instead, he was down on one knee to her left, with tears in his eyes and holding a small ring box adorned with the world-famous Tiffany logo.

He flipped open the box to reveal a beautiful diamond engagement ring. The reflection of the candle hit the diamond and shone up through Jacqueline's water glass.

"Jacqueline. I love you and would treasure nothing more than spending the rest of my life with you. Would you please do me the honor of becoming my wife."

Jacqueline was shell-shocked. She scanned the restaurant, and every face was looking at her, waiting for her response. Some people were even taking pictures.

"Oh Jack," she said. "How wonderful, and what a beautiful ring. I would like to accept and thank you. It will be my honor as well."

The two of them embraced (Jack still down on one knee) and the restaurant erupted in cheers. The violinist switched to a quick rendition of "Here Comes the Bride," and the rest of the evening was splendid.

They tentatively set a 90-day period before getting married and decided to have the ceremony in Scottsdale. It was a place they'd visited frequently over the past few years and were planning on retiring there in a few more.

Chapter 69

JAT Is in Play

Jeremy spent the next few days building a management presentation and creating a data room. He uploaded all the relevant tax returns, financial accounts, dashboard and legal documents.

Once it was complete, he sent Sarah an NDA, and after it was signed, sent her the management presentation and data room link. He offered several times over the next few weeks to arrange a meeting, preferably in person but on Zoom if required.

Sarah replied saying she would review the documents with Ross and the management team and get back to him.

The following morning, Ross, Jess, Sarah and Chris all sat in the boardroom. The summary financial picture was displayed on the giant TV screen.

JAT Financial Summary

$	2024 A	2025 A	2026 F
Revenue	26,301,036	30,246,191	34,783,120
Y-Y Growth, %	N/A	15.0%	15.0%
COGS	-4,163,461	-3,327,081	-3,478,312
Gross Profit	23,047,926	26,919,110	31,304,808
GM, %	87.6%	89.0%	90.0%
Overheads	-14,276,087	-16,332,943	-18,782,885
EBITDA	8,771,840	10,586,167	12,521,923
Margin, %	33.4%	35.0%	36.0%
Acquisitions	4	5	5

DEALMAKER WEALTH

The business was booming. The 2025 actuals were solid, and although it was only early September, 2026 was looking to be even better. Sarah passed around the nine-month financial period to the end of August, and the business was well on track to hit its numbers.

"Where's the 2027-to-2030 forecast?" asked Ross.

"There isn't one. I think it was always their intention to sell the business at the end of this year. Besides, the forecast will change depending on whoever the buyer is, right?"

"Right," said Ross. "We'll blow this up. We're the best in the world at this. What do you think the business is worth?"

"Well, I prepared a valuation summary," Sarah said, putting it up on the screen.

Empire Valuation of JAT

$	2024	2025	2026
Revenue	26,301,036	30,246,191	34,783,120
Overheads	-14,276,087	-16,332,943	-18,782,885
EBITDA	8,771,840	10,586,167	12,521,923
Margin, %	33.4%	35.0%	36.0%
3-Year Average			10,626,643
Multiple			8.0
EV			85,013,146
Debt load			-12,304,939
Equity Value			72,708,207

DEALMAKER WEALTH

"I think the business is worth an 8X multiple of the three-year average EBITDA of $10,626,634, assuming they hit their full-year numbers. We would probably close in 90-days, so mid-December, and we can track the financials until then.

"They're carrying a $12-million-and-change debt load from all their acquisitions, so netting that out of the enterprise value, it's worth $72 million."

"Okay, how would we fund that?"

"I suggest we offer $65 million. $50 million at closing and a $15 million seller note. Maybe even a $10 million note and $5 million earn-out."

"Okay, that works. Let's go see them. Did they give you dates?"

"Yes, I think we should all go next Tuesday. I'll call Jeremy to confirm."

After the meeting, Sarah called Jeremy and suggested next Tuesday for a meeting at the JAT office in Chicago. Ross wanted to inspect the business in person.

"That will work," said Jeremy. "I can have Terence and also Bryan, our Chairman and GM, and Phillip in attendance. But before I lock that down, can you give me an indication of price? Did you look at the numbers?"

"Sure. We're probably in the $65 million range, based purely off the numbers."

"Really? That's not going to fly. We're in the $80 million to $100 million range. That's the range the various investment banks have indicated to us. We've not received any offers, but they're all confident of hitting at least $80 million. I just don't want to waste your time."

"Okay. Let me get back with Ross and come back to you."

Ross had left the office for the day. He was driving home in his Lamborghini Urus SUV. The electric blue car was as shiny as a diamond weaving through the traffic up to Steiner Ranch, where he lived. The call came through to the car.

"Ross, it's Sarah. JAT wants at least $80 million, maybe as high as $100 million. I think we can get to $80 million if pushed, but $100 million would be overpriced, in my opinion. We can't have the meeting until we underwrite at least the $80 million."

"Well, if we did $65 million at closing and a $15 million note, that still is only half of what we have in capital available, so, yes I think we can underwrite that. Besides, we may not like the business, and nothing is binding. Tell them 'yes' to $80 million for now, and let's lock down that trip."

Sarah called Jeremy back and confirmed $80 million could work, subject to due diligence and legals, but that they would not be prepared to make an offer of any sort until after the meeting.

"That works, Sarah. Thank you. Make the plans, and we'll see you next Tuesday."

Chapter 70

Empire Visits JAT

Ross, Sarah, Jess and Chris all took the JSX from Austin to Chicago. They took a large Uber black SUV to the hotel, had dinner, then prepped the questions for the meeting tomorrow morning.

Ross would ask the "why sell" questions and, since he was a master of seller psychology, would feel Terence and the board out on the exit.

Chris would dig into the sales and marketing function. Sarah would handle all the financial questions and Jess would direct all operational questions. JAT had offices in Chicago, Gary, Indiana and Cleveland, Ohio. There was also a satellite office in New York via a JV they had with a Madison Avenue advertising agency.

Ross was sipping an Old Fashioned when he queried the team, "Why do you think these guys are selling? This business has come from nowhere in three years. They could go and do what we've done, raise nine figures and continue acquiring. Clearly, they know what they're doing. I just don't get it."

Neither did the team. Maybe the Chairman was forcing this. "We'll find out tomorrow," Sarah said.

The team retired early and met for coffee at 7 a.m. the following morning to fine-tune the sequencing of the questions.

Uber collected them at 8 a.m., and they arrived just a few minutes before the 8:30 start. As promised, a breakfast of pastries and fruit was waiting for them.

JAT consisted of Terence, the CEO; Bryan, the Chairman; Jeremy, the CFO; and Philip, the GM. The office was amazing. Far more glamorous than the Austin base of Empire. It was almost Google-like. There were snooze pods, a full cafe, pool tables and even Pelotons.

The board room was huge, with the latest technology and wall-to-wall glass. Awards hung everywhere on the walls. This clearly was a stellar business, and they were proud of it.

Terence kicked off the introductions, and after a good 30 minutes of rapport building, launched into the management presentation. Terence went through all the strategic projects underway, the capital structure and the timeline of the five acquisitions, including how they were integrated and currently managed.

JAT operated in a classic hub-and-spoke model. Chicago was HQ and had all the central services. The other offices served purely as sales and fulfillment.

Jeremy went through the numbers, and Sarah grilled him for what seemed like an hour. Chris and Terence went back and forth on how JAT acquires customers and the strength of the sales pipeline, recurring revenue projects and referrals from key clients.

Jess and Phillip jammed on the operations, and then Ross wrapped up the meeting with the big question.

"So, Terence. This is an excellent business and would be a great acquisition for us. There's a lot of things you do well that we can incorporate into Empire. Also, I believe some of our best practices could benefit JAT as well.

"I'm curious though. You're on a roll and could keep going. Why sell now? Why not raise more capital, make more acquisitions then sell out in a few more years or even do an IPO?"

"This was always a three year project for me, Ross," explained Terence. "When I brought the Chairman on board, we mapped out a three-year plan to an exit for at least $80 million. We believe our numbers and current performance justify no less than that. It's time for us now to make that exit."

"What are you going to do next? Would you consider staying on board part-time?"

"Yes, I would. Bryan and Jeremy want to retire, but I'm only mid-40s. I don't want a full-time gig, but I'd be happy to consult for a few years if that's something that interests you."

"Yes, it is. I think we'd work really well together."

After that, the meeting wrapped, and Sarah confirmed Empire would make an offer in the next few days. The Empire team took the Uber back to the airport and flew United first class back to Austin. On the flight Sarah and Ross workshopped the offer:

$65 million closing payment
$10 million seller note over four years at 10% interest

$5 million earn-out based on a 50/50 split of EBITDA above $12 million per year $80 million total

Terence would be retained on $200,000 per year for 20 hours per week for three years and would receive 2% of Empire, a percentage which in itself was worth $7 million. Jeremy had calculated Empire to be worth something in the region of $350 million and had heard it was going to shoot for a billion-dollar valuation as a public company on the Nasdaq.

That $7 million today would be worth $21 million in the future, so it would be a massive incentive to Terence.

On studying the operating agreement, Ross realized Terence had control of the business and had drag rights over the other shareholders. This meant Terence could exit on his terms, and all other shareholders would have to follow suit.

Ross instructed Sarah to make the offer tomorrow morning.

The United flight landed. The team members had just carry-on luggage, so all were through Austin airport in under 30 minutes and into Ubers for their respective trips home.

Chapter 71

Empire Makes an $87 million Offer to Buy JAT

Combining the $80-million deal structure for JAT and the $7 million of equity for Terence in Empire, the total consideration was $87 million.

Jeremy received the offer and called a board meeting on Zoom.

Terence, Bryan, Jacqueline and the attorney all logged in. Jacqueline had only 30 minutes to spare. The fitting for her wedding dress was scheduled later that morning. Her wedding in Scottsdale was only 42 days away, and this was the first fitting. She was excited about the wedding and had heard from Terence last night that an offer was on its way from Empire.

Surely they haven't made an offer so soon? she thought.

Bryan chaired the meeting.

"Ladies and gentlemen, we have an offer from Empire. It's definitely in the ballpark. Before I present it to you, I wanted to update you on my private equity conversations. I did speak to several of the large private equity funds, and all indicated an appetite for acquiring JAT but in the $60 million to $70 million range.

"Empire has offered $87 million, comprising as follows:

$65,000,000 cash at closing
$10,000,000 seller note
$5,000,000 earn out

$7,000,000 in retained equity for Terence in the Empire top-co. This is 2% of the current valuation of $350 million
$87,000,000 total

"Now, as you know, our operating agreement gives Terence the right to exit and drag us all with him. However, he wanted you all to see this offer and get your feedback and opinions."

"I'll go first," said Bryan. "I think it's a great offer and subject to a few tweaks, I like it."

Jacqueline and Jeremy concurred.

The attorney, Kyle Parsons, who didn't own equity but was a full board member nonetheless, served as external counsel to JAT. He would run the legals for the deal. He liked the valuation but didn't like the earn out. He also thought the closing payment should be higher.

"Colleagues, I think $87 million is a fair price, but I would like to see $70 million at closing and a $10 million note paid over two years. No earn out. We'll have to skew the exit proceeds to reflect Terence receiving the $7 million of equity. If they agree to that, I think it's a great deal."

Terence concluded the meeting and thanked everyone. He instructed Jeremy to go back with the counter offer, which he promised to do later that day.

After lunch and a brisk walk around the park, he dictated the email back to Sarah.

From: Jeremy Brown
To: Sarah Lewis
SL: Counter offer for the proposed acquisition of JAT

Hi Sarah,

We met as a board this morning and have a counteroffer for you. We are happy with the $87 million total consideration; however, we request the following changes to the deal structure.

$70,000,000 cash at closing
$10,000,000 seller note over two years
$7,000,000 in retained equity for Terence in the Empire top-co
$87,000,000 total

The current net working capital of JAT is $2 million, so that will remain. We will also discharge the current $12,000,000 of debt from the closing payment.

I look forward to your response.

Regards
Jeremy

        He hit send, and it pinged Sarah's phone less than five seconds later.

        She opened the email, scanned it, forwarded it to Ross, then walked into his office down the hall.

        "Check your email, boss," she said as she barged into his office.

        He opened it, read it twice then said, "Do it. Let's go."

        Sarah called Jeremy immediately to accept the counteroffer and promised to follow up with a binding LOI within 24-hours.

        Jeremy went to see Terence and told him the news. He was elated.

Chapter 72

A Smooth Closing

Terence was amazed that the initial acquisition of JAT three years ago was so problematic but that all other deals since then had gone much more smoothly. Almost six weeks had passed since signing the LOI and that time had gone in a flash.

He walked into Brittany's office at 9:30 a.m. on Friday. As controlling shareholder, he had the proxy to sign for all shareholders, including Bryan, Jeremy, the employee trust and Jacqueline, who was in Scottsdale preparing for her wedding tomorrow. Terence would be flying up later that day with his family, but first he would go get the cashier's check for Jacqueline's share of the sale proceeds. The money would come from the attorney's client account. The check would be ordered, and Terence would collect it before heading to the airport. Jacqueline didn't know he was doing this. It would be an amazing surprise for her wedding day.

Ross and Sarah had flown in for the closing and wanted to immediately go meet the troops afterwards. Both were in the attorney's office waiting for Terence. Chris and Jess were in the Starbucks near the office. They would join everyone at JAT afterwards.

Everyone signed the documents, and JAT was now officially owned by Empire. It was a very proud moment for Terence. In just over three years, he had created over $75 million in shareholder value. All from a $100,000 equity investment from his savings. His original founding shareholders (who helped fund the original downpayment for JAT) had been exited about 18 months ago for 6X their original investment. They were happy.

Terence looked through the exit proceeds table:

Exit Proceeds

Exit Proceeds	Shareholding	Closing Payment	Seller Note	Equity
Debt repayment	N/A	11,209,382	N/A	N/A
Closing costs	N/A	182,773	N/A	N/A
Terence Turner	60.8%	28,633,570	6,080,000	7,000,000
Bryan Scott	17.4%	13,304,908	1,740,000	0
Emplyee Trust	15.0%	11,469,748	1,500,000	0
Jacqueline Turley	6.8%	5,199,619	680,000	0
Total	100.0%	70,000,000	10,000,000	7,000,000

DEALMAKER WEALTH

He would be wired $26,633,570 before the end of the day. He would also receive another $6,080,000 within the next two years, guaranteed, and he also owned $7,000,000 of stock in Empire.

Bryan would receive a total of $15,000,000 and change. It was a 7.5X return on investment from his original $2 million investment. He was thrilled.

As were all the employees. Daniel, Jeremy, Lucy and Phillip were now all millionaires.

Jacqueline couldn't believe it either. She would receive just over $5 million tomorrow via check and a further $680,000 in the next two years.

JAT had been an amazing team effort, and the entire team had benefited financially from its success.

Terence called Jacqueline on his walk back to the office to introduce Ross and the Empire team to his former troops.

"We did it, partner," he proclaimed loudly.

"I'm so proud of you, Terence. You've been an amazing business partner and trusted custodian of JAT, and I'm thrilled to see what Empire does with it. They're the perfect buyers."

"Thank you for selling me the business three years ago. I guess I've been lucky."

"You're not lucky, Terence."

"So what am I, Jacqueline?"

"What are you?" she replied and paused. "You are the creative dealmaker."

Epilogue
Three Years Later

Terence was attending the InvestorCon annual event in Las Vegas. He flew in a few days early with Julie. The children were staying with Julie's parents, so Terence was combining attending the two-day event with some couple-time.

In the three years following the sale of JAT, Terence had become an angel investor. He had invested in over ten deals (mostly from within the Protégé community), and—apart from attending monthly board meetings and at least one Protégé call per week (he was still in the program and the Upper Echelon Mastermind)—he had retired, as he promised Julie he would. He played tennis at least three times per week, and, as she also played tennis, they often played mixed doubles with Jacqueline and Jack.

They had purchased a holiday home in Spain, in a beautiful, quaint village called Alcalali, nestled in the hills between Valencia and Alicante, about 30 minutes north of the budget vacation spot, Benidorm. They rented it out most of the year through VRBO and AirBnB, but they visited it together with the children at least twice a year. In fact, they had spent all six weeks of the school break there this past summer.

Terence and Julie checked into the Encore, the sister hotel from the Wynn. Still with tens of millions of dollars in the bank, Terence upgraded to a villa for $1,400 per night. He left Julie unpacking and went downstairs to hit the black jack table.

He was playing $25 per hand. Despite his wealth, he wasn't going to play at the high roller tables.

He had read a book on the plane about basic blackjack strategy. He already knew to sit as far down the row as possible so he could make his moves based on the previous cards the dealer presented to his co-gamblers before him. This wasn't in the strategy book, but Terence considered it a good idea.

He was up about $500, and he sensed the table was cooling down. *Perhaps a few more hands,* he thought.

He decided to put a $100 chip down on the table, in the circle near where his cards would be dealt.

He had six additional $100 chips and approximately $1,000 in $25 chips.

The dealer dealt hands to all six players. Terence was number five in the sequence.

Everyone else had terrible cards apart from player two, who had 21. "Blackjack," the dealer shouted. "Winner winner, chicken dinner," the player replied, copying the scene in the amazing card-counting movie, *21*. Card counting wasn't possible at this table. It was an automatic card shuffling machine, rather than the five-deck or six-deck shoes dealers would use in the past, although these were still utilized in the off-strip casinos.

The dealer had a four, plus the blind card.

Terence had two eights. A perfect chance to split, according to the strategy book.

The dealer arrived at Terence, and he duly split the pair of eight's. He placed another $100 chip next to the ante stake.

The dealer dealt him a three, making eleven on hand one and a two for the other hand, making ten.

Ten and eleven playing a four.

Basic strategy would say double down, so he did it, not once but twice. He placed two more $100 chips down.

The dealer hit his eleven with the king of spades. 21. Perfect.

The dealer then hit his ten with a five. Fifteen. Not great, and he couldn't take any more cards.

The dealer turned over her blind card and it was the nine of hearts.

Thirteen. The dealer has to play until at least 17.

Then the next card, the three of clubs.

16.

Then the next card, which felt like an eternity, was the seven of diamonds.

23.

Busted.

Terence had won both hands. He had wagered a total of $400 and had won $400. He asked the dealer to color him up.

Quit while on top, he thought.

His original $1,000 kitty had amassed to $2,125.

The dealer gave him two $1,000 chips, a $100 and a $25.

Terence rose from the table, walked to the cashier and turned it all into cash.

Feeling smug, he walked past the Gucci boutique on his way to the lift.

Inside the window was a stunning, small-clutch purse. He walked into the store and asked the assistant how much it was.

$1,950, so probably $2,125 including tax.

I'm buying it for Julie, he thought.

The assistant went into the back and came back with a new one, all boxed up, and placed it inside one of the iconic green Gucci bags.

"Sir, that will be $2,113.41."

Rather than pull out his card, he slapped his entire $2,125 onto the counter.

"Got lucky in the casino, sir?" the assistant asked.

"Yes, I did. This is a treat for my wife."

Terence placed the $11 and change into his pocket and took the elevator to his villa.

Julie was thrilled. "Thank you, my love. What a lovely surprise."

"You're welcome, my dear."

"Are you ready for dinner?"

"Yes, reservation is at 8 p.m. at Sushi Samba over at the Venetian. I've scheduled an Uber for 7:45, so we have 30 minutes to grab a drink in that nice lounge bar we walked past on our way to check-in."

The Turners thoroughly enjoyed the evening, and at 7:30 the next morning, Terence took an Uber to the MGM for the event.

Terence walked in and registered. He was only going to spend the first day there. Carl Allen was speaking along with other speakers on real estate and land flipping. Terence wanted to diversify his investments outside of business acquisitions.

Carl did his presentation on how to buy profitable small businesses, using other people's money.

As he was wrapping up his presentation, he spotted Terence in the eighth row.

"Ladies and gentlemen, this isn't a setup, I've just seen one of my finest students in the audience. I didn't know he was here. With your permission, I would like to get him onstage and ask him some questions about his deals."

Terence froze. He had not prepared for this, but as the audience started hollering, he took to the stage and sat next to Carl on one of the polished, chrome stools.

Terence relived his journey for the audience. They were riveted. The initial acquisition of JAT and its last minute complications. The subsequent bolt-on acquisitions and capital raise. The exit to Empire PR, of which he was still a minority shareholder. Empire had listed on the NASDAQ via IPO and now had a market capitalization of $2 billion. He owned 2% (following dilution) so he was sitting on $40 million of equity.

Carl did the mental math (which he was great at). "So, Terence, you've amassed over $80 million of wealth from that very first deal where you invested $100,000. That's an 800X return over seven years. Amazing! Congratulations."

"Thank you, coach. I couldn't have done it without you and the support of the amazing Protégé community."

Carl's wife, Julia, was also at the event. She looked on with pride at how he was changing people's lives. In fact, she, Carl, Terence and Julie went out for dinner that very night. Not only were Carl and Terence mentor and mentee, they had become friends. The girls got along like wildfire. They were comparing Gucci purses.

After dinner, they all said their goodbyes, and Carl and Julia walked back along the strip to their hotel, the Bellagio. "You're changing lives, my love, and I'm very proud of you," she said.

Carl stood still, put both hands in his pockets, turned to Julia and smiled.

About the Author

Carl Allen is a serial business acquirer with more than 30 years of experience both in corporate M&A and Main Street deals. He's been involved in more than 400 transactions as a buyer, seller, investor, advisor, coach, and mentor.

Carl is the founder and CEO of Dealmaker Wealth Society, a coaching and mentoring community for entrepreneurs, small business owners and investors who want to creatively buy businesses. He's also a private equity investor with a current portfolio of 22 businesses in online coaching, professional services, construction, eCommerce, marketing and events.

Carl has pioneered the art of translating seller psychology and rapport into creative deal structures.

Carl resides with his family in the UK and also on the Space Coast of Florida.

Printed in Great Britain
by Amazon